MW00641416

The
New England Pulpit
and the
American Revolution

*When American Pastors Preached
Politics, Resisted Tyranny, and
Founded a Nation on the Bible*

Formerly titled
The New England Clergy and the American Revolution
ALICE M. BALDWIN

EDITED AND INTRODUCED BY
JOEL McDURMON

AMERICAN VISION PRESS
POWDER SPRINGS, GEORGIA

The New England Pulpit and the American Revolution:
When American Pastors Preached Politics,
Resisted Tyranny, and Founded a Nation on the Bible

Copyright © 2014 Joel McDurmon. All rights reserved.

Published by The American Vision, Inc.
    The American Vision, Inc.
    PO Box 611
    Braselton, Georgia 30517
    www.AmericanVision.org

Written permission must be secured from the publisher to use or reproduce any part of this book, except for brief quotations in critical reviews or articles.
Printed in the United States of America.

Cover design by: Chad Trotter

ISBN: 978–1–936577–33–0

This edition is dedicated to

Kevin Clauson

in the fight for Faith and Freedom.

Other books by Joel McDurmon

American Fascist: The Real Theodore Roosevelt

Noah: The True Story

*In the Midst of Your Enemies: Exposition and Application of
1 Samuel*

Restoring America One County at a Time

The Bible & War in America

*Jesus v. Jerusalem: A Commentary on Luke 9:51–20:26,
Jesus' Lawsuit Against Israel*

God versus Socialism: A Biblical Critique of the New Social Gospel

Biblical Logic: In Theory and Practice

Zeitgeist—the Movie: Exposed

The Return of the Village Atheist

*Manifested in the Flesh: How the Historical Evidence for Jesus
Refutes Modern Mystics and Atheists*

Contents

Foreword

by Joel McDurmon

We have a terrible problem in our land today, and the truth contained in Dr. Baldwin's book is a welcome antidote—should we be willing to take it. The problem is that our pulpits and preachers today have abandoned the fullness of what Christ commanded us: to disciple nations and to teach them all of His commandments. That Great Commission includes the call, which our forefathers ably demonstrated, to speak truth to the public realm: to call out rulers, governments, laws, abuse, and to demand liberty and justice. In all our preaching today about iniquity and sin, we neglect to address inequity and tyranny.

And worse: should one dare to mention that broader social and political scope of the Great Commission today they are likely to be harangued not only by humanists and leftists, but by the vast majority of Christians and clergy. The response will be almost unanimous, almost in perfect chorus: "Christians should not preach politics!" "We should preach the 'Gospel' only!" Of course, this assumes that the Great Commission applies only to the inner, private lives of people and the salvation of their souls for the next world alone. In short, it limits the definition of the Christian calling in such a way as to exclude its social aspects up front.

Dr. Baldwin's wonderful book illustrates how preachers of a bygone, but crucial and formative, era thought and practiced *just the opposite*. After mountains of research in colonial sermons, tracts, pamphlets, archives, and other publications, she relates how the substantial pulpits of colonial America rang constantly with teaching on all aspects of the public square: good rulers, good laws, good forms of government, the blessings of liberty. We especially hear of those choice values of biblical order that became the hallmarks and battle cries of American independence. These are best summarized in Baldwin's own Conclusion:

> Out of reading and discussion, preaching and practice there had grown up a body of constitutional doctrine, very closely associated with theology and church polity, and commonly accepted by New Englanders. Most significant was the conviction that fundamental law was the basis of all rights. God ruled over men by a divine constitution. Natural and Christian rights were legal rights because a part of the law of God. The peculiar privileges of Englishmen were guaranteed by the constitution. Every part of the government was limited in power by the constitution. Any act contrary to the constitution was illegal and therefore null and void.

> Probably the most fundamental principle of the American constitutional system is the principle that no one is bound to obey an unconstitutional act. The present study reveals that this doctrine was taught in fullness and taught repeatedly before 1763. The enquiry is sometimes made why the courts in America have the power of declaring laws void, why, in other words, the courts have accepted the principle that no one is bound by an unconstitutional act. No single idea was more fully stressed, no principle more often repeated, through the first sixty years of the eighteenth century, than that

governments must obey law and that he who resisted one in authority who was violating that law was not himself a rebel but a protector of law.[1]

She goes so far as to note that we cannot properly understand the nature of the American system without understanding the message preached by the American pulpit constantly over the decades leading up to independence. Commenting on the classic paraphrase of "life, liberty, and property," she proclaims,

> No one can fully understand the American Revolution and the American constitutional system without a realization of the long history and religious associations which lie behind these words; without realizing that for a hundred years before the Revolution men were taught that these rights were protected by divine, inviolable law.[2]

And it will surprise many—especially those who focus too much on the influence of the Enlightenment—just how these great preachers derived their doctrines.

The Bible and the Law of God

Baldwin's work is a phenomenal resource by which to learn of the true influence of Christianity and the Bible in the founding of this nation. It serves as a flat refutation of secularist critics who wish to kill and bury our Christian heritage. But the book also serves as a corrective to some overzealous advocates of America's Christian heritage who sometimes cannot seem to remove from intense focus on the brief period of the framing of the national Constitution, 1787–1789.

It has been my argument that in order to see the real Christian roots of our heritage, you must turn back before the framing era

---

1. Pp. 212–213. (All such references following, except otherwise noted, are to page numbers below.)
2. P. 51.

and focus instead upon the colonial era leading up to it. In *Restoring America One County at a Time*, I make the point:

> In order to find the *true* Christian foundations of this
> country, we need to look back before those who are often
> mistakenly called "founders" to discover the clear biblical
> ideas that existed in society and government *before* their
> era—principles which were lost, neglected, marginalized,
> or even suppressed during the later "founding" era. Much
> of what we have come to associate with "Christian Amer-
> ica" was actually the product of a late nineteenth-century
> progressive, imperialism which was Christian in name
> only and rarely if ever could cite the Bible to confirm its
> political and social policies. Aside from some Christian
> rhetoric—which was more political than biblical—there
> has remained a gap between Sunday school lessons and
> any comprehensive application of biblical ideals to society
> from the Pilgrim and Puritan era until today.[3]

Part of the difficulty has been the misunderstanding of a tremendous study undertaken by political scientists Donald Lutz and
Charles Hyneman concerning the intellectual influences of the
"founding era" which they described as 1760–1805. The results
were published in 1984, and they made clear the pervasive impact
of the Bible upon the American political culture in part of that era.
But they were a bit misunderstood to say something they did not:
some related the results so as to give the impression that the later
constitutional framers had widely cited the Bible in their writings—especially the book of Deuteronomy! But this was not what
the data showed. The data showed that the vast quantity of quotations from the Bible, including a bulk from Deuteronomy, had
appeared in publications during the *earlier* part of that era—years
before the Philadelphia Convention. What should have eradicated

---

3. Joel McDurmon, *Restoring America One County at a Time* (Powder Springs,
GA: American Vision, 2012), 2–3.

any misunderstanding was the author of the study's own comment that as the era crept closer to the time of the Convention, "The Bible's prominence disappears" in the data.

I have done more detailed analysis of this study elsewhere.[4] I relate it here only to highlight the crucial important of Dr. Baldwin's book which follows. What Lutz and Hyneman uncovered from the generations of preachers leading up to American independence was here revealed in startling relief already in 1928. Baldwin wasted no time getting to the point:

> It must not be forgotten, in the multiplicity of authors mentioned, that the source of greatest authority and the one most commonly used was the Bible. The New England preacher drew his beliefs largely from the Bible, which was to him a sacred book, infallible, God's will for man. Of necessity it colored his political thinking. His conception of God, of God's law, and of God's relation to man determined to a large extent his conception of human law and of man's relation to his fellows. If his ideas of government and the rights of man were in part derived from other sources, they were strengthened and sanctioned by Holy Writ. This was of course especially true of the clergy. They stood before the people as interpreters of God's will. Their political speeches were sermons, their political slogans were often Bible texts. What they taught of government had about it the authority of the divine.[5]

This reality leads Baldwin into a study of the political and governmental concepts these pastors actually derived from Scripture, as summarized above, and chief among them is the application of God's Law to life. While the preachers often referred to "the law of nature," Baldwin notes that in their minds, this was not distinct

---

4. Joel McDurmon, "The Framers and their allegedly frequent Bible quotations," http://americanvision.org/6415/the-framers-and-their-allegedly-frequent-bible-quotations, Sept. 28, 2012 (accessed Nov. 18, 2014).

5. Pp. 16–17.

from the "law of God." Were there any question at all, the preachers turned to the written revelation of God's Law, including Old Testament law, to make it clear:

> The revelation in the Old and New Testaments helped to make clear the law of nature and to disclose its full extent. In the Old Testament God gave to man a "positive law." It was true that some of its statutes applied to the Jews only, but there were also great moral principles which applied to all phases of man's activity, now as formerly, and were equally binding. Thus even in that part of Old Testament law which no longer applied to Christians and in the history of God's dealings with His chosen people there were many examples for men of today.[6]

To be sure, the relationships between certain theological terms, and the uses to which they were put, were not always uniform or even purely biblical. In fact, some of the preachers themselves departed from orthodoxy in someways. But in large measure, the most important doctrines of American liberty arose from a biblical understanding and application of God's Law. Thus Baldwin could conclude, "There was no conflict in their minds between the divine and natural law. They were the same"; and thus, "from the law of God they derived their political theories."[7]

Application of Biblical Law

These men truly held the Bible in high esteem, and as a result, they expected to see it actually *applied* in all areas of life, including politics and government. As such, they required their governing officials to be Christians, and not only Christians, but ardent students of that divine book, the Bible, and its laws. Baldwin relates this understanding and how the preachers of the era were at the forefront of making it a real-world demand:

---

6. P. 21.
7. P. 29.

Rulers must study carefully the law of God, both natural and revealed. In the Bible are found all the maxims
and rules of government: there the natural laws are
made clearer, there the ruler learns his due authority
and its limitations, there the people learn how far they
must submit. Rulers must also thoroughly understand
the constitution and the civil law, that they may learn
their obligations and the people's rights. Even when
God dealt with the Jews who were under His immediate government, He had their rulers write down the
constitution in a book and read it constantly. It was
evident that knowledge and ability were necessary, and
the clergy were unanimous in requiring these qualities
in civil rulers and for the most part in their ministers
as well.[8]

These relationships between God and government, between
God and people, and between government and people, were established through the biblical concept of *covenant*—a theme which
surfaces frequently in this study. This, too, was derived directly
from Old Testament revelation, and formed the basis of both theology and government for the New England minister:

His theology depended upon it, it was the foundation
of his church government, he believed it to be at the
root of all God's dealings with men. When he searched
the Bible he found, so he believed, that even the Jewish
government, which was peculiarly God's own, rested
on compact. When he questioned Reason and Nature,
which to him were the voice of God, again he found
the compact or covenant. When he read the wise men
of the past and of his own day, once more he found
it. When he looked at his own environment he found
it there. The charters were considered compacts, and

---

8. Pp. 46–47.

when men set up new towns they drew up a town covenant. It became in practical experience the only way to
form a corporate body.[9]

She further relates how this concept had *deep* historical roots
reaching all the way back to the covenant theology of the earliest colonists. Yet even as late as 1780, one of the more prominent preachers, Samuel Cooper, was preaching this doctrine—with explicit reference to the ancient Hebrew republic—before the Massachusetts
House of Representatives and Governor John Hancock.[10]

But the application of biblical law did not stop at theoretical
constructs or generalities. Preachers routinely went on to preach
on specific principles with real-world consequences—including
armed resistance and civil disobedience where necessary. In fact,
echoing the teachings of Reformers from centuries before them,
many of these preachers decreed laws, or even whole governments,
invalid should they defy biblical order or biblical laws. For example,
as Baldwin summarizes, Elisha Williams preached in 1744 that

> [G]overnments which did not originate from the people
> and in which they did not make their own laws were not,
> properly speaking, governments at all, but tyrannies and
> "absolutely against the Law of God and Nature."[11]

Examples abound. Stephen Johnson's Fast Day Sermon of
1765 was one of the more potent. As Baldwin relates it, "No obedience was due to any edicts which were unconstitutional. . . . Where
executive and legislative authority exceed the bounds of the law of
God and the constitution, then their acts are *ipso facto* void."[12] This
was hard-core nullification doctrine long before it was cool.

---

9. Pp. 32–33.

10. See Eran Shalev, "'A Perfect Republic': The Mosaic Constitution in Revolutionary New England, 1775–1788," *The New England Quarterly* 82/2 (June
2009), 235–263, for this and many more examples of the application of Old
Testament Law to the American formative era.

11. P. 41.

12. Pp. 128–129.

Preaching in 1757 at one of my favorite venues of the time—annual "artillery elections"—James Cogswell gave a stirring call even to arms in defense of religion:

> There is a Principle of Self-Defence and Preservation, implanted in our very Natures, which is necessary to us almost as our Beings, and which no positive Law of God ever yet contradicted. . . . *When our Liberty is invaded and struck at, 'tis sufficient Reason for our making War for the Defence or Recovery of it.* Liberty is one of the most sacred and inviolable Privileges Mankind enjoy; . . . what Comfort can a Man take in Life when at the Disposal of a despotic and arbitrary Tyrant, who has no other law but his Will: . . . To live is to be free: Therefore when our Liberty is attacked, and clandestine, underhand Machinations, or open Violence threaten us with the loss of so dear a Blessing, 'tis Time to rouze, and defend our undoubted and invaluable Privileges . . . *When our Religion is in danger . . . it will warrant our Engaging in War.* . . . Religion is a treasure never to be parted with . . . we fight for our Properties, our Liberties, our Religion, our Lives.[13]

Note the almost seamless, organic relationship between religious and civil freedom in this argument. Such was fundamental throughout the era.

All of these doctrines stemmed from the understanding that the Christian life should not be confined merely to private devotions and the four walls of a closet, or even of a church building. Instead, the liberty which Christ purchased for us included within it also political liberty. Preachers demanded this be recognized and applied. Preaching the annual Thanksgiving Sermon in 1766, Joseph Emerson made this view explicit. He openly gave thanks for a political victory in the form of the repeal of the Stamp Act:

---

13. P. 110, footnote 16; emphases added.

And what is the great, the mighty deliverance we have experienced? . . . Is it of such value as to demand a whole day
to be spent in praising God for it? Yes, our lives,—yea,
eternity,—as *it is what our Savior purchased for us*, and as
there are such glorious things, of a spiritual nature, connected with it. And what is it? A deliverance from slavery;—nothing less than from vile ignominious slavery.[14]

Again, the pulpits' appeal to liberty was hardly uncommon.
Just the opposite. As Baldwin notes, "There is hardly a Massachusetts sermon of these days which does not mention liberty."[15] And
while there may have been varying degrees of radicalism in regard
to liberty, the vast majority wanted more of it.

In the defense and advance of liberty, pulpits did not fear
to thunder against specific legislation—a "no-no" under today's
501(c)3 arrangement. Among the most memorable instances
was widespread denunciation of the Stamp Act of 1765. Baldwin
notes the ministry of the prominent minister Jonas Clarke, who
not only routinely imbued his flock with biblical principles for
natural rights and liberty, but directly attacked the Stamp Act for
infringing upon them.[16]

One of the most prominent clergymen, Charles Chauncey,
was not even to the point of advocating independence yet (most
were not in 1765), and yet noted such an esteem for civil liberty
among the colonists that he proclaimed the Act could never be
enforced without bloodshed.[17]

In another instance, Emerson attacked the use of admiralty
courts as a destruction of English Common Law and liberty upheld as anciently as Magna Charta. Imagine hearing a sermon
today on the evils of civil jurisprudence—of the evils of things
like administrative courts, child protective services, tax courts, and

---

14. P. 123, footnote 44 below; emphasis added.
15. P. 138.
16. See pp. 120–121.
17. P. 117.

xvi   The New England Pulpit and the American Revolution

more. The comparison would not be too dissimilar.

The pulpits' interest in governmental acts continued even more intensely after independence, into the formation of state constitutions:

> The ministerial eye was fixed watchfully upon the legislature, and when a constitution was presented to them that had not been formed in this fashion they led their townspeople to reject it, proceeded to give their reasons, and continued their demands upon the Assembly. For example, when the town of Billerica began in 1775 to consider the form of government to be adopted, it chose as one of its committee its beloved and democratic minister Henry Cummings, who had directed its earlier action against Great Britain.... Cummings was but one of many clergymen who were active in procuring the rejection of the constitution of 1778 by their towns.[18]

In these efforts, note, the clergymen used every outlet open to them. They were active in many public committees, town halls, public venues, and published often in newspapers and pamphlets, not to mention the constant use of their most familiar tool, the pulpit. By faithfully proclaiming the whole counsel of God to every area of life, these men shook a tyranny to its foundations and helped rebuild a free society upon its ruins. And it all began by patiently, persistently molding the hearts and minds of an entire generation before.

Shaping the Public Mind

This point must not be lost on us. These preachers did not appear on the scene only when tyranny suddenly arose. They had been working constantly in teaching and training their flocks, and the broader public, in the biblical message of freedom and political liberty. It was through steady and purposeful labor over time that

18. P. 173.

their influence pervaded the populace and laid the foundations for resilience in the midst of crisis.

Baldwin notes this labor in the background, for example, in the preaching of the aforementioned Jonas Clarke: "For years before the Stamp Act he is said to have preached Sunday after Sunday and explained in many a town meeting the doctrines of natural and constitutional rights and the right of resistance."[19]

She comments further, with a note of lament for our own time, but underscoring the same principle:

> It seems a most significant fact, and one never sufficiently realized by historians, that for the seven years before the beginning of the trouble with England the people had heard continually from the pulpit such ringing words upon the unspeakable value of their chartered privileges and their rights as Englishmen; of law and constitution as contrasted with tyranny and arbitrary government; of the danger of becoming slaves and losing all their freedom, civil and religious, under such a government; of the justification of war in defense of their cherished rights and liberties.[20]

In fact, she continues, "It is true that hardly any idea in any sermon had not been presented through an unbroken continuity of nearly a hundred years. . . ." By the time the crises came, the doctrines of liberty and resistance were "familiar old themes," "common convictions," and "nothing new."[21] The foundations had for so long been laid, it was natural for the people to think in terms of them. And when the tyrants began to encroach, it was natural for the people to view them as progressive enemies, and themselves as the "true conservatives" who were doing nothing more than "supporting the traditions of the past."[22]

19. P. 120.
20. P. 113.
21. See pp. 113, 105, 131.
22. P. 133.

The influence of these ministers spread just as broadly as their worldview and their devotion to it. Far from treating only personal piety, the broad vision and rousing passion of the preachers inspired men to change a nation in many ways. It was said, for example, that the preaching of Stephen Johnson in the 1760s inspired the organization of the Sons of Liberty—famed for their execution of the Boston Tea Party.[23]

When fighting later broke out, ministers served, and sometimes led. They led recruiting efforts, often drawing volunteers with stirring sermons where regular recruiters had failed.[24] Ministers served in various ways, including fighting. Baldwin has an entire chapter (11) on these varied services which often included opening their homes to masses of workers, and in some cases, sacrificing financially from their already-meager salaries.[25] There are even anecdotes of ministers preaching in church with muskets loaded at their side, and stores of gunpowder hidden in the pulpit.[26] (Talk about "fire and brimstone"!)

The pulpit lay behind all of these acts and sacrifices of liberty. It is not surprising, therefore, to find that the pulpit declared independence long before the state actually did. Independence was ringing to various degrees from many pulpits already in 1774. The fiery John Cleaveland anticipated the language of the famous 1776 Declaration in his own words over a year before, declaring all the political connections broken and allegiance to Britain totally dissolved.[27]

Preaching and teaching the people in such a way meant having a populace readied and trained for acts of liberty. This would culminate, of course, in the efforts for new constitutions. Drawing upon their lessons about representative government and government by covenant or compact, the colonists naturally moved to

---

23. P. 126, footnote 52.
24. P. 153.
25. P. 209.
26. P. 207.
27. P. 165.

practice what had been preached. As a result, Baldwin says, "The constitutional convention and the written constitution were the children of the pulpit."[28]

Push and Pull

There was certainly some opposition to these preachers in their day. Those who were loyal to Great Britain simply observed in shock and dismay as preachers led hordes of trained Bible-believers into sacrificial acts of bravery and defense of liberty. The loyalist establishment had not considered how decades, even centuries, of applying God's Law to government in the hearts and minds of the people would manifest in fierce loyalty to freedom in the face of tyranny. When the time came, however, that those covetous of power tried to enforce wicked laws, they found themselves confronted by an army of parishioners led by preachers.

It is no wonder, then, that such loyalists would consider these ministers the driving force behind what they viewed as rebellion. James Otis, Jr. (not a minister), had won popularity by withstanding unlawful searches and seizures of property granted by intrusive and unchecked "writs of assistance" (search warrants) in 1761. Looking back on the era, loyalist Justice and historian Peter Oliver viewed the clergy as nothing more than Otis's henchmen—in fact, a veritable militia of their own. Referring to their black Geneva gowns, he called the preachers the "the black regiment," saying "it was in vain to struggle against the Law of Otis, & the Gospel of his black Regiment."[29]

As we compare, once again, their day and ours, we can hear an eerie note of correspondence, and it is not flattering. The parallel appears not in the fierce cries from the pulpit against tyranny, courts, taxes, and legislation, but rather from the loyalists who

---

28. P. 170. Here she is speaking in general of written constitutions and conventions, most likely with the Massachusetts state assembly in mind, which culminated in 1780. She is not speaking of the later national convention of 1787–1788, although the concepts apply in a more secularized form.

29. P. 124, footnote 48.

supported the tyranny! And what was their demand of the clergy at the time?

It was none other than the same cry as our own preachers to-day: "Don't preach politics!" Stick to "the Gospel" only! Indeed, the same Peter Oliver complained that "The Clergy had quite unlearned the Gospel, & had substituted Politicks in its Stead."[30] Likewise, a sermon by Boston preacher William Gordon elicited loyalist pamphlets in response, one of which scolded the "reverend politician" and sighed, "I most heartily wish . . . that he and many others of his profession would confine themselves to gospel truth."[31]

It is understandable that a tyrant would wish to censor the whole counsel of God, especially as it moves populations to resist tyrants. But the sadness of our time is that we do not even need tyrants to intimidate us into silence. Our preachers and Christians do it to themselves.

Since around the 1780s, and really gathering steam around the 1800s, a sappy piety crept in and overtook the hearts and minds of American Christians, and especially of their pulpits. We turned away from our heritage of covenant theology along with its emphases on great and godly social institutions—family, church, and state—and a corresponding love of God's Law in those institutions. We have instead turned inwardly to private, personal devotions and songs on Sundays. In doing so, we have lost the great heritage of godly civilization passed down to us.

The church in our era has neutered its own pulpit and silenced itself. No, we do not need tyrants to censor us. We have censored ourselves with poor theology, fear of law, fear of consequences, and a perverse longing for escape through rapture.

If there is any note struck in this book that should move us— and there is hardly a note which should not—it ought to be the prescient fear voiced in the early "College Hall Addresses" in New Hampshire when independence was debated and deliberated. The great fear of that people was that they might throw off the yoke of

---

30. P. 154, footnote 1.
31. P. 164, footnote 30.

tyranny only to replace it with a worse one of their own making. Baldwin quotes from one of their memorials:

> [I]t is a thousand pities, that when we are engaged in a bloody contest, merely to oppose arbitrary power without us, we should have occasion to contend against the same within ourselves; especially by those who profess to be friends of liberty.... As for ourselves, we are determined not to spend our blood and treasure, in defending against the chains and fetters, that are forged and prepared for us abroad, in order to purchase some of the like kind of our own manufacturing.—But mean to hold them alike detestable....[32]

Whereas this was a note of warning to themselves in 1776, it is a resounding trumpet of condemnation to us today.

One preacher, like the men of Issachar, showed particularly keen understanding of his times. Commemorating the Battle of Lexington (merely a year later), and yet still a couple months before the fateful July 4, 1776, Jonas Clarke declared from the pulpit: "From this day will be dated the Liberty of the world." From "this day"—the day of the Battles of Lexington and Concord, in which British soldiers attempted to raid the artillery and disarm the American people. Preachers had been preparing those soldiers for years prior, preaching on rights, arms, politics, law, and government, tyranny and war. And it was at that Battle that, reportedly, the preacher himself—the same Jonas Clarke—had led riflemen to repel the British.

Where are such preachers today? What do we hold dear? For what are we willing to fight and die? Are we willing even to *preach* the doctrines of government, liberty, and God's Law? Where are the sermons, tracts, and pamphlets circulating today from America's preachers condemning taxes and tyranny? Preachers in the 1760s spoke out, and some spilled their blood, to fight the

---

32. P. 191.

erosion of jurisprudence and the onset of admiralty courts! Today we have a vast array of this type of court tyrannizing nearly every area of life, and hardly a pulpit even knows, let alone cares, let alone preaches. We had ministers leading men in the sacrifice of their lives and money over intrusive search warrants and seizures of property. Today where are even the sermons on these things?

Pulpits across this land should be ringing with denunciation of warrantless wiretaps, extrajudicial drone strikes, no-knock warrants, militarization of police, civil forfeiture, the surveillance state, the welfare-warfare state, fiat money, tyrannized markets, executive orders, national emergencies, and a thousand other infractions so extreme and overt they would have driven King George III to join the rebellion himself. And the pulpits are silent.

The pulpits are silent, the flocks left untrained, the people unmotivated, and liberty all but dead. And we have no one to blame but ourselves.

If liberty is ever to be restored in this, or any, nation, it will only come through a return to the message enshrined in Christ and His commandments. God may see fit to circumvent the rebellious and stubborn preachers who stand idly and cower today. It may please Him to replace them with a more faithful movement in some way. Yet it is most natural for us to call the preachers to repentance, and back to faithfulness, in hope that the pulpit will once again fulfill its role as the voice of liberty in the land.

A substantial first step toward that end would be to recover the lost history of our pulpits—of a time when America's pastors preached politics, resisted tyranny, and founded a nation on the Bible. Dr. Baldwin's nearly-forgotten book is a perfect source from which to start relearning. I strongly recommend it to every pastor and every Christian—and I recommend they follow the example of its subject matter even more.

Preface
(to the original)

*T*he first half of this study, in somewhat different form, was submitted under the title *The Influence of the New England Clergy upon American Constitutional Doctrine* in partial fulfillment of the requirements for the degree of Doctor of Philosophy at the University of Chicago; and it is with sincere gratitude that I acknowledge my indebtedness to Professors Andrew C. McLaughlin and Marcus Jernegan for their suggestions, criticism, and constant encouragement during the preparation of my thesis. In the difficult process of transforming the thesis into a book, I have been greatly aided by Professor W. K. Boyd of Duke University. And for her help in the reading of proof and in various ways I am indebted to my assistant, Miss Louise Seabolt.

I wish further to express my appreciation both of the generosity of the Duke University Press in publishing this monograph and of its staff in seeing it through the troublesome transition from manuscript to print; and also of the courtesy shown me by the librarians of the many libraries whose collections I have used, especially by Mr. G. S. Godard of the Connecticut State Library, by Mr. A. C. Bates of the Connecticut Historical Society, and by Mrs. Shepherdson and Mr. J. H. Tuttle of the Massachusetts Historical Society.

Finally, the following study has not been for me one of merely academic interest. My grandfather, Rev. Josiah Lyman, of

Easthampton, Massachusetts, my father, Dr. Fritz W. Baldwin, and my uncle, Dr. Albert J. Lyman, were all Congregational clergymen; and it was through them that I first learned to appreciate, in some measure, the ministers of New England. To their memory, also, therefore, I owe an expression of my indebtedness.

A.M.B.

Introduction

*I*n recent years, historians have realized as never before the complexity of the American Revolution and that its roots stretch far back into the earlier days. To weigh fairly the different causes and factors—geographic, economic, social, political, and religious—is a difficult task, and there is still controversy as to the emphasis which each should have. One factor which was recognized by contemporary writers as especially significant but which, until recent years, has been touched but lightly by later authors is the religious. Men of the time asserted that the dissenting clergy and especially the Puritan clergy of New England were among the chief agitators of the Revolution and, after it began, among the most zealous and successful in keeping it alive.

Similar statements have been made by later writers and certain of the more prominent clergy, especially Mayhew, Cooper, and Chauncey, of Boston, have been mentioned frequently as Revolutionary leaders. A few of the more famous political sermons have been collected and republished.[1] Biographies, town histories, histories of American literature, etc., have given us bits about the work of this or that individual and have discussed, to some extent,

---

1. J. W. Thornton, *The Pulpit of the American Revolution*; Frank Moore, ed., *The Patriot Preachers of the American Revolution*; J. S. Loring, *The Hundred Boston Orators, 1770–1852.*

1

his political theories. Among modern historians Cross in his careful study of the project of an Anglican Episcopate,[2] Van Tyne in his studies on the American Revolution,[3] and J. T. Adams in his first two volumes on New England history,[4] are especially notable for their emphasis upon the significance of the religious factor and the work of the clergy. But the first deals with one phase only of the subject, and the limits of Van Tyne's single volume and short article preclude any detailed treatment. Adams, although he gives great weight to the clergy, especially during the seventeenth century, does not recognize sufficiently the part they played in teaching political theory to the people both before and after 1763 and in giving to the theories religious sanction, nor does he emphasize sufficiently the bearing of the ecclesiastical quarrels and religious movements of the eighteenth century upon the development of a spirit of independence, a love of liberty, and the use of arguments with which to support it.

In short, the intimate relation of the New England minister to the thought and life of eighteenth-century New England has never been adequately developed. That is the purpose of this study: first, to make clear the similarity, the identity of Puritan theology and fundamental political thought; second, to show how the New England clergy preserved, extended, and popularized the essential doctrines of political philosophy, thus making familiar to every church-going New Englander long before 1763 not only the doctrines of natural right, the social contract, and the right of resistance, but also the fundamental principle of American constitutional law, that government, like its citizens, is bounded by law and when it transcends its authority it acts illegally. The author believes that here can be traced a direct line of descent from

---

2. A. L. Cross, *The Anglican Episcopate and the American Colonies.*

3. C. Van Tyne, *The Causes of the War of Independence*; also, "Influence of the Clergy and of Religious and Sectarian Forces on the American Revolution," in *Amer. Hist. Rev.,* XIX. 44–64.

4. J. T. Adams, *The Founding of New England; Revolutionary New England, 1691–1776.*

seventeenth-century philosophy to the doctrines underlying the American Revolution and the making of written constitutions. It is hoped that the study may explain, in some measure, why these theories were so widely held, so dearly cherished, and so deeply inwrought into American constitutional doctrine. And, finally, an attempt is made to present, in some detail, the activities of the clergy in the events of the Revolution and in establishing the institutions of the new-born states.

Further, it should be remembered that throughout the colonial period the great majority of the people in all the New England colonies except Rhode Island were Congregationalists, who sometimes and in some places approached so closely to Presbyterianism that it is hard to distinguish accurately between the two sects. Such distinction was frequently not made at all at the time of the Revolution by their adversaries, who applied the name Presbyterian to both indiscriminately. There were, however, churches definitely organized into Presbyteries and, as the eighteenth century progressed, an increasing number of Baptists and Episcopalians.[5] This study deals primarily with the Nonconformist clergy, making

5. Ezra Stiles, in his *Discourse on Christian Union*, 1760, p. 130, estimates that there were at that time 300 Congregational churches in Massachusetts, 170 in Connecticut, 43 in New Hampshire—530 in all. Charles Chauncey, in *A Letter to a Friend*, 1767, note p. 8, says that at the lowest computation there were not less than 550 regularly ordained ministers in New England, some Presbyterian, mostly Congregational. Clark, in *Congregational Churches in Massachusetts*, p. 193, computes that in 1770 there were in Massachusetts 294 Congregational churches, 11 Episcopalian, 16 Baptist, 18 Quaker. The proportion was approximately the same elsewhere in New England, perhaps more Episcopalians in Connecticut and more Baptists in Rhode Island. Guild, in *Chaplain Smith and the Baptists*, note p. 157, says that in 1764 there were less than 70 Baptist churches in America, with possibly 5000 members. They grew rapidly in numbers, especially after 1774. Briggs, in his *American Ptesbyterianism*, pp. 342–43, says that at the time of the Revolution there were five Presbyteries in New England with thirty-two ministers. Certain of the Presbyterian churches, notably in the Grafton Presbytery, had been Congregational. The churches sometimes shifted from one to the other several times. In Connecticut, the consociated churches based on the Saybrook Platform, approached closely to Presbyterianism.

such distinction between the various sects as may be necessary when essential differences of opinion in theology or politics appear. Unless, then, the sect is mentioned, the term "clergy" is to be understood as applying to the Non-conformists and especially to the Congregationalists and Presbyterians.

One

The Eighteenth-Century Minister, His Power and Learning

*T*he New England clergy of the eighteenth century occupied a position of peculiar influence and power in the life of their own communities and of the several colonies. It is true that they had lost something of the respect and reverence as well as much of the political power which they had enjoyed in the first sixty years of settlement and expansion. Nevertheless, it is unsafe to conclude that their parishioners did not on the whole respect them and that their influence was small. There is abundant evidence to the contrary.[1]

They were for the most part a "learned clergy," graduates of Harvard or of Yale.[2] Shortly after graduation the young ministers

---

1. See Adams, *Founding of New England*, pp. 450–51; *Revolutionary New England*, pp. 169–73; Sabine, *Loyalists of the American Revolution*, I. 59; and various other references throughout this study. Certain of the election sermons of the early eighteenth century, especially in Connecticut, lament the disaffection of the people to the ministry. See Chauncey, 1719, pp. 48–50; Marsh, 1721, pp. 38–39; Williams, 1723, pp. 48–51. Some of the reasons for this criticism will be explained later.

2. Of 52 settled Congregational ministers in New Hampshire in 1764, 48, says Stackpole, were college graduates. From 1748–1800, nine-tenths were college graduates (*History of New Hampshire*, II. 304). Many of the Baptist and Separate Congregational clergy were not educated men. In 1764, Guild says, there were but two liberally educated Baptist ministers in New England (*Chap-*

were settled in their new parishes, where they often remained throughout their lives. Sometimes they were given land, money, or some other special inducement to settle and were usually promised a salary which, when paid regularly and in specie, meant comfort at least. But frequently the salary was in arrears or paid in depreciated currency and at the best was none too large to meet the demands of such a position. For the most part the ministers lived in small towns or smaller villages and stretched their salaries to the family needs by farming or by taking into their homes a few boys whom they fitted for college or trained for the ministry. Here they lived among their people, on week days settling disputes and occasionally, in the remoter districts, serving as doctor or even as village lawyer or school teacher,[3] on the Sabbath preaching to men and women whose lives they intimately shared. They were sober and industrious in their ways, usually dignified in their bearing, and they spoke as men having authority. "You must expect if you come to Danbury to be a good deal noticed & perhaps gazed at," wrote young Ebenezer Baldwin in 1763 to his sister Bethiah, "for to be the Minister's sister you know in a Country Town is a considerable thing."[4]

In those days of few newspapers and fewer books and of little travel, the ministers who perhaps attended the annual ministerial conventions, or at least the meetings of the local associations, who read more than most of their neighbors, who corresponded with their fellow-ministers and men of other towns and colonies, who had often been the classmates and remained the friends of the rising young lawyers and merchants, were likely to be a means of contact between their parishioners and the outside world. As teachers who prepared the more ambitious boys for college, they had an opportunity to impress them with their own beliefs. As

lain Smith, p. 49). Before 1783 there were a good many more.

3. The latter was rare. For examples and discussion, see *Centennial Papers of the General Conference, Connecticut, 1867*, pp. 28–30; B. Emerson, *The Ipswich Emersons*, pp. 91, 94, 95; Stackpole, *History of New Hampshire*, p. 307; Holland, *History of Western Massachusetts*, p. 279.

4. *New Haven Colony Hist. Soc. Papers*, IX. 164.

preachers they had at least a weekly opportunity to reach most of the people living in the parish, who if not church members were usually church attendants. They preached not only on Sunday but on many special occasions prescribed by the churches or ordered by the colonial assemblies, such as days of fasting and prayer and days of thanksgiving. If special news arrived, such as the death of the King, a defeat or victory in war, the minister was likely to make the most of it, and to his country audience a sermon on such a theme must have been especially welcome. Here was a fine opportunity to impress upon the community his political beliefs. Moreover, not only were doctrinal and political sermons heard from the pulpit, but also bits of important letters, decisions of ecclesiastical councils, proclamations from the seat of government, news from the army.[5]

In the larger towns there was also a weekly lecture, less religious in character, at which a sermon was preached. And in the chief cities there had long been special occasions which gave the clergy opportunities to get their ideas before the public. There was the annual ministerial convention which came, in Massachusetts at least, at the time of the election of the Council. In Massachusetts there was the annual artillery election. In Connecticut, in Massachusetts, in Plymouth so long as it remained a separate colony, and in Vermont after 1778, there was the general election day, coming always in the spring, when the Council was elected and a special minister was chosen to preach the sermon which was, as a rule, printed by order of the Assembly and distributed, usually, it would seem, one copy to each member of the Assembly and sometimes at least one or more to the minister or ministers of the towns.[6]

5. Wheelock's *Memoirs*, p. 217. He read a letter of Dennis de Berdt during the French and Indian War and said he would read others of interest. See also Love, *Fast and Thanksgiving Days of New England*.

6. See Bibliography; also Walker, *A History of the Congregational Churches in the United States*, pp. 244–45, and Thornton, *Pulpit of the American Revolution*, pp. xxiii–xxvi.

There seems to be some question as to the frequency of their publication at the expense of the General Court. Many say in the frontispiece that a copy was

Some of these election sermons discussed the government of
the ancient Hebrews and its excellencies; many were theoretical,
concerned with the origin and end of government; some dealt more
particularly with their own charters and the dearly-won rights of
Englishmen; some, with great freedom of speech, gave practical
advice to the Assembly about well-known evils and desirable laws;
the majority discussed in greater or less detail the qualities and re-
sponsibilities of magistrates. Year after year the same themes were
discussed; often the same phraseology was used. Usually enough
of the writer's own attitude appears to enable the reader to judge of
his conservatism or liberalism. Now and again there was an election preacher who was exceptionally direct and thorough-going
in his discussion either of government or of the agitations of the
day, or of both. But whether stereotyped or original, conservative
or radical, for a hundred years before the Revolution and year by
year throughout the long conflict, these sermons dealt with matters of government. They were heard by large audiences of clergy
and laymen; they had the prestige of well-known names and of
the colonial assembly attached to them; they were sent to friends
in other colonies and in England and were distributed regularly
to the country towns where they became, as Winsor styles them,
"text-books of politics."[7] Thus they passed from hand to hand

---

desired by the Assembly for the printer. In 1684 the General Court thanked
Mr. Hale for his Election Sermon, desired a copy for the press, and desired that
"effectual care" be taken "that ye same be printed at ye publique charge" (*Mass.
Archives*, XI, no. 33a). Joseph Belcher's Election Sermon of 1701 was printed
by order and 500 copies distributed among the towns. At least four imprints
of this sermon were made. In 1775, Mr. Langdon's sermon was printed and a
copy sent by order of Court to each minister and member of Congress (Swift,
p. 426). If a sermon by its boldness displeased the Court there was occasionally some hesitation about printing it. See Sewall, *Letter Book*, II. 236–37,
note. Foxcroft's sermon before Court was printed by the Court (Sewall's *Letter
Book*, II. 232). With very few exceptions, however, these sermons were printed,
whether at public or private expense. The first election sermon was preached
in Mass., 1633; in Conn., 1674; in N.H., 1784; in Vt., 1778. The custom was
peculiar to New England and was continued into the 19th century.

7. J. Winsor, *Memorial History of Boston*, III. 120, says that the small village

and from colony to colony. Their theories and even their phrases reached the ears of townsmen and countrymen. Possibly men may often have been unheeding because of the constant repetition, but that very repetition through so many years must have driven the ideas and phrases home until they became part of the warp and woof of New England thought.

It is not only in the election sermons that one must search for the political theories of the clergy. Other sources, less determined by the long tradition of the occasion, are the political sermons preached to a minister's own people in towns and especially in country villages, the letters and articles written to newspapers, and the correspondence with friends, as well as the town and county documents which they frequently helped to draw up. Especially important are the doctrinal sermons and the pamphlet literature occasioned by the frequent religious and ecclesiastical controversies of the eighteenth century. In these controversies, which often involved laymen as well as clergy, can be seen the reaction of the layman to the ministerial teaching and his application to ecclesiastical matters of the doctrines which he later applied to political questions. Here one sometimes finds striking analogies between

pulpits rang throughout the year with the sentiments of the election sermons, that they served as text books in politics, and that thus the New Englander had become "enlightened in speculative and practical politics to a degree unknown any where else in the world." J. Mayhew, *Observations on the Charter and Conduct of the S. P. G.*, 1763, p. 39, says "the common people of New England, by means of our schools, and the instructions of our 'able, learned, orthodox ministers,' are, and have all along been, philosophers and divines in comparison of the common people in England, of the communion of the church there established. This is commonly said by those who have had an opportunity personally to inform themselves."

That the election and other sermons were widely distributed and read is evident from the frequent mention of them both by the laymen and clergy and by the numerous quotations in other sermons. See note, p. 10; also frequent references in Sewall's *Letter Book* to sermons sent to England, to Conn., to Mass., and other colonies; Cotton Mather, "Diary," (*Mass. Hist. Soc. Coll.*, 7th Ser., VIII. 128–29); *Mass. Hist. Soc. Coll.* LXXIV. 73, 88. See later references to sermons distributed by Mayhew, Chauncey, and others, and to the use of election sermons.

religious and political creeds. Indeed, as one studies this everyday literature of the time, it becomes increasingly evident that the New England ideas of government were intimately connected with the interpretation of the Bible. Although theology was of less importance to the average New Englander in the eighteenth than in the seventeenth century, it still had a far more important place in his life than it has today.

The sources from which the New England ministers developed their theories may be learned partly from the quotations and footnotes which frequently are to be found in sermons and pamphlets, partly from diaries, letters, and other documents. The references by name to ancient and more modern authors did not always mean, however, that the ministers had read their works, but rather had found them referred to or quoted in the works of some historian or Biblical commentator.

The most common source was the Bible. The Old Testament furnished many illustrations of covenant relations, of the limitations placed upon rulers and people, of natural rights, of the divine constitution, etc. The New Testament gave authority for the liberties of Christians, for the relation of Christians to those in authority over them, and for the right of resistance. Indeed, there was never a principle derived from more secular reading that was not strengthened and sanctified by the Scriptures.

Another source seems to have been the writers of classical and late Roman days to which reference was made from the seventeenth century throughout the entire period under discussion. Those most frequently referred to were Thucydides, Aristotle, Plato, Cicero, Vergil, Seneca, Tacitus, Sallust, Plutarch, Pliny, Josephus, and Eusebius; while others such as Socrates, Demosthenes, Caesar, Horace, Lactantius, Juvenal, Suetonius, and the church fathers were occasionally mentioned.

The next great source was the works of John Locke, his essays on religious toleration and human understanding as well as those on government. He was quoted by name as early as 1738, but his influence is to be seen in earlier works. Especially after 1763 the references to him are numerous, not only by the more prominent ministers of the larger towns but by those of country villages as well. And in many works in which no direct reference is made one finds his theories, sometimes his very phrases, and this is true for years before 1761 as well as afterwards.

Other writers to which frequent reference was made before 1761 as well as later were Luther, Calvin, Hoadly, Sydney, Puffendorf, Sir Edward Coke, Milton, Burnet, Butler, Wollaston, and Tillotson,[8] while Voltaire was mentioned only by Mayhew, and Hobbes by Eliphalet Williams and James Dana of Connecticut, the latter quoting him as referred to by Whitby. A common source was the histories of the colonies, of England, and of other countries. Most frequently mentioned after 1761 and sometimes as a source from which Locke's words were taken were Neal's histories of the Puritans and of New England. Others were Rapin's *History of England*, Rider's *History of England*, Perrin's *History of the Waldenses*, and after 1766 Hutchinson's *History of Massachusetts*. Another source of political theory was the commentaries and

---

8. Benjamin Hoadly, *The Common Rights of Subjects Vindicated*, 1718; *Measures of Submission to the Civil Magistrate Considered*, 1705; Algernon Sydney, *Discourses Concerning Government*, a new edition of his works, 1772; Samuel Puffendorf, *The Law of Nature and Nations*, 1703; also, *The divine feudal Law, or Covenants with Mankind represented, together with the Means for uniting of Protestants*, trans. into Eng., 1703; also, *De Officio Hominis et Civis, juxta Legem Naturalem*, 1763 (all had several editions); Bishop Gilbert Burnet, *The History of the Reformation of the Church of England*, 1679, 81; *History of His Own Time*, 2 vols., 1724–34; various pamphlets and sermons; Bishop Butler, *Analogy of Religion, Natural and Revealed, to the Constitution and Course of Nature*, 1736; Sir Ed. Coke, *Institutes of the Laws of England*, 1628; Wm. Wollaston, *The Religion of Nature delineated* (10,000 copies sold by 1738; seven editions between 1728 and 1750; see Lowndes, *Biographers' Manual*, p. 2976); John Tillotson, *Sermons* (vol. I was pub. in 1671; many others later and in many editions; an edition of his works with life pub. in 1752). Colman said that the works of Thos. Bradbury of London were well known and loved (*Colman Papers*, II. no 63). A new edition was published in 1768 and quotations given, especially a sermon in 1713. Stoughton, *History of Religion in England*, V. 397–99, says Bradbury, about 1714, made his pulpit a tribune for assertion of ecclesiastical and civil liberty. A famous sermon of 1712 was very radical.

annotations on the Bible. Those most frequently mentioned were Whitby, Henry, and Pool. After 1761 other authors quoted or referred to by several different men were Harrington, Montesquieu, Lord Somers, Bacon, Blackstone, Dr. Watts, and Dr. Warburton, while occasional reference was made to Junius, Vattel, Burlamaqui, Fortesque, Bracton, and others.[9]

The ministers frequently quoted earlier election sermons, not only in their own election sermons but in other sermons, and in pamphlets, letters, and newspaper articles. They also quoted other works by ministers such as the Magnalia, the pamphlets of John Wise,[10] Stiles's *Christian Union*, the pamphlets of Mayhew and

---

9. Daniel Whitby, *A Paraphrase and Commentary on the New Testament*, 2 vols., 1700, many editions; also sermons, treati ses, and other works; Henry Matthew, *An Exposition of the Old and New Testament*, 5 vols., 1st collective ed. 1710 (many later editions); *Miscellaneous Works*, lst ed. 1726; Matthew Pool, *Synopsis Criticorum aliormnque S. Scripturae Interpretum*, 5 vols., 1669–76; *Annotations upon the Holy Bible*, 1683–5, 2 vols. (various editions); James Harrington, *Oceana*, 1st ed. 1656; *Political Discourses*, 1st ed. 1660; *Works* (many editions); Lord John Somers, *A Collection of scarce and valuable Tracts*, 16 vols., 1748–52; *The Judgement of whole Kingdoms and Nations concerning the Right Power and Prerogative of Kings, and the Rights, Properties and Privileges of the People, etc.*, 1771 (Bohn says this was erroneously attributed to Somers); Isaac Watts, D. D., *Logic, or the right Use of Reason in the Enquiry after Truth*, 1725 (many editions); *Sermons*, 1721–23 (many editions); *Philosophical Essays*, 1734 (a 6 vol. ed. of his works was pub. in 1753); Bishop Wm. Warburton, *The Alliance between Church and State*, 4th ed., 1741; *The Principles of natural and revealed Religion*, 2 vols., 1743–54; *The Divine Legation of Moses, Demonstrated*; many letters and other works; Junius, *Letters*, P69 (some reprmted in Amer. newspapers); Emer de Vattel, *The Law of Nations, or Principles of the Law of Nature applied to the Conduct and Affairs of Nations and Sovereigns*, 1760; J. J. Burlamaqui, *Principles of natural and politic Law*, 2 vols., 1748 (several editions; quoted by Dr. Samuel Cooper in letter to Pownall, 1773; cf. Amer. Hist. Rev. VIII. 327–28); Sir John Fortescue, *De Laudibus Legum Angliae*, 1616. Latin and Engl. ed. 1675; also *The Difference between an absolute and limited Monarchy* (both went through several editions); Henri de Bracton, *De Legibus et Consuetudinibus Angliae Libriquinque*, 1569 (various editions).

10. John Wise, *The Churches Quarrel Espoused*, Boston, 1772, first pub. 1710; *A Vindication of the Government of New England Churches*, in same ed. as above, first pub. 1717. In a copy of the 2nd ed. of 1772 of Wise's books there

Chauncey relating to the work of the S. P. G. After 1765 there was frequent quotation of the political sermons, both election and others.[11] Occasionally political pamphlets not written by clergymen were mentioned. Among these were Paine's *Common Sense*,[12] the articles of the "Farmer,"[13] works by J. Quincy, Jr., and Dr. Price, *The Interest of Great Britain Considered with Regard to Her Colonies*, the *Excellencies of a Free State, Consideration on the Measures Carrying on with Respect to the British Colonies in North America*, and various letters and pamphlets from England, such as the sermons of the Bishops of Llandaff and of St. Asaph.[14]

To illustrate more fully the reading of the ministers it may be interesting to choose a few—of different periods, colonies and position—and list the books to which they referred. Azariah Mather of Haddam in his Connecticut Election Sermon of 1725 referred to "Famous Bolton," Seneca, and Aesop. He quoted from Fuller: "A good Ruler is one that looks on Salus Populi to be Maxima Charta"; from Cicero: "Salus Populi est Finis imperii"; and from Henry: "Good Rulers will be in Pain, when Subjects are in Tears."

---

is a list of subscribers from P–Z; and among them were six ministers, one of whom took six copies.

11. Stiles preserved the political articles published in 1765 by Rev. Stephen Johnson of Lyme in the *New London Gazette*. The Fast Day Sermons of 1765 by Johnson and of 1774 by Sherwood were quoted, among others.

12. Read by Samuel Cooper of Boston. See *Calendar of Franklin Papers*, I. 179. Thos. Allen of Pittsfield also read it.

13. Richard Salter, Connecticut Election Sermon, 1768, p. 39; S. Sherwood, Fast Day Sermon, 1774, p. vii.

14. See Hollis Papers. Various ones sent to Andrew Eliot were read and distributed by him. See also letters between Samuel Cooper and Benj. Franklin. Franklin sent numerous pamphlets to Cooper, such as Beaumont's *Réflexions d'un Etranger désinteressé*, four Irish pamphlets, Molyneux's *Case of Ireand*, etc.; cf. Writings of B. Franklin, V. 254–55, 203–05, 259, 262, 298–99, etc. A pamphlet of 1691, *English Liberties or the Freeborn Subjects' Inheritance*, by Henry Care and Wm. Nelson had its 6th ed. in 1774. Many copies were subscribed for, 466 names being given, many taking several copies; 14 clergymen in Mass. and Conn. are mentioned. In Windham Co., Conn., 120 copies were taken, chiefly by farmers. Six ministers in five out of the eight towns subscribed. See *English Liberties . . .* , 1774, and Larned, *History of Windham County*, II. 140–41.

Jared Eliot of Killingworth, Franklin's friend and correspondent, in his Election Sermon of 1738 referred to Sir William Temple's Memoirs (also mentioned by others), to "Whitby in Loc," Jerome, Tertullian, Locke, "Shuckford's Conect," Rapin, and Puffendorf.[15]

Jonathan Mayhew of Boston had read Harrington, Sydney, Locke, Milton, and Hoadly.[16] Before 1759 Thomas Hollis of London had sent him Sydney's discussion on government and Milton's Eikonoklastes;[17] and in 1764 a new edition of Sydney;[18] in 1764, the new edition of Locke's treatises on government[19] and in 1765 a new edition of Milton's prose works and Andrew Marvel's *Rehearsal Transpos'd*.[20] In his published works Mayhew not only referred to these authors but to Epictetus, Bishop Butler, Dr. Warburton, Voltaire, Sir Thomas More, sermons and addresses by Hobart and other ministers, and various other works of less significance.

Andrew Eliot, another Boston clergyman of prominence, said that Sydney was "the first who taught me to form any just sentiments on government."[21] He also received and read many books

---

15. Mather, pp. 12–15. Robert Bolton was a learned Puritan scholar of the 17th century who wrote many sermons, etc.; Dr. Thomas Fuller wrote sermons, pamphlets, histories, etc. One pub. in 1658 was *The Soveraign's Prerogative and Subject's Privilege*. Dr. Samuel Shuckford in 1728–54 pub. in 4 vols. *The sacred and profane History of the World*, "connected from the Creation of the World to the Dissolution of the Assyrian Empire." This went through several editions.

16. Tudor, *Life of James Otis*, p. 145; Mayhew, *Sermons*, 1748, pp. 37–38, and various references in his other works. John Adams married the daughter of Rev. Wm. Smith of Weymouth. She and her sisters were said to have been versed in Shakespeare, Milton, Tillotson, Berkeley, etc., and not unacquainted with Butler and Locke. See John Adams, *Life and Works*, I. 61, 63. Adams, as a boy, used to listen to Rev. Lemuel Bryant, "a liberal scholar and divine," and the schoolmaster, Joseph Cleverly, argue about government and religion (X. 254). In early days he talked with his cousin, Rev. Zabdiel Adams, about Newton, Bacon, Locke, and many other authors (II. 105).

17. *Hollis Papers, 1759–1770, Letter of Aug. 16, 1759*.

18. *Ibid.*, Nov. 21, 1763.

19. *Ibid.*, no. 35.

20. *Ibid.*, no. 49. Marvell wrote in the 17th century various works on popery and arbitrary government. *The Rehearsal Transpros'd*, was published 1672.

21. *Ibid.*, no. 109.

and pamphlets from Hollis and speaks in his letters of Harrington, Sydney, Locke, Milton, of whose *Defensio pro populo Anglicano* he never wearied,[22] Trenchard's *History of Standing Armies,*[23] and the *Excellencie of a free State.*[24] In his Election Sermon of 1765 he referred to Burlamaqui, Montesquieu, Livy, Horace, Prince's Election Sermon of 1728, and to Dr. Stephen Hales, an eighteenth-century writer on natural philosophy.

A much more obscure person was the Reverend Dan Foster, of Connecticut, who in 1774 wrote six sermons on civil government in order to enlighten his people on the issues of the day. He referred to Cicero, translated by Roger L'Estrange, Prideaux's *Connection,* "Lord Sommers," "Monsieur Meveray, as I find him quoted," and Neal's *History of the Puritans.*[25] Another less well known minister was Peter Whitney of Northborough, Massachusetts, who in two sermons delivered July 14, 1774, quoted Locke, the treatise *Vox populi, vox Dei,* Montesquieu, Bishop Burnet, quoted from Hutchinson's history, Mayhew, and the Election Sermons of Eliot, Cooke, Turner and Haven.

22. *Ibid.,* no. 121.

23. *Ibid.,* no. 171.

24. *Ibid.,* no. 109. See *Writings of B. Franklin,* ed. Smyth, IX. 104. Hollis sent works on government such as the above to Harvard, Yale, Princeton, and the college of Bermuda as well as to individuals; therefore the students graduating after 1760 must have had an opportunity to read them. Many of the. graduates were of course ministers in 1770. Many of the books referred to in preceding lists were in Dartmouth College Library in 1775. Of the works dealing primarily with government and political theory the only ones were those of Locke. See the typed list in Dartmouth College Library.

25. Humphrey Prideaux, D.D., *The old and new Testament connected in the History of the Jews and neighboring Nations,* 3 vols., 1716 (many editions). I have not learned what Meveray was meant. Rev. David Barnes of Scituate is said to have been a great reader, and eager "for every new publication on politics, religion, ethics, or philosophy." He was very liberal (Bradford, *Biog. Notices,* p. 56). Rev. Peter Thacher, of Malden, was unusually well read in civil and ecclesiastical history. He could quote freely from the essays, sermons, and memoirs of the times of the Stuarts and Cromwell—"from the manly testimonies of Ludlow to the crude excrescences of Goodwin and Hugh Peters" (*Mass. Hist. Soc. Coll.* 1st Ser., VIII. 283).

Now and then in a diary can be found a list of the books read. The wide reading of Ezra Stiles needs no mention. A much less travelled and learned man was the Reverend Ebenezer Parkman of Westborough, Massachusetts, who went when he could to the ministerial convention of Boston and rode to Lexington to hear Jonas Clarke preach. He speaks in his diary of reading Dr. Scott's Sermons, Lord Chesterfield's Letters, a sermon by Mr. Flavel, an author often referred to by others, Bacon's *Advancement of Learning*, Lord Somers on Government, Montesquieu, whose *Spirit of Laws* he bought in 1765, a sermon of 1779 by Israel Evans, Dr. Swift, *The Scotch Scourge*, Hutchinson's *History of Massachusetts*, and, just before his sermon on the Stamp Act preached early in September of 1765, "Bp. Hoadley's Measure of Submiss[n]. to y[e] civil Magistrate." After reading Hoadly, Parkman wrote that he was "prepar[d], on y[t]. Subject."[26]

Illustrations might be multiplied, but enough have been given to show something of the extent and variety of the sources from which the ministers drew their theories. It must not be forgotten, in the multiplicity of authors mentioned, that the source of greatest authority and the one most commonly used was the Bible. The New England preacher drew his beliefs largely from the Bible, which was to him a sacred book, infallible, God's will for man. Of necessity it colored his political thinking. His conception of God, of God's law, and of God's relation to man determined to a large extent his conception of human law and of man's relation to his fellows. If his ideas of government and the rights of man were in part derived from other sources, they were strengthened and sanctioned by Holy Writ. This was of course especially true of the clergy. They stood before the

---

26. Parkman's Diary was printed in 1899. See Bibliography. The Dr. Scott referred to might have been Dr. John Scott, whose sermons and other works were pub. in 1718, a later Dr. John Scott, whose work on Genesis appeared in 1753, or a Dr. Thomas Scott of the 17th century, who wrote political tracts which brought him into conflict with the government. The Mr. Flavel was John Flavel, a nonconformist minister whose works went through many editions, the first appearing in 1701. [The abbreviation, punctuation, and superscription are original, being conventions often used in letters and diaries at the time—JM.]

people as interpreters of God's will. Their political speeches were sermons, their political slogans were often Bible texts. What they taught of government had about it the authority of the divine. To understand, therefore, something of the source and strength of their political faith and its influence upon those whom they taught, it is essential to review briefly certain of their theological doctrines and also their ecclesiastical polity.

Two

The Legalism of Theology
and Church Polity

"**G**od having made Man a Rational Creature, hath (as it were) Twisted Law into the very Frame and Constitution of his Soul. . . ."[1]
Some such belief as this axiom of Timothy Cutler seems to have lain deep in the mind of the New England Puritans. They were legally-minded men. Their theology and church polity were legalistic[2] and had a large share in determining the character of their political thinking. The law of God did not concern religious and ecclesiastical matters alone, but affected politics as well.

They conceived the universe to be a great kingdom whose sovereign was God, whose relations with His Son and with men were determined by covenant or compact, "covenant-constitutions,"

---

1. Timothy Cutler, Connecticut Election Sermon, 1717, p. 15. Cutler was minister of Stratford, Connecticut. See also Colman, *Sermons*, 1717, p. 94. The election, artillery, convention and other sermons were sometimes printed under a special title, sometimes simply as Election or Convention Sermon. In this and the following footnotes, italics are not used unless a definite title is given. Because of the number and length of the footnotes it has seemed best at times to give only the name of the author and the pages referred to, if the meaning is obvious. For full names and titles, see Bibliography.

2. [By "legalistic" here, Dr. Baldwin does not mean the theological legalism or "works salvation" sometimes referred to as the "Judaizer" heresy. Rather, she simply refers to a system of order based on the rule of law. A church polity based on rule of law can easily become the basis for a similar political theory.—JM]

which were always conditional and implied strict obligations on each side.[3] God had made a covenant of works with Adam and Eve, who wilfully broke it. Then in His mercy He made a second covenant of grace "ordaining the Lord Jesus . . . according to a covenant made between them both, to be mediator between God and Man."[4] This covenant made by Christ with His Father was entirely voluntary, a compact made between them in council.[5] By it, salvation was promised to men in return for faith in the Christ. Christ, by His sacrifice, paid the penalty for a broken covenant which a just God, who ruled by law, could not but demand. In return, God gave into the hands of His Son, as His delegate, the government of the world.[6] This conception of a covenant or compact as the foundation of divine and human relations is of basic importance in New England thought.

---

3. J. Cleaveland, *An Essay to defend* . . . , pp. 18–19. Also S. Willard, *Sermons*, 1682, pp. 172, 185; 1699, pp. 35, 418; *Confession of Faith of Massachusetts Churches*, 1680, pp. 246–47 in 1772 ed.; Colman, *Sermons*, 1717, p. 108; Dunbar, Massachusetts Election Sermon, 1760, pp. 20–21; Wakeman, Connecticut Election Sermon, 1685, p. 16. Baptists were at one with Congregationalists in this matter. The Presbyterians did not always agree with the Congregationalists concerning covenants. The church covenants were not always considered necessary and, although they believed in God's covenant with man, not all of them believed that the consent of man was necessary to make it binding. God made the covenant and man's consent was required. It was binding not merely because of consent but because of God's authority. N. Whitaker, *Confutation*. . . ., 1774, pp. 12–17.

4. *Confession of Faith of Massachusetts Churches*, 1680, pp. 245–47 (1772 edition). This was frequently the topic of sermons. See Mayhew, *Sermons*, 1748, pp. 147–48; *Sermons*, 1755, p, 102; Davenport, Massachusetts Election Sermon, 1669, p. 3; J. Barnard, Convention Sermon, 1738, pp. 18–19.

5. Typical are the words of Samuel Belcher: "that blessed compact which passed between the Father and Son, when the Terms of Man's Redemption were agreed upon, in the Council of God" (Massachusetts Election Sermon, 1707, p. 12).

6. Pemberton, Massachusetts Election Sermon, 1710, p. 53: "He had lay'd this Government on the Shoulders of His Only Son, who is the Man upon the Throne above the Firmament, according to whose direction the Wheels and Living Creatures move below. Now God has made him Head over all things for the Church. . . ." See J. Cotton, *The Doctrine of the Church*, 2nd ed., 1643, pp. 8–9.

God, the Sovereign, was also a lawgiver. He had established laws for his people, "perfectly wise, just and good," which were "founded upon the Nature and Relation of Things, and are of universal and perpetual Obligation. . . . Immovable as the Mountains and Immutable as God himself."[7] And Christ also gave laws to His subjects, determined the form His church should take, and commissioned His officers.[8]

To the New Englander this divine law became a "divine constitution,"[9] a fixed, fundamental law, sacred and inviolable. Throughout the seventeenth and eighteenth centuries it was a frequent theme of discussion, and to determine its nature and meaning and to make it clear to their people was one of the chief aims of the clergy. They conceived of it as three-fold, including the law of nature, the law of the Old Testament, and the law of Christ.

One of the most interesting features of the sermons and pamphlets before 1763, as well as afterwards, is the treatment of the law of nature. By this is meant the general principles of justice and equity under which men were conceived to have lived before the founding of any society or civil state and which gave men therefore their so called "natural rights." This law had been planted by God deep in the hearts of men, "written as with a pen of iron and the point of a diamond," before the fuller revelation of the written law, and was still to be found there.[10] There seems little evidence that

---

7. Appleton, Massachusetts Election Sermon, 1742, pp. 11–13. This belief was expressed repeatedly in the sermons of the 17th and 18th centuries. Cf. Pemberton's Election Sermon, 1710, p. 28; Burnham's Connecticut Election Sermon, 1722, p. 12; Hancock's Massachusetts Election Sermon, 1722, pp. 3, 5; Mayhew's Sermons, 1755, p. 314; Ezra Stiles' *Installation Address*, 1770, p. 22.

8. Woodbridge, Connecticut Election Sermon, 1727, pp. 16–17. T. Barnard, Convention Sermon, 1738, pp. 17, 22, 25. The whole sermon is on Christ "the only, and Supream Head of the Church." The term "divine lawgiver," was often used by the clergy both of God and Christ, and there were continual references to His right to govern and to His laws.

9. This was a common phrase of the ministers. Certain laymen also used this or similar phrases. Examples: T. Barnard, Artillery Sermon, 1758, p. 7; "Remarks" of Layman on Pres. Clap's *"Brief History and Vindication. . . ."* 1757, p. 59; Tucker, Convention Sermon, 1768.

10. Mayhew, Sermons, 1755, p. 258.

the clergy, at least, thought of it as distinct from the law of God. Rather it gained greater force as a part of God's law. Thus in 1669 John Davenport in his Election Sermon said, "the Law of Nature is God's law."[11] Again and again the clergy made this assertion and clearly regarded the laws of nature as sacredly and legally binding as any other part of the divine law. Samuel Hall in his Connecticut Election Sermon of 1746 put it thus: "I think there can be no doubt about this; but that in all cases where the matter under Determination appertains to natural Right, the Cause is God's Cause."[12] John Barnard in his Massachusetts Election Sermon of 1734 phrased it somewhat differently but with equal assurance: "This Voice of Nature is the Voice of God. Thus 'tis that vox populi est vox Dei."[13]

This law of nature was an unwritten law. The revelation in the Old and New Testaments helped to make clear the law of nature and to disclose its full extent.[14] In the Old Testament God gave to man a "positive law." It was true that some of its statutes applied to the Jews only, but there were also great moral principles which applied to all phases of man's activity, now as formerly, and were equally binding. Thus even in that part of Old Testament law which no longer applied to Christians and in the history of God's dealings with His chosen people there were many examples for men of today.[15]

---

11. Davenport, Massachusetts Election Sermon, 1669, p. 4.

12. Hall, Connecticut Election Sermon, 1746, p. 80

13. Barnard, Massachusetts Election Sermon, p. 9. See Bulkley's Connecticut Election Sermon, 1713, p. 29. Home's Proposals of Some Things, p. 11; Bellamy's *The Law our School-Master*, p. 37; Mayhew's *Sermons*, 1755, p. 262.

14. Peter Clark, Convention Sermon, 1745, p. 23. See Woodbridge's Connecticut Election Sermon, 1752, pp. 10–11, and Williams' Connecticut Election Sermon of 1741, p. 180 Williams says "There never was, nor can be any Wisdom among men, but what is communicated from God; nor is there any Law of Nature, or Rule of Natural and Moral wisdom, which we speak of, as implanted in the Mind of man, but what is found in the Bible, and cultivated and improved by that Revelation...."

15. Appleton, Massachusetts Election Sermon, 1742, pp. 11–13, 49. The moral law of the Old Testament lays down such rules of justice and truth and goodness "as are a sufficient Directory for us in every Station of Life, whether

In the New Testament were the special laws made by Christ for His followers and His church. These did not in any way contradict the great laws of nature and the moral laws of the Old Dispensation; rather they fulfilled them, but they did away with the exacting religious regulations which had bound the Jews so closely. It was Christ, entrusted by His Father with government over men, who was the great legislator for Christians.[16] In His Gospel were laws binding upon a Christian which were not included in the natural law.[17] Here was to be found the "perfect law of liberty." Just what was meant by this Christian liberty was a matter of the greatest moment, and among both clergy and laymen there was often a difference of opinion, but as men's conception of their rights broadened so did their interpretation of the phrase. Whatever it included, those liberties were sacred, a part of the "divine constitution."

This law of God, natural and written, was not only moral but also rational, and God expected obedience not so much because of His authority as because of its reasonableness and the benefits to be derived therefrom.[18] The good of His people and the rights of men were the end of His government and His law was framed with that in view.[19] God, it was true, was an absolute, all powerful

private or public, whether in natural, civil, or sacred Authority. . . . These are the judgments of God that are given to us as well as unto the Nation of Israel." Cutler, Connecticut Election Sermon, 1717, p. 17: "The Religious Laws of that People as in Contradistinction to the Laws of Christianity, are Ceased, we have a more Perfect Institution now. The Moral stand in full Force and Obligation on us to Observe them. The Political Deserve the greatest Reverence, as the Result of Perfect Wisdom and Rectitude; and are most Reasonable to be Observed by us where our Circumstances Run Parallel with theirs."

16. N. Eells, Connecticut Election Sermon, 1748, p. 25; Mayhew, *Sermons*, 1755, pp. 258–59. Two other sermons speak of Christ as having a "natural right" to the government of men, as a result of His covenant with God (Woodbridge's Connecticut Election Sermon, 1724, p. 3, and Webb's Massachusetts Election Sermon, 1738, p. 5).

17. Mayhew, *Sermons*, 1755, pp. 260–64.

18. Woodbridge, Connecticut Election Sermon, 1727, p. 2; Colton, Connecticut Election Sermon, 1736, pp. 32–36, esp. p. 33.

19. Colton, Connecticut Election Sermon, 1736, p. 36; J. Bulkley, Connecticut Election Sermon, 1713, pp. 30–32; E. Pemberton, Massachusetts

sovereign. Even the unorthodox Mayhew declared that "No one but God, has an absolute, unlimited authority over us."[20] But nevertheless God did not act in an arbitrary and unjust fashion. He could not. The very nature of God forbade it; He was Himself perfect and His every act must be perfectly just. Indeed, it was from this excellency of His nature that His fitness and His right to govern the world were evident.[21] The laws of nature and the revealed law, being God's law, were expressions of this perfection and God, by His very nature, was bound by them. Thus God by the perfection of His own being was limited by inviolable law.[22] "God himself (with reverence be it spoken) cannot punish his own creatures without a law broken."[23]

This conception of a moral God self-limited does not seem to be confined to those who denied predestination and who believed in the free will of men. So strict a Calvinist as John Cleaveland, of Ipswich, declared that "the law must be a transcript of God's moral

---

Election Sermon, 1710, p. 53; R Colman, Sermons, 1717, p. 94; Webb, Massachusetts Election Sermon, 1738, p. 18; J. Allen, Massachusetts Election Sermon, 1744, the "Good of His subjects is the very end of Christ's government over us," pp. 28–29.

20. Mayhew, *Sermons*, 1755, pp. 313–14.

21. W. Williams, Massachusetts Election Sermon, 1719, p. 10.

22. G. Bulkeley, *Will and Doom*, 1692, Preface, pp. 94–95; J, Bulkley, Connecticut Election Sermon, 1713, p, 17: "the Divine Government is managed by fixed and steady Rules." Pemberton, Massachusetts Eiection Sermon, 1710, p. 29: "He governs not by unaccountable Will or inconstant humour, which are imperfections his Nature can't suffer, but by Stable Measures, as may best suit the Nature and Circumstances of the Subjects and the noble End of his Government." See also Williams, Massachusetts Election Sermon, 1719, p. 10; Colton, Connecticut Election Sermon, 1736, pp. 32–33; Chauncey, Connecticut Election Sermon, 1719, p. 20; Webb, Massachusetts Election Sermon, 1738, p. 14; Stiles, *Installation Address*, 1770, pp. 10–11; Jesus also governed His church by the "strictest Rules of Justice and Righteousness." Mayhew, *Sermons*, 1748, pp. 13, 96–97; *Result of a Council of Consociated Churches at Windham, 1747*, p. 6; He "always acts and disposes of all Things according to the strict Rules of infinite and inviolable Justice."

23. G. Bulkeley, *Will and Doom*, 1692, Preface, p. 94; see also B. Colton, Connecticut Election Sermon, 1736, pp. 32–33.

nature, it must at least, be just, holy and good; it must be very pure; it must be perfect."[24] After the Great Awakening and the work of Jonathan Edwards had widened and defined the breach between strict Calvinists and Arminians, it is true that the former accused the latter of denying the absolute sovereignty of God and of vilifying the holy law. They themselves so "magnified the Law" that they believed God could not forgive Adam who had transgressed the law and broken the covenant, nor his descendants who shared his guilt, without the penalty being paid in full.[25] "The punishment of sin cannot be remitted without shaking the pillars of the universe. . . . The earth and sublunary heavens may pass away, but the law shall not pass away, till the whole be fulfilled."[26]

The Arminians, of whom Mayhew was perhaps the most extreme, could not accept this strained and distorted legalism but they assuredly did not deny God's absolute sovereignty.[27] Nor did the Calvinists believe God other than perfectly moral and just, unable by His very justice and perfect morality to make any but just and perfect laws. Mayhew in 1750 only expressed more directly the views of earlier orthodox clergymen when he declared:

> God himself does not govern in an absolute arbitrary
> and despotic manner. The Power of this almighty King
> is limited by law—by the eternal laws of truth, wisdom,
> and equity, and the everlasting tables of right reason.[28]

---

24. J. Cleaveland, *An Essay answering Mayhew*, 1763, p. 25.

25. Adam's descendants were legally accounted sinners because their persons were legally in him, as the person of the debtor is in the surety, or the person of the prince is in the ambassador (Cleaveland, *An Essay to defend*, etc., p. 104, note quoted from Dr. Wigglesworth).

26. E. Stiles, *Installation Address*, 1770, p. 36. See also B. Colman, Sermons, 1717, p. 108, and Cleaveland, *An Essay to defend*, p. 104, note.

27. See Mayhew's own words, p. 32.

28. Mayhew, Sermon, 1750, in Thornton, p. 81. This becomes still clearer from the analogies drawn between civil and divine government. Later sermons, after 1763, voiced the same conviction. Doubtless there were those who admitted God's theoretical power to act unjustly and to enforce submission, if He would, but believed Him so perfect as to render such an act on His part impos-

Both Calvinist and Arminian, then, believed in a divine law; a fundamental constitution, which was binding upon God and man. In this, long before 1760, they included the so-called laws of nature as well as Christ's "law of liberty."

The significance of the belief in the binding character of law upon God and man seems to have escaped many who write of the Revolutionary philosophy. It is fundamental to any understanding of American constitutional thought. God's government is founded on and limited by law and therefore all human governments must be so founded and limited, if patterned after His. A government, therefore, which exercises its authority unconstitutionally acts illegally. Here is one great source of the American doctrine of government by law.

This legalistic conception was also dominant in matters of church government, although there was a greater diversity of opinion and practice than in doctrine. All believed, indeed, that the way intended by Christ was shown in His gospel and was a part of the law established for His churches; but men did not interpret

---

sible. See Stiles, *Installation Address*, 1770, p. 22.

That before 1760 there was discussion among the clergy concerning the existence of laws of nature outside God's jurisdiction is evident from the following from a sermon by Nathaniel Potter, of Brookline, preached in 1758, p. 11: "'But admitting (what is contrary to Scripture, Reason, and the Common Sense of Mankind, and involves in it an Idea of God, utterly unworthy a wise and good Governor) that the whole Frame of Nature is ruled and managed by certain invariable Laws which omnipotence itself cannot enforce or suspend."

Adams in *The Founding of New England*, p. 77, says that the pivot of the Puritan's creed was the absolutely unconditioned will of God, and in Revolutionary New England, p. 170, attributes to the Arminians the doctrine of His self-limitation in dealing with free agents. That the two were not deemed incompatible is evident from Mayhew's words given above and on p. 32, and from Gershom Bulkley's preface to his *Will and Doom*, 1692. On p. 93 he says, "That absolute and unlimited sovereignty to do and command what he will, because he will, and to be obeyed without reserve, is the incommunicable right and prerogative of Jehovah," and on p. 94: "Laws are essential to government. God himself (with reverence be it spoken) cannot punish his own creature without a law broken. . . . He that governs without or against law arrogates a higher prerogative than God doth."

the gospel alike, and the different opinions caused constant and often bitter discussion. In these controversies clergymen and laymen shared; and, however trivial and futile their discussion may seem to us today, they assuredly were the occasion of long arguments on government, liberty, and the rights of men.[29] Here also, as in sermons on the "divine constitution," inferences were often made concerning the nature of civil government, and analogies were drawn.

Both the Old and New Testaments and even the light of nature were searched for precedents and arguments. The Congregationalists and Baptists who made up perhaps four-fifths of churchgoing New England believed that the church could only exist by covenant, a sacred and binding agreement or compact made by the members with each other and with God. Everywhere they found precedents for this method. The Old Testament gave them many examples; the "light of nature," to which men turned in the seventeenth as in the eighteenth century, showed, so they believed, that the only way in which men could be joined into one body was by covenant. In the New Testament there were passages which they interpreted in the same fashion. In forming a church, therefore, the members voluntarily covenanted with God and with one another and believed that only so could they be given power eventually one over the other.[30] The church so constituted became "as a citycom-

---

29. For further details, see Chaps. 5–7.

30. J. Cotton, *The Way of the Churches*, 1645, pp. 2–4, 61–64; I. Backus, *Truth is great*, p. 33, note; *Platform of Church Discipline*, 1648, chap. iv; I. Mather, A *Disquisition concerning Ecclesiastical Councils*, 1716, p. 5; J. Barnard, Convention Sermon, 1738, pp. 10–11; J. Davenport, *The Power of the Congregational Churches*, 1672, p. 35: This voluntary covenant "is the strong knitting glew whereby persons are joyned together in all such voluntary relations." Dexter, Congregationalism, what it is, p. 5, says Baptists were purely Congregational in principles of church order and government; and Backus, in *Truth is great*, p. 33, note, says: "Government in church, as state, is founded in compact or covenant, implied or expressed; and they are equally binding upon officers and privates to act towards each other according to the nature of the compact, as far as their ability and opportunity will admit of."

Certain of the Presbyterians did not consider this covenant necessary. Whitaker, *Confutations*, 1774, pp. 12–17, says this implies that the consent of

pacted together," a new body with rights of self-government, a new organism formed by the joining together of all the members by free consent.[31]

It seems also to have been the custom for the minister to enter into a covenant with his people, which was binding unless dissolved by mutual consent.[32] These covenants were sacred and binding, and to break them was a serious offense. Their nature and their sanctity were the constant theme of the clergy for more than a hundred years before the Revolution. If a man had any confidence in his minister's ability and in the truth of his teaching, he must have become convinced that voluntary, conditional, binding compact lay at the bottom of the most important relations of men.[33]

The church members, thus joined together, had power to choose their own officers,[34] to whom they were then willing to

the people is necessary to Christ's authority. He declares men are bound to accept God's covenant, not by their free consent, but by God's authority. Man's refusal is "'high rebellion." This difference does not seem to have been general. Some Presbyterian churches signed covenants. The chief difference was in the power given to Synods.

31. Davenport, *Power of the Congregational Churches*, p. 37; *Platform of Church Discipline*, chap. iv, sect. 3; Hooker, *Survey of the Summe of Church Discipline*, p. 46; *Answer of Elders and Messengers*, 1662, pp. 75, 113–14; J. Barnard, Convention Sermon, 1738, pp. 10, 12. Cf. Wise, *Vindication*, 1717, p. 17.

32. Sprague, I. 719. Illustrations are numerous; e.g. in Eccles. Papers, VII, no. 263 a, no. 268; VIII, 44 a (C. S. L.); MS Letter from E. Wheelock, 1759.

The ecclesiastical records of Mass. and Conn. give instances of the difficulties that occasionally arose in consequence. If a pastor left his people without their consent it was looked upon as breaking the compact and was considered a great grievance, no doubt partly because it meant paying out a fairly large sum of money to settle a new pastor. On the other hand, the church and parish might vote his dismissal but he did not have to leave unless he concurred. Councils were often called and sometimes the Assembly was petitioned. If a man were dismissed for delinquency it was not violation of contract, but was allowed in the Platform. There was much controversy over authority of Council in such a matter.

33. For the attitude toward social compact, see Chap. 4. For examples of various kinds of covenant, see Appendix A.

34. J. Cotton, *Way of the Churches*, p. 63: "That Christian libertie which the Lord Jesus by His bloud hath purchased for His Church, and for all His children, giveth them all libertie to choose their owne Officers, and their owne

submit, but "in case of manifest unworthiness and delinquency," they had "power also to depose them, for, to open and shut, to chuse and refuse, to constitute in office and remove from office are acts belonging to the same power ."[35] Sometimes a controversy arose as to this power of choice and dismissal and then the reasons pro and con were argued at great length.[36] Always the right was maintained; it was officially stated in the Cambridge Platform of 1648 and was jealously guarded by those churches which adhered to the Platform and as jealously by many of the clergy. In the churches which clung to the "Congregational Way" the power of action both in choosing officers and in transacting all business lay with the majority, and the equality of all members was recognized. Though the advice of a council might be asked and accepted, there was no legal appeal to an authority higher than the individual church.[37] On the other hand, the churches which inclined toward Presbyterianism gave legal authority to the action of councils.

On these questions of the local independence of the churches, the right of the majority to rule, the amount of power to be given to the church "rulers," the relation of the church to the state, the complete freedom of judgment in matters of religion and similar problems, there arose very early differences of opinion which continued more or less throughout the entire colonial period, at times becoming sharp and involving laymen as well as ministers. It is not my intention to discuss these controversies except in so far as they brought forth arguments which bore upon the political thinking of the time or as they illustrate the application of theories of government. Certain of them will be mentioned in later chapters.

---

fellow-Members . . . " I. A. Mather, *A Disquisition*, pp. 5–6; J. Barnard, Convention Sermon, 1738, pp. 11–12. This was true of all but Episcopalians, and sometimes of them in America for lack of bishops.

35. *Platform of Church Discipline*, 1648, p. 206; Dexter, *Congregationalism, What it is*, pp. 2–3.

36. See Chapters 5, 6.

37. Dexter, *Congregationalism*, p. 3. See also Chapters 5 and 7.

Three

Concepts of Government

"The Original of Government is Divine. It is from God, by His Sovereign Constitution and Appointment."[1] Thus wrote, in the beginning of the eighteenth century ,one Ebenezer Pemberton of Boston. Fifty years later, the same sentiment was reiterated by another divine when he said: "Liberty both civil and religious is the spirit and genius of the sacred writings."[2]

Long before 1763, the New England clergy had developed and taught an elaborate theory of government. As they founded their theology and church polity upon the law of God as revealed in the natural law and the written word, so from the law of God they developed their political theories. They read histories, ancient and modern, pored over commentaries and studied the works of philosophers when they could get them, but even the most learned turned to the infallible Scripture to learn what God intended government should be. Men might and did differ as to the interpretation of the Bible, but its authority they never questioned. Through constant reiteration and reinterpretation certain ideas and texts, from time to time filled with new meaning as men's thinking

---

1. Pemberton, Massachusetts Election Sermon, 1710, p. 11. The whole sermon is on government and its divine original.

2. B. Stevens, Massachusetts Election Sermon, 1761, p. 8.

29

broadened, became unwritten principles of government.

Civil government, so the clergy taught, was of divine origin. Sometimes they founded their arguments on reason or the light and law of nature, sometimes on the Bible, sometimes on both, but it amounted to the same thing in the end. It was ordained of God,[3] and its purpose, like the government of Christ and of God Himself, was the good of the people.[4] Here the analogy between theology

---

3. J. Davenport, *A Discourse about Civil Government*, 1663, p. 6; Massachusetts Election Sermon, 1669, p. 4: "Power of Civil Rule, by men orderly chosen, is God's Ordinance, For 1. It is from the Light and Law of Nature, and the Law of Nature is God's Law. 2. The orderly ruling of men over men, in general, is from God, in its root, though voluntary in the manner of coalescing . . ." J. Bulkley, Connecticut Election Sermon, 1713, p. 13: Religion "Asserts the Divine Original of Government, and Founds it in Divine Institution," not any particular form, but government, in general; p. 23: "all Civil Power is a Derivative, comes from God, and is a ray of His. . . ." Solomon Williams, Connecticut Election Sermon, 1741, p. 1: Civil government of divine institution, "all the just measures, Rules and Maxims of its Administrations are derived from the same source which is the fountain of that Power . . ." I have more than forty such references before 1761 and many thereafter. There are many others, where, if not definitely stated, the same thing is implied.

4. This is stated in very many of the sermons and pamphlets read and in many is elaborated and applied. A few quotations are given below. I have more than thirty such before 1761. After 1761 such statements are very numerous. J. Davenport, *A Discourse on Civil Government in a new Plantation*, 1663, p. 17: "the end of all Civil Government & Administrations . . . is the publick and common Good. . . ." Samuel Whitman, Connecticut Election Sermon, 1714, p. 32: "You very well know that the Publick good is the End of Government. . . ." A. Mather, Connecticut Election Sermon, 1725, pp. 13–14: "The great subordinate End is the Publick good; the Means and Laws of Government must be calculated to work and bring about that End & Effect. And a good Ruler knows these Maxims are not only founded in Nature, but expressly asserted in God's Word: . . . All shall be Sacrificed to subserve the Publick." Mather quotes Cicero and others to this effect. N. Appleton, *Funeral Sermon . . . Preach'd at the Publick Lecture in Boston*, 1757, p. 18: Government was instituted by God for the good of mankind. If a ruler acts selfishly or oppressively, "He acts quite contrary to the original Design of Government and contrary to the express Will of Him from whence all Power and Authority are derived." Mayhew, Massachusetts Election Sermon, 1754, p. 6: "After the glory of God there can be no other end of government" than the good of man, the common benefit of society; p. 8: "The end of government,

and political theory is very close and very significant. Even the most conservative of the clergy admitted it. The more liberal emphasized it. A government which did not have the good of the people at heart did not have the sanction of God. There could be no other end whether government were considered as a divine ordinance, instituted indirectly by God or as more immediately the ordinance of man, founded in common consent.[5] Neither God nor man had any other purpose in founding government. This was the starting point for the necessity of law and order, for the limitations upon rulers, and for the inviolability of the rights and liberties of the people. From it sprang the argument, identical with that of Locke, that governments are limited by the purpose for which they were founded, viz. the good of the people. The good of the people might be interpreted variously, but whatever else it meant it assured the protection of their natural rights. Without government there would be no security for those rights which God intended man to enjoy, no assurance of life, good order, liberty, and prosperity.[6]

Except in the case of the Jews, God did not specify the particular type of government to be set up. Men might choose, provided always that the type chosen answered the end of government and

---

then, as it is a divine ordinance, must be human felicity . . . must be the common good of all, and of every individual, so far as consistent therewith. . . ."

5. Mayhew, Massachusetts Election Sermon, 1754, pp. 6–9.

6. Typical of many are the following: Davenport, *A Discourse about Civil Government*, 1663, p. 17: the end of government is the natural, moral, civil and spiritual good of men. Belcher, Massachusetts Election Sermon, 1701, pp. 31–32: without government men are "in a state of war." Hancock, Massachusetts Election Sermon, 1722, p. 7: without government, the world is a chaos. Samuel Checkley, Sermon, 1727, p. 5: without government, anarchy and confusion. Jared Eliot in his Connecticut Election Sermon, 1738, p. 31, says that the question whether civil government "be from Fear or Love of Society, or from both, has been a matter of Dispute," and quotes Rapin, Puffendorf, and Locke.

For the necessity of government to preserve life, liberty, and property, typical references may be found in the Massachusetts Election Sermons of 1710, p. 16; 1729, p. 8; 1734, p. 24; 1747, p. 8; 1761, pp. 54–55, 70–71; in the Connecticut Election Sermons of 1712, p. 9; 1752, p. 23; in Williams' *A Seasonable Plea*, 1744, p. 4. See also later references.

was not inconsistent with the divine laws.[7]

Civil government, though ordained by God, did not come immediately from Him, but mediately through the people. Whatever form it might take, the clergy almost unanimously agreed that if it were a just government it had been founded on compact.[8] This compact relationship was a matter of vital importance to the New England minister. His theology depended upon it, it was the foundation of his church government, he believed it to be at the root of all God's dealings with men. When he searched the Bible he found, so he believed, that even the Jewish government, which was peculiarly God's own, rested on compact. When he questioned Reason and Nature, which to him were the voice of God, again he found the compact or covenant. When he read the wise men of the past and of his own day, once more he found it. When he looked at his own environment he found it there. The charters were considered compacts, and when men set up new towns they drew up a town covenant.[9] It became in practical experience the only way to form a corporate body.

7. Davenport, *The Power of the Congregational Churches*, 1663, p. 129; J. Checkley, Sermon, 1727, pp. 19–20; Election Sermons, Pemberton, 1710, pp. 12–14; Bulkley, 1713, pp. 13–14; Woodbridge, 1727, pp. 19–20; Barnard, 1734, pp. 10–11; Allen, 1744, pp. 25–26; Phillips, 1750, pp. 6–7; Mayhew, 1754, p. 4; Haven, 1761, p. 8. Some preferred and believed that God preferred a definite kind of government. Gershom Bulkeley, a Presbyterian who had become a lawyer and justice and who opposed the independent action of Conn. during the Revolution of 1688, declared that monarchy was the best type (*Will and Doom*, p. 93). John Wise, who had been imprisoned by Andros for refusal to pay taxes, believed in democracy in Church and State (*Vindication*, 1717, p. 39 of 1772 ed.). Many before 1761 eulogized the British government, and some discussed at length the advantages of a mixed or balanced government of the British type. Many declared that there was no reason to believe that God preferred monarchy and that therefore no claim to divine right or hereditary accession could be based upon such preference.

8. A few did not believe it. Gershom Bulkeley in 1692 wrote that all civil authority came directly from God, that the king of England was the fountain of all power, with his power limited only by God. God, however, did limit it, did guard the rights of the people, and insist on the observance of law by the king.

9. See Appendix A.

Thus the social compact seems to have been accepted without question by the ministers of both the seventeenth and eighteenth centuries. It was used to support the church covenant which was so dear to them. From it and the inferences drawn therefrom they found authority for the Revolution of 1688 and the Hanoverian succession. Both the social and the church covenants were used to explain and defend the rights of the ople in church and state, and not only of the people but of rulers also.

Throughout the century before 1763 the analogy between religious and civil covenants was clearly recognized and frequently expressed. In 1645, John Cotton, attempting to prove the necessity of the church covenant, argued thus from the covenants in the Old Testament and the veiled references to covenants in the New, and also from the light of nature:

> for it is evident by the light of nature that all civill Relations are founded in Covenant. For, to pass by naturall Relations between Parents and Children, and violent Relations between Conquerours and Captives; there is no other way given whereby a people (Sui Juris) free from naturall and compulsory engagements, can be united or combined together into one visible body, to stand by mutuall Relation, fellow-members of the same body, but only by mutuall Covenant; as appeareth between husband and wife in the family, Magistrates and subjects in the Conmon-wealth, fellow Citizens in the same City. . . .[10]

The Cambridge Platform of 1648 and the *Answer of Elders and Messengers* of 1662 made the same comparison.[11] So again in 1663 John Davenport, in discussing the power of the Congregational church, said that as all citizens are admitted into *jus civitatis* by voluntary entering into covenant whereby they become a political

10. J. Cotton, *The Way of the Churches*, 1645, p. 4, also pp. 2–3, 61–62.

11. *Platform of Church Discipline*, chap. iv, section 3. Comparison to a city is drawn from the Bible. *Answer of Elders & Messengers*, 1662, p. 17.

body, so it is in the church. All voluntary relations, he said, are by covenant.[12] He spoke of the

> analogy and agreement that is between the Spiritual power of a Congregational Church of Christ, and the civil power of the most free and perfect Cities, which Thucidides saith have three privileges, viz. to use, 1. Their own Laws. 2. Magistrates. 3. Judgments. . . .[13]

This is explained more at length in his remarkable Election Sermon in 1669 before the Massachusetts Court. Civil rule, he said, is "God's Ordinance" because "It is from the Light and the Law of Nature and the Law of Nature is God's Law"; men being

> combined in Family-Society; it is necessary that they be joyned in a Civil-Society; . . . the power of making Laws, followeth naturally, though the manner of Union, in a Political Body, is voluntary . . . the designation of these or those to be Civil Rulers, leaving out others is from God, by the People's free Choice, at least by the Suffrages of the major part of them, wherein the rest must acquiesce. This Power of Rulers of the Common-wealth is derived from the People's free Choice . . . for the Power of Government is originally in the People . . . the People so give the Magisterial Power unto some, as that they still retain in themselves these three Acts, 1. That they may measure out so much Civil Power, as God in his Word Alloweth to them, and no more, nor less. 2. That they may set bounds and banks to the exercise of that

---

12. Davenport, *The Power of the Congregational Churches*, p. 36.

13. *Ibid.*, p. 123. See also pp. 27–28, 46–49. The church covenant is "not a yoke of bondage, but of precious liberties. . . . In like manner it bindeth the members of the Church to all the duties of their Church-relation mutually, both Officers and People . . . And therefore I cannot but wonder, that some, who do approve and plead for all other Covenants, viz., National, Conjugal, Social Covenants, should yet dislike and oppose Church-Covenants" (pp. 48–49). See also *A Discourse about Civil Government in a New Plantation*, 1663, p. 6.

Power, so as it may not be exuberant, above the laws, and due Rights and Liberties of the People. 3. That they give it out conditionally, upon this or that condition; so as, if the condition is violated, they may resume their power of chusing another.[14]

Here is government set up by the people and resting upon their consent; magistrates chosen by the majority and strictly limited in power to what is allowed by God, so hedged about that their power cannot be used against the rights and liberties of the people, removable by the people if the conditions set by them be violated. Magistrates and people are bound by law, and that law is determined by the divine law which carefully guards the rights and liberties of the people.

There are interesting likenesses and differences between these political theories of the theocratic John Davenport and those of the more radical Thomas Hooker and Roger Williams. As early as 1638, Thomas Hooker, in a sermon preached at Hartford had declared,

> 1. That the choice of public magistrates belongs unto the people by God's own allowance. . . . 3. They who have power to appoint officers and magistrates, it is in their power also, to set the bounds and limitations of the power and place unto which they call them. *Reasons.* 1. Because the foundation of authority is laid, firstly, in the free consent of the people.[15]

Roger Williams agreed with him:

> The sovereign, original, and foundation of civil power

---

14. Davenport, Massachusetts Election Sermon, 1669, pp. 4–6 (*Mass. Col. Soc. Pub.*, X.).

15. Notes on two sermons by Hooker made by Henry Wolcott, Jr. (*Conn. Hist. Soc. Coll.*, I. 20). Hooker, in a letter to Winthrop in 1638, speaks of the covenant made by the people of Agawam and others in Connecticut with their elected magistrates and does not see how such a covenant can he cast away at pleasure without sin (*Conn. Hist. Soc. Coll.*, I. 14).

lies in the people; and it is evident that such governments
as are by them erected and established, have no more
power, nor for no longer time, than the civil power or
people consenting and agreeing shall betrust them with.
This is clear, not only in reason, but in the experience of
all commonweals, where the people are not deprived of
their natural freedom by the power of tyrants.[16]

The chief differences between these leaders of different sects
seem to lie in Davenport's statement that the people can give the
magistrate no more and no less power than is allowed by God,
whereas Hooker and Williams make the people the judge of the
power to be given. Under the former, the law gains a peculiar sanctity and inviolability, whether interpreted so as to extend the power of magistrates, or, as might happen, the power of the people.
They agree, however, that government is set up by the people and
rests upon their consent; that magistrates are chosen by the people
and are strictly limited both in power and in the exercise of it and
are removable if they violate the conditions of their power. [17] And
they are arguing already from the law of nature and from reason.

With the coming of the eighteenth century there was a greater
elaboration of the social compact and of that between rulers and
people. Sometimes this was due to the desire of certain of the
clergy to oppose a tendency toward Presbyterianism and to support the power of the local church against a Council or Synod, or
the power of the brotherhood against a too authoritative minister;
sometimes it was due to a demand for religious toleration; sometimes to a more purely political purpose. Ministers might wish to
warn those in power of the unlawful nature of oppressive acts or

16. *The Bloody Tenent*, p. 137, quoted by Backus, *Church History of New
England*, I. 62 of 1839 ed., as a statement of belief of Baptists.

17. Illustrations might be given of the application of their theories by the
clergy in the 17th century. For example, in 1644 they demanded that the magistrates maintain the liberties of the people and refuse to surrender a vessel in
Boston harbor at the demand of the English commission, affirming "salus populi suprema lex" (Barry, *History of Massachusetts*, I. 328).

warn the people of the need of submission to lawful authority. In either case the aim was to inculcate obedience to law and to show the basis therefor. To do this the ministers set forth the origin and end of government and discussed the meaning of the social compact. And this led them to a discussion of the state of nature and the rights of man, both those given up and those retained.

The most complete account of the process by which compacts were made was that of John Wise, of Ipswich, who had defied Andros, refused to pay taxes levied, as he believed, without authority, and had suffered imprisonment.[18] Heartily opposed to the effort certain ministers were making to establish a Synod in Massachusetts, he published in 1717 his famous treatise, *A Vindication of the Government of New England Churches.* It is a striking argument for democracy in church and state and had then and later a remarkable effect.[19] Wise considered man first in his natural state, enjoying the liberty which belonged to him, a liberty which made him subject to no other human being. In consequence, all men in this state were equal in authority and each had a right to judge for himself what was most conducive to his happiness and welfare. This liberty and equality of men, so Wise believed, could not be lessened until, in order to form a civil state, they gave up certain rights, at the same time preserving and cherishing as much as was consistent with the public good. The people were, therefore, the original of all power, but when they combined in society they delegated a part of their power and authority to others. Wise vividly pictured the voluntary formation of a new commonwealth by such free and equal men.[20] He concluded that a democracy was the type

18. Dexter, *Congregationalism as seen in its Literature,* pp. 494–95. Wise was the son of a serving man.

19. *Ibid.,* pp. 498–502; Walker, *Congregational Churches in the United States,* pp. 209–12. In 1710 Wise had published a satire called *The Churches Quarrel Espoused.*

20. J. Wise, *Vindication,* pp. 17–39 of 1772 ed: "Let us conceive in our mind a multitude of men, all naturally free and equal; going about voluntarily, to erect themselves into a new common-wealth.

"1. They must interchangeably each man covenant to join in one lasting society, that they may be capable to concert the measures of their safety, by a public vote.

of government which the "light of nature" often directed men toward. "A democracy, This is a form of government, which the light of nature does highly value, and often directs to, as most agreeable to the just and natural prerogative of human beings . . . ."[21]

The connection, in Wise's mind, between democracy in church government, based on covenant, for which he was arguing, and democracy in the state is shown clearly in his conclusion, that the

> people or fraternity under the gospel, are the first subject of power . . . a democracy in church or state, is a very honorable and regular government, according to the dictates of right reason. And therefore . . . these churches of New England, in their ancient constitution of church order; it being a democracy, are manifestly justified and defended by the law and light of nature.[22]

"2. A vote or decree must then nextly pass to set up some particular species of government over them. And if they are joined in their first compact upon absolute terms to stand to the decision of the first vote concerning the species of government: then all are bound by the majority to acquiesce in that particularform thereby settled, though their own private opinion, incline them to some other model.

"3. After a decree has specified the particular form of government, then there will be need of a new covenant, whereby those on whom sovereignty is conferred, engage to take care of the common peace, and welfare. And the subjects on the other hand, to yield them faithful obedience. In which covenant is included that submission and union of wills, by which a state may be conceived to be but one person. . . . A civil state is a compound moral person. Whose will (united by those covenants before passed) is the will of all . . . the aforesaid covenants may be supposed, under God's providence, to be the divine Fiat, pronounced by God, let us make man. . . ."

21. *Ibid.*, pp. 17–39 of 1772 ed.

22. *Ibid.*, p. 44. Adams, *Revolutionary New England*, pp. 97–98, speaks of Wise as drawing his arguments solely from the law of nature rather than from the Scripture. He thinks that the political thought of the 18th century was divorced from theology and based rather upon Reason. The clergy, it is true, were influenced by Locke, Sydney, Hoadly, etc., but they of the 18th century as those of the 17th believed Reason and Nature but the voice of God and the laws of Nature as truly those of God as the laws found in the Scripture. This they said repeatedly and thus gave a sacred significance to the laws of nature and the arguments from Reason. As John Barnard said in 1734, "this Voice of Nature is

This is the most detailed account of the social compact found in the works of any of the New England clergy before 1763. One of its significant features is the demand for a second covenant, the first to form a society, the second to determine what would be the form of government. This distinction has not been found clearly stated elsewhere. Wise's two pamphlets must have been extensively read by clergy and laymen.[23] The clergy were sharply divided over the issue of Synods, and the quarrel was prolonged. Those who wished no Synod ultimately won, owing at least in part to the impetus given to popular rights by John Wise.[24] But although many disagreed with

the Voice of God. Thus 'tis that *vox populi est vox Dei."* And Chas. Chauncey in his Election Sermon, 1747, p. 9: "As it originates in the reason of things, 'tis, at the same time, essentially founded in the will of God. For the voice of reason is the voice of God." Moreover, they found in the Bible much to confirm what Nature and Reason taught them. S. Williams in his Connecticut Election Sermon, 1741, pp. 18–21, 23–25, voices the common conviction. "In the Law of God they will find the best Maxims and Rules of Government they can ever be furnish'd with.... There never was nor can be any wisdom among men, but what is communicated from God; nor is there any Law of Nature, or Rule of Natural & Moral wisdom, which we speak of, as implanted in the Mind of man, but what is found in the Bible., and cultivated and improved by that Revelation ... Here you learn, That every man has an indisputable right to all the good things which God gives him by Nature and Providence, his own Labour or regular Compacts, Agreements and Constitutions made between men; and that these are to be inviolably secured to every man till he forfeits them. Here Rulers are taught to seek the virtue and happiness of their People, as the end of Government.... Besides, it teaches them the just measures of their authority & all the true Uses of it as 'tis derived from the Supream Lord for the good of the People, and to be used for Him, to promote their Felicity, according to the just, natural & covenanted Rights of the people...." This will become still more evident in later chapters.

The evidence shows that neither the clergy, including Wise, nor the laymen as a whole turned so completely from theology and the Scripture in their political thinking as Adams implies. There was no conflict in their minds between the divine and natural law. They were the same. For further references to social compact, etc., see S. Williams, Connecticut Election Sermon: 1741, pp. 23–25; E. Holyoke, Massachusetts Election Sermon, 1736, p. 112; Frink, Massachusetts Election Sermon, 1758, pp. 73–74; S. Haven, Sermon, 1761, p. 9.

23. Each went through two editions.

24. For further details, see Chap. 5; Dexter, *Congregationalism as seen in its Literature*, pp. 513, gives an account of the quarrel. Walker, *Creeds and Platforms*,

Wise's conclusion as to the power of the individual church and highly disapproved of democracy in church or state, preferring rather a balanced government, they yet agreed with him that compact was the method by which the people set up government.

There was, however, some difference of opinion as to whether all governments of whatsoever kind originated in compact. Joseph Moss in his Connecticut Election Sermon of 1715 said that all just governments originated either in compact or conquest, the latter where the war was a just one.[25] John Barnard in 1734 said that all governments "upon a more Thorow Examination" resolved themselves into compact and agreement.[26] In 1738 in a remarkable sermon on government, in which he quoted Locke, Puffendorf, Rapin, and others, Jared Eliot declared that civil government was set up by force, by fraud, or by compact, which was the most ordinary and most regular government;[27] that the government was a legal one once a people was reduced, whether the method be by conquest or by covenant.[28] The majority believed as did Elisha Williams that all governments which did not originate from the people and in which they did not make their own laws were not, properly speaking, governments at all, but tyrannies and "absolutely against the Law of God and Nature."[29] There was no medium between common consent and lawless force and violence.[30]

---

pp. 492–93, thinks Wise's pamphlets of less influence than the opposition of the General Court.

25. J. Moss, Connecticut Election Sermon, 1715, pp. 6–7.

26. J. Barnard, Massachusetts Election Sermon, 1734. Cf. Wm. Welsteed, Massachusetts Election Sermon, 1751, pp. 11–12: all right to rule over men, even that founded in conquest, "must finally be resolved into Compact, Consent, and Agreement...."

27. J. Eliot, Connecticut Election Sermon, 1731, p. 31. This is the first direct mention of Locke found in the writings of the clergy.

28. *Ibid.*, p. 11.

29. E. Williams, *A Seasonable Plea*, 1744, pp. 4–5, 63, quotes Locke on Government very freely.

30. Mayhew, Massachusetts Election Sermon, 1754, pp. 5–8. B. Stevens, Massachusetts Election Sermon, 1761, p. 16, says the Jewish like all other free governments was founded on compact.

Four

Theories Concerning
Rulers in Church and State

Samuel Stoddard in an Election Sermon of 1703 made the assertion that "The abuses that are offered unto a People by their Rulers, and the abuses that are offered unto the Rulers by the People are deeply resented by God."[1] Over half a century later Benjamin Stevens, in a similar sermon, declared that "The Majesty of laws must be revered, where the liberties of a people are secured."[2] Thus the New England ministers applied the concept of compact obligations, natural law, and God-given rights to their conception of the relative power and duties of rulers and people. This was a subject which was sure to catch men's attention and arouse controversy, especially in the first half of the eighteenth century when certain of the older traditions and ways of life were breaking down under the impact of new economic and social conditions.

By 1715 a period of rapid growth in the New England colonies had set in. Men began to move into the western part of Massachusetts and the less settled regions of Connecticut and up along the rivers into Vermont and New Hampshire. They were eager for land, even to the extent of buying it when they had no intention of settling. New towns were founded, old ones were divided. There were quarrels between absentee proprietors and settlers, quarrels

1. Stoddard, Massachusetts Election Sermon, 1703, p. 4.
2. Stevens, Massachusetts Election Sermon, 1761, p. 63.

over land titles, quarrels over church affairs and over many other matters There were wars, bitter party strife, struggles between the lower and upper houses of the legislature, disputes with the governors, depreciation of the currency, speculation, greater differentiation in wealth, hard times for the poor.[3] There was widespread discontent among the people. Men were inclined to ignore distinctions of rank and to criticize the government, to talk vaguely of equality and liberty, of oppression and the burden of heavy taxes. There was what the clergy were pleased to call a "levelling spirit"[4] loose in the land, especially in Connecticut.[5] In church as well as in state the common man was inclined to insist on his rights.

To many of the clergy the spirit of the day seemed disorderly and lawless and they feared for the welfare of the government. They believed it their peculiar business to be "watchmen on the tower," to scent out and warn against danger and to set men right as to the principles upon which they were to act and the views they were to hold.[6] Some blamed the people and emphasized the need of submission to government and to authority. These believed it the special charge of gospel ministers "to put their Flock in mind to be Subject to Principalities and Powers and to obey Magistrates."[7] Others did not hesitate to lay a large share of the trouble at the

---

3. For a full account see Adams, *Revolutionary New England*. Much can be learned from the sermons of the period, though one must always take into account the traditional character of the election sermons and the natural tendency of the clergy, especially the older ones, to exaggerate the evils of the day.

4. [The "Levellers" were a faction during the days of Cromwell. They demanded greater religious toleration and expanded equality before the law, including expanded suffrage for non-property owners. Their views were radical for their time and widely feared by established powers who saw the demand to share power as a revolt against constituted authority (see, for example, the quotation on p. 79 below). While the Levellers were long gone by the era under discussion, the "levelling spirit" was still widely exclaimed as a political bogeyman.—JM]

5. For causes of this, see Chaps. 5–7.

6. N. Appleton, Convention Sermon, 1743, pp. 27–30.

7. Pemberton, Massachusetts Election Sermon, 1710, p. 87; various other illustrations might be given. S. Whittelsey, Connecticut Election Sermon, 1731, p. 35.

door of the rulers and to enlarge upon the duties of rulers to people. The Bible, so these said, was far more concerned with the good of subjects than with the splendor of rulers.[8] But conservatives and liberals felt the necessity of defining clearly what a just government should be and the respective rights and duties of rulers and people. So the main topic of the political sermons and of many of those more purely religious was what constituted lawful authority. And again the clergy searched the scriptures and the law of God as well as the writings of philosophers, ancient and modern.

There were certain texts which were used constantly. In the Bible rulers are "Gods," or "ordained of God." The people are bidden to be "subject to the higher powers," to "render unto Caesar the things that are Caesar's and unto God the things that are God's." But they are also told that rulers are "ministers of God for good," that "One is your Master even Christ," "You are called to liberty," and are commanded to "Stand fast in the liberty wherewith Christ hath made you free." How were these and other phrases to be interpreted and reconciled, and what must a government be like if it were based upon divine precepts? Moreover, the law of nature and the voice of reason also spoke God's will. What had they to tell about the relation of ruler and subject?

The ministers of New England believed that "rulers," among whom they included king, parliament, colonial governors and assemblies, and all in authority, were God's delegates and derived their power from Him.[9] But not directly. It were folly to think that and to base thereon any claim to absolute authority or divine right.[10] Rather their power came, as did civil government itself,

---

8. J. Eliot, Connecticut Election Sermon, 1738.

9. Typical references may be found in the Massachusetts Election Sermons of 1710 by Pemberton, p. 18; of 1744 by Allen, pp. 20, 25–26; of 1750 by Phillips, p. 3; in the Connecticut Election Sermons of 1713 by Bulkley, pp. 14–25; of 1719 by Chauncey, pp. 1–2; in a sermon at Portsmouth, N. H., by Haven, in 1761, p. 8.

10. Mayhew, *Sermon*, 1750, in Thornton, pp. 85–86. Massachusetts Election Sermon, 1754, pp. 4–5: "These notions are not drawn from the holy scriptures, but from a far less sure and sacred fountain. They are only the devices

only mediately from God but directly from the people.[11] It was not left to rulers to be oppressive and arbitrary, not even if their power came by conquest. God, from whom their power ultimately was derived, had limited that power.[12] Since rulers were called "Gods," they must conform to God's pattern and must labor to imitate

---

of lawned [land-owning—JM] parasites, or other graceless politicians, to serve the purposes of ambition and tyranny." E. Williams, 1744, *A Seasonable Plea*, p. 26: The Powers that be are of God, etc., "no doubt relates to Civil powers; . . . A Text often wrecked and tortured by such Wits as were disposed to serve the Designs of arbitrary Power, of erecting a civil Tyranny over a free people, and as often wrested out of their hands by the Force of Truth." There were numerous other such statements throughout the period. Occasionally, however, one finds a different belief. For other references see Appendix A.

11. J. Bulkley, Connecticut Election Sermon, 1713, p. 14: "In elective states, where Persons are Advanc'd by the Suffrage of others to Places of Rule, and vested with Civil Power, the Persons Chusing give not the Power, but God . . . And hence it is, that Humane Laws bind the Conscience; Not simply as Humane, but as made by that Authority which is Divine in its Original, and to which Obedience is Commanded in the Divine Law." J. Moss, Connecticut Election Sermon, 1715, pp. 7, 32, speaks of agreement between rulers and ruled, of compact and of virtual covenant between General Court and people. J. Barnard, Massachusetts Election Sermon, 1734, p. 17: "So that after all is said, the Right to rule takes its Rise from the Consent, and Agreement, that is the Choice and Election, of the Community, State, or Kingdom . . . and He, and He only, has the Right to rule, to whom the Government commits the Power, and Authority." J. Mayhew, Massachusetts Election Sermon, 1754, p. 6: "from man, from common consent, it is that lawful rulers immediately derive their power." Thomas Frink, Massachusetts Election Sermon, 1758, pp. 73, 74: "by Compact, Consent or Choice of the Persons governed." "The individual Person becomes the higher Power, by the Consent, the Choice or Contract original or actual, of the Community." S. Haven, Sermon, at Portsmouth, 1761, p. 9, speaks of "the mutual contract between the prince and the subjects." There are many other similar references. A few emphasize the derivation of power from God and make the King the fountain of all power. Cf. Bulkley, 1692. E. Adams, Connecticut Election Sermon, 1733, stresses power as derived from God and therefore not to be resisted, as does Throop, Massachusetts Election Sermon, 1758.

12. Pemberton, Massachusetts Election Sermon, 1710, pp. 18, 97; Wise, Massachusetts Election Sermon, 1729, pp. 18–19; J. Ingersoll, Connecticut Election Sermon, 1761, pp. 17–18; Haven, Sermon at Portsmouth, 1761, pp. 8–9. There are many similar statements; see Appendix.

God's government.[13] Here the analogy between theology and political philosophy is striking. God and Christ govern men for their good, therefore so must human rulers.[14] For that and that only do they exist. "The tye is Sacred and Deep to manage this great betrustment faithfully," said John Hancock in 1722.[15]

God and Christ govern always by fixed rules, by a divine constitution, and therefore so must human rulers.[16] The fundamental constitutions of states may differ; men's rights under them may be greater or less, but certain great rights are given by Nature and Nature's God to the people. These are a part of every constitution and no ruler is permitted by God to violate them. Rulers cannot change the constitution; that can be done only by the people. But the constitution and the laws must be consonant with the divine law.[17] Therefore rulers must study carefully the law of God, both natural and revealed.[18] In the Bible are found all the maxims and rules of government: there the natural laws are made clearer, there the ruler

13. Appleton, Sermon, 1742, p. 49: "The Grand Charter which the Sovereign of the World has given to Magistrates, impowers them to make Orders and By-Laws (for human Laws are no other) for the well-ordering and governing civil Societies, but it is with this Limitation and Proviso, that they be not repugnant to the Law of God, which is the Law of Justice, Truth, Mercy and Goodness, your Laws then must be tempered after the same Manner." J. Allen, Massachusetts Election Sermon, 1744, pp. 28–29: "great end of government is the good of the subject: This is the very design of Christ himself in his rule over us. . . . Now in this the God of heaven is a pattern to our earthly Gods. . . ."

14. Belcher, Massachusetts Election Sermon, 1701, pp. 32–35, shows how Joshua, Moses, David, and Solomon had only the good of the people at heart.

15. Hancock, Massachusetts Election Sermon, 1722, p. 15.

16. References for most of these statements will be found in connection with later quotations.

17. Davenport, *Power of Congregational Churches*, p. 129; Fitch, Connecticut Election Sermon, 1674, p. 14; Cutler, Connecticut Election Sermon, 1717, pp. 16–17. Laws must not cross antecedent obligations we lie under to laws of Nature and of God; and must he such as to make it no sin to obey them. Cf. also Ingersoll, Connecticut Election Sermon, 1761, pp. 17–18.

18. Moss, 1715, pp. 13–14; Breck, 1728, p. 22; Buckingham, 1728, p. 42; Appleton, Sermon, 1742, pp. 11–13; Worthington, 1744, p. 29; Woodbridge, 1752, pp. 10–11; Mayhew, 1754, pp. 6–8.

learns his due authority and its limitations, there the people learn how far they must submit. Rulers must also thoroughly understand the constitution and the civil law, that they may learn their obligations and the people's rights.[19] Even when God dealt with the Jews who were under His immediate government, He had their rulers write down the constitution in a book and read it constantly. It was evident that knowledge and ability were necessary, and the clergy were unanimous in requiring these qualities in civil rulers and for the most part in their ministers as well.[20] If the instructions of its clergy for a hundred years had any weight, it is no wonder that New England wanted its leaders well-born and able.

Not only are the rulers strictly limited by law, but the people are as well. To submit to lawful authority is required of them by God.[21] This does not mean a lessening but rather a preservation of

19. Moss, 1715, pp. 18–19, 25–28. They must have leisure and good pay for this purpose. Mather, 1725, p. 7; Buckingham, 1728, p. 42; Wise, 1729, p. 11: "They should be well seen into the fundamental Laws of the Constitution, by which the Liberties and Privileges of the Subject are secured; as well as the Prerogative of the Prince is ascertained. For if the Rulers of a People don't rightly understand the Constitution, or duly consider whether it be an absolute Monarchy, . . . or a mixt Monarchy, where the Prerogative is bounded and limited by Law; and the Subjects Liberty and Property secured by legal Fences. If they don't duly consider how dearly their Privileges have been purchased, how highly they are esteemed, how valuable they are in themselves, and how jealous a People justly are of them, the Rulers may not be so careful to keep the Constitution, and establish Laws and Rules made for the Defence of these invaluable Privileges." Worthington, 1744, p. 28: the "very Principles and Foundation of Governments and the Secrets of Politicks," the statutes and common law, etc. T. Barnard, Sermon, 1763, p. 25; and many others. Swift, in *Mass. Col. Soc. Pub.* I. 405, says that four-fifths of all Massachusetts Election Sermons deal with the character of the good ruler.

20. At first Separates and Baptists laid little stress upon an educated clergy, but before the Revolution the Baptists had founded Brown University to supply the growing demand.

21. A commonplace throughout the whole period; even Mayhew, who was so outspoken against arbitrary power and so devoted to freedom, said, "However, it is not to be forgotten that as in all free constitutions of government, law, and not will, is the measure of the executive Magistrate's power, so it is the measure of the subject's obedience and submission" (Election Sermon, 1754, pp. 20–21).

their liberty, for law is the basis of liberty. The restraint put upon
Christians by Christ is for the very purpose of increasing their liberty, and so it is in civil government. Without law and obedience to
law there would be no liberty; lawlessness on the part of the people
is quite as likely to destroy it as tyranny and oppression on the part
of rulers. Neither tyranny nor anarchy is pleasing to God.[22]

One of the most striking features of the political philosophy of
the ministers is this emphasis upon fundamental law and its binding quality. Many of the election sermons discussed it and some
were remarkably detailed, but it was also the subject of sermons
less political in their nature. It came up repeatedly in ecclesiastical
controversies and in the struggle for religious toleration. Only the
language used by the ministers themselves can give any vivid conception of their convictions.[23]

Gershom Bulkeley, who in 1692 published his *Will and Doom*
already referred to, resented the fact that all those who did not
agree with the independent action of Connecticut were accused
of being enemies to lawful government. He believed that the king,
was the fountain of all power but that he was strictly limited by
God. No human law can be contrary to the law of nature and right
reason, he said, for an unreasonable law is a law against law, and
unlawful authority is no authority. All lawful authority comes
from God and must be obeyed, but unlawful or usurped authority
may be resisted.[24] Cotton Mather was just as definite. Speaking of
the Declaration of Indulgence by James II, he said:

> If it assumed an illegal power of dispensing with laws, yet
> in relation to them, it only dispensed with the execution

22. A common idea in the sermons, with varying emphasis; Belcher, Massachusetts Election Sermon, 1701, p. 31, says that tyranny unless very extreme
is better than anarchy.

23. These sermons are to be found in various New England libraries but
they are so little read that it seems wise to quote certain ones at some length.
See Appendix A.

24. G. Bulkeley, "Will and Doom," *Conn. Hist. Soc. Coll.* III. 93–97. See also
"The People's Rights to Election or Alteration of Government in Connecticut,"
Conn. Hist. Soc. Coll., I.

of such infamous laws as were *ipso facto* null and void before; laws contrary to the laws of God, and the rights and claims of human nature. . . .[25]

One of the early sermons mentioned and quoted by other ministers was the Massachusetts Election Sermon of 1710 by Ebenezer Pemberton. God, said Pemberton, is the source of all power and all rulers are accountable to Him. God rules "not by unaccountable will but by stable measures," therefore earthly rulers likewise govern by "unalterable principles, and fixed Rules." Pemberton grew impatient with those who "with a Nodd" tried to inflame the people and upon some slight complaint rouse rebellion. Yet he acknowledged , that the people must have some regular remedy when the "Fundamental Constitution" was overturned and their liberties and property invaded.[26]

Shortly afterwards, in 1713, there was preached an election sermon in Connecticut by John Bulkley which, aside from the two pamphlets of John Wise, is the most interesting of these early eighteenth-century political discourses. He discusses the mutual serviceableness of religion and civil government, religion being as essential to a due observance of good laws as to the making and due execution of them.[27] Religion inculcates good principles, es-

---

25. Cotton Mather, *Parentator*, p. 102, quoted from *Letter Book* of S. Sewall, I. 56, note.

26. For fuller quotation see Appendix A. See also Woodbridge, Connecticut Election Sermon, 1752, p. 10: both "Light of Nature and Revelation agree . . . that he that ruleth over men must be Just." Appleton, Sermon, 1742, pp. 35–36, 57–58, thinks the people, though sometimes led away, can judge as to the justice of rulers and whether they are oppressed and injured. Sermon 1757, p. 18: If a ruler oppresses the people, "He acts quite contrary to the original Design of Government and contrary to the express Will of Him from whence all Power and Authority has derived."

27. See also Connecticut Election Sermons by Moss, 1715, pp. 13–14; Whittelsey, 1731, pp. 9–10; Williams, 1741, pp. 1, 8, 18–21, 23–25, 31; Worthington, 1744, pp. 4–5, 7–8; Whitman, 1745, p. 1–2; Woodbridge, 1752, pp. 10–11, 17–18; also Appleton, Sermon, 1742, pp. 11–12 and Mayhew, Sermon, 1754, p. 8. Various others are referred to elsewhere.

tablishes maxims of government, forces both ruled and ruler to a faithful performance of duty. He speaks strongly against "levelism" as tending to destroy government, but also declares that rulers must not be arbitrary but must "labour to imitate the Divine Government; which is manag'd by fixed and steady Rules," and government can be successful only as those rules are attended. God has in his Word fixed the bounds and limits of government; and though the various degrees of persons ruling and the limitations upon their power be left to men, yet they must have due regard to the general laws by which God describes and determines the bounds of human authority; and no power can be vested in men which is not proportioned to the public good. He says,

> Its not in the Power of Rulers to make what Laws they please, Suspend, Abrogate or Disanul them at pleasure. ... As for Mens Civil Rights, as Life, Liberty, Estate, &c. God has not Subjected these to the Will & Pleasure of Rulers. They may not Enact any Laws to the Prejudice of them, nor Disanul such Laws of the State as tend to Secure these Interests.... Tis already Determin'd in the Divine Law (with relation to these Interests of a People) that the Enjoyment of them be free & undisturb'd and Rulers may not make any Determinations repugnant here to: Or, if they do, they are of no force. No Law of the Civil Magistrate can bind in Opposition to the Divine.... And as to such things being indifferent in their own Nature, and not already Determin'd in the Law of God, nor by Principle deducible therefrom, altho' they are subject to the Determination of Humane Authority, yet all must be done in due Subordination to those Laws of God that have made it a Sin in any to invade these Rights of a People."[28]

---

28. J. Bulkley, Connecticut Election Sermon, 1713. pp. 3–30. Like references are very numerous.

That rulers must preserve the life, liberty, and property of the people inviolate or else act in opposition to God's law is an idea repeated constantly in the sermons and pamphlets written by the clergy. From the middle of the seventeenth century this is a common phrase, especially liberty and property. The significance of this is great and cannot be overemphasized. No one can fully understand the American Revolution and the American constitutional system without a realization of the long history and religious associations which lie behind these words; without realizing that for a hundred years before the Revolution men were taught that these rights were protected by divine, inviolable law.

The first of the eighteenth-century ministers who made the rules which are binding upon the ruler depend upon compact was Joseph Moss in his Connecticut Election Sermon of 1715, two years before Wise published his famous *Vindication*. All just government, he says, is founded either in compact, or in conquest where that is just. If founded on compact between ruler and ruled, some laws must be formulated binding the former, which must be impartially executed;[29] even if founded in conquest, God requires

---

29. "As none can make a just Claim to any Natural Original Right to Rule over others, (Family Rulers only excepted) so Mankind never did nor will, Submit themselves voluntarily to the Government of others their Fellow-Men; but upon some Agreement of what Rules the Ruler or Rulers should observe in Government; which Rules are the Laws of that Kingdom or State so Covenanting to be under Government; and in such Government founded thus Originally in Compact; the right Execution of the Civil Rulers Office lyeth in the impartial & upright Administration of Justice . . . according to the Rules," (J. Moss, Connecticut Election Sermon, 1715, pp. 6–8, 32, 40). T. Buckingham, Connecticut Election Sermon, 1728, p. 43, says there must be some fixed rules of government duly published; that a constitution of good laws is absolutely necessary for both people and rulers. Jeremiah Wise, Massachusetts Election Sermon, 1729, pp. 11–19, says rulers should know well the fundamental laws of the constitution by which the liberties and privileges of the subject as well as the prerogative of the prince are secured. Rulers are to govern by fixed rules, those of God's Word and human laws agreeable thereto. Rulers cannot invade the rights and the liberties of the people. God does not permit it. He quotes Bishop Burnet. Such quotations before 1760 could be multiplied.

the conqueror to make good laws and to observe them faithfully. Moss believed that the people must submit to rulers so long as they kept within their legal limits.

In 1722 the man who delivered the election sermon at Boston was John Hancock of Lexington, the predecessor of Jonas Clark of Revolutionary fame, and the grandfather of the more famous John Hancock. His whole sermon is on rulers as benefactors, and he is most emphatic in his denunciation of those who abuse the rights and liberties of the people. When rulers so abuse their power, he says, they are "the greatest Burdens unto Mankind, and the greatest Plagues and punishments to the World. . . ." He then addresses the Court directly:

> if you should abuse your Power, and go over all the bounds of your Duty & Obligations; oppress & vex this People, and lay heavy burdens upon them, and grievous to be born; you'd forfeit the gratitude and regard due to Benefactors; and become obnoxious not only to the resentments of the People groaning under their burdens, but also to the Divine Displeasure; . . . As Oppression makes a wise man mad, so it makes a righteous God angry.[30]

One of the ministers whose convention and election sermons defined good government and the power of rulers both in church and state was John Barnard of Marblehead. In his Election Sermon of 1734 he discusses the origin of government and the right to rule in compact and then turns to the constitution of a state. Righteousness in a ruler, either executive or legislative, means acting upon and preserving the constitution.

It is certain, (with a proper Salvo to the natural Rights

---

30. J. Hancock, Massachusetts Election Sermon, 1722, pp. 13–14, 24–25; Stoddard, Massachusetts Election Sermon, 1703, p. 15: "When People are put to unnecessary charge, they are Oppressed, and when they are Oppressed, they are abused; it is directly contrary to the Office of Rulers, to lay heavy burdens on the People . . ." Cf. also N. Hunn, Connecticut Election Sermon, 1747, pp. 14–15.

of Mankind, which it is the End of all Government to
preserve,) none can have any Right to act contrary to the
fundamental Laws of that State, till all Parties concerned
agree upon such Alterations as are thought needful, and
then those Alterations become wrought into the Constitution, and are a certain Rule for all the Parts of the
Government to go by, in their future Administrations.[31]

This careful observance of the constitution is especially necessary in a "mixed government," that no part may overstep its authority but that each may preserve its rights inviolate. Barnard
also declares that the natural and civil rights of subjects must be
zealously guarded by rulers, but he deplores the fact that persons
of boundless ambition often foment popular clamor about liberty
and property and delude people into thinking they are in danger
when all they want is uncontrolled sway. Such designs, he says,
must be guarded against.

During the period before 1740 the Connecticut ministers
seem to have been less concerned with the rights of the people
than were those of Massachusetts, and they were more afraid of
"levelism." They drew a dark picture of conditions in that colony,
of "great swelling words" against government and against dignitar-
ies in church and state which even went to the extreme of condemning all government and breathing sedition.[32] The complaint

---

31. J. Barnard, Massachusetts Election Sermon, 1734, pp. 23–24. For fuller
quotations, see Appendix A. In his Convention Sermon of 1738, Barnard quotes
Hoadly on the right's of the people. This is much like Chauncey's Sermon of 1747.
See also Holyoke, Massachusetts Election Sermon, 1736, pp. 12–13.

32. Connecticut Election Sermons, Wakeman, 1685, p, 27; Buckingham,
1711, seems to be quoted in part from Wakeman; Whitman, 1714, p. 28; Cutler, 1717, pp. 49, 55, says there is still reason to complain of Injustice, Fraud,
and Oppression; Estabrook, 1718, p. 23; Marsh, 1721, pp. 25–28, speaks of
a mighty spirit, both in and out of the Assembly, for land; Williams, Sermon,
1741, pp. 38–39, same; Williams, 1723, pp. 16–20, says some are saying: "All
men are of the same flesh and blood, and why should any exercise Government
over others?" and suggests that rulers may be largely to blame; J. Allen, Thanksgiving Sermon, 1722; A. Mather, 1725, pp. 26–27, 19–20, hopes that under a

seems to have been most bitter during the regime of Governor Saltonstall, who was instrumental in having the Saybrook Platform made law. But though less extreme, it continued, and certain of the clergy themselves were accused by their brethren of stirring up sedition. During this period the ministers chosen to give the election sermon described strongly the dangers of "levelism." It would mean, so they said, the destruction of all government and was contrary to the will of God, who has decreed that there shall be differences of degree among men. Some, however, implied and a few declared that the rulers were themselves to blame. Thus Eleazar Williams, in 1723, after lamenting the licentious and levelling spirit of the day and the mighty desire for land among all classes, suggested that the rulers see whether there were not fault among them to account for their being "the song and common talk of the Drunkard over their Cups."[33] Many other ministers stated in general terms the duty of rulers to safeguard the rights of the people in church and state.

It was the desire to show clearly how greatly it was to men's interest to support government, to fulfil their obligations to civil rulers, that led Jared Eliot, the pastor of Killingworth and the friend and correspondent of Benjamin Franklin, to undertake in 1738 a careful consideration of the nature of government. This is the first work by any one of the New England clergy, so far as can be learned, which quotes freely from Locke, Puffendorf, and Rapin, at the same time mentioning them by name. Eliot begins

---

new governor he will hear no more of "Arbitrary Power & Despotic Proceedings among us." Russel, 1730, p. 14; Whittelsey, Sermon, 1731, pp. 30–32, says some would "Raze to the Foundation the whole Constitution, rather than submit to a supposed Injury"; Adams, 1733, pp. 57–58, 63, 65 speaks of some ministers who head "uneasie parties" against Government; J. Marsh, 1736, p. 19; Eliot, 1738, p. 44. Others after 1740 are referred to in Chaps. 5 and 6.

33. E. Williams, Connecticut Election Sermon, 1723, p. 41. In using election sermons one must take into account their tendency to conform to type, as well as the fact that the ministers who delivered them were chosen by the General Assembly and that it seems to have been a matter of long custom to bewail the evils of the time.

his sermon by discussing man in a state of nature and says that an exact account of such an one is given in the account of Ishmael. He dilates upon the checks and balances of the British government, upon its growth since the days of the Anglo-Saxons, and lauds it as a legal government, the corner-stone of which is that "no man's Life, Limb, Name or Estate, shall be taken away but by his Peers, and by the known Law of the Land." The governments in the British plantations are but as "little Models" of that at home, with the same liberties but with the additional liberty of electing their own rulers from among themselves. He discusses sovereign authority and declares it a fundamental principle of government that it must lodge somewhere. The community, he says, has placed it in the legislature[34] and therefore individuals have nothing to do to judge of the expediency of the laws. There is no government where there is absolute liberty. Statutes are a restraint upon natural liberty, but for the purpose of preserving all such liberty as is good for the whole. Law indeed is the very basis of civil liberty.[35] Thus one sees how mistaken are the men who think of government as only "the contrivance of artful and designing Men, who would make themselves great at the Expence of their poor Neighbours; who would oppress the Poor, and grind the face of the Needy." Eliot defines a "Legal, Limited & well Constituted Government" as one in which the ruler limits himself for the good of the subject, an act in itself of sovereign power.[36] If, however, laws should be made by this gov-

34. Jared Eliot and Samuel Hall, also of Conn., are the only two read who bestow upon the legislature absolute sovereignty. Hall in 1746 says that "the Legislature is Accountable to none: There is no Authority above them; none can call them to an Account, but only that God by whom Kings reign and Princes decree Justice." Eliot believed that in extreme cases, where the Government disregarded divine law, it might be opposed.

35. See also Dickinson, Connecticut Election Sermon, 1755, p. 11; Stevens, Massachusetts Election Sermon, 1761, pp. 70–71; Mayhew, Massachusetts Election Sermon, 1754, pp. 20–21. Various others give expression to the same idea, a common one.

36. J. Eliot, p. 36. See also pp. 11–39. See Appendix A. An example of a different conception, one much more common, is in Frink, Massachusetts Election Sermon, 1758, p. 73: "It remains . . . . that this Authority be conveyed to

ernment which are inconsistent with the laws of God or which sap the foundations of the commonwealth, men must exercise their right of discretion and must obey God rather than men, as the Apostles did.[37]

Among those who dwelt long upon the nature and advantages of a balanced government and who were outspoken in laying the evils of the day upon the general Court was Charles Chauncey, of Boston, the same Chauncey who was the friend of Samuel and John Adams and of the other Revolutionary leaders, one of the most ardent and influential in the American cause. His sermon of 1747 won so much criticism from the General Court that there was some question of printing it. "It shall be printed," he said, "whether the General Court print it or not. And do you, Sir, . . . say from me that, if I wanted to initiate and instruct a person into all kinds of iniquity and double dealing, I would send him to our General Court."[38] And printed it was.

Much of this sermon is like many before its day, recommending the election of able men who understand the laws and constitution, the nature of government and the privileges of the people; discussing the origin of government in the reason of things and at the same time its foundation in the will of God, since reason and the voice of God are one; stating that God wills that some rule and some be in subjection and this for the purpose of guarding "men's lives, liberties and properties"; that rulers must confine themselves within the limits of the constitution by which their power is delegated to them. "Especially," he says, "is this an important point of justice, where the constitution is branched into several parts . . . in order to preserve a

---

this or that individual Person or Family, by Compact, Consent or Choice of the Persons governed . . . And this is what men call a legal Right or Title to the Crown, i.e., a Title by the Laws & Constitution of the Land." Quoted from Whitby's *Annotations*.

37. J. Eliot, Connecticut Election Sermon, 1738, pp. 13–14. Stevens, Massachusetts Election Sermon, 1761, p. 36, also mentions the Apostles as claiming their rights and privileges as men and as Christians and obeying God rather than man.

38. Sewall, *Letter Book*, II, pp. 236–237, note.

ballance in the whole . . . They have severally and equally a right to that power which is granted to them in the constitution."³⁹

Chauncey discusses also the rights and privileges of the subject. In all governments, he says, there is a reserve of certain rights, in some few and small, in some many and great, and it is no wonder that the people keep a jealous eye upon these rights and think to defend them at any cost, especially when they had been won through great hardships by their ancestors. "Shall such valuable, dearbought rights be neglected, or invaded by the rulers of a people,"⁴⁰ one of whose chief ends is to perpetuate and secure a full enjoyment of them? Nay, rulers must defend them against all threat, either by arbitrary rulers or seditious people. Like certain other ministers, Chauncey talks of the danger to a people's liberties from men who "strike in with the popular cry of liberty and privilege,"⁴¹ thus working themselves into the good opinion of the populace as lovers of their country when all they are aiming at is their own power. Such he regards as dangerous enemies to the community.

It was only three years later that Jonathan Mayhew, of the West Church, Boston, preached his famous sermon on *Unlimited Submission and Non-Resistance to the Higher Powers.* This sermon is the one most frequently quoted, but his election sermon of 1754 has many of the same ideas and phrases.

Although Mayhew was bolder in speech than many of the other ministers, there is nothing in either of these sermons which may not be found in many others. Their fame is due partly to their vigorous language and partly to Mayhew's renown as a young, radical preacher, engaged in the theological controversies of the day, who drew young men to him, who played a conspicuous part in the trouble over an American Episcopate, and whose sermons were read widely, both in England and America. He was a bold and passionate advocate of civil and religious liberty. From 1748 until his

39. C. Chauncey, Massachusetts Election Sermon, 1747, pp. 14–15.
40. *Ibid.*, p. 33. See also E. Williams, *A Seasonable Plea*, 1744, and Hunn, Connecticut Election Sermon, 1744. p. 14.
41. Chauncey, p. 34.

death in 1766 he preached and wrote for the cause so dear to his heart. He had studied Locke, Milton, Sydney, and others and was instrumental in having many books on government sent to Harvard and elsewhere by his friend, Thomas Hollis, of London.[42]

The occasion for Mayhew's sermon was the order to observe the birthday of Charles I, but the liberal Congregationalist was aroused by the activity of the Society for the Propagation of the Gospel and the growth of Episcopalianism. He was doubtless influenced also by the growing antagonism of the day to any kind of arbitrary control, English or Colonial. This famous sermon was a fiery thing which must have stirred the blood of his hearers in the old West Church. "There is nothing in Scripture which supports this scheme of political principles," he asserts of the doctrine of unlimited submission.

> Neither God nor nature has given any man a right of dominion over any society independently of that society's approbation and consent to be governed by him. . . . [D]isobedience is not only lawful but glorious [to those that] enjoin things that are inconsistent with the demands of God![43]

The people themselves are to judge when resistance is right, nor will they be inclined to judge unwisely. A ruler is as much bound by law and the constitution as are the people. But Mayhew, like his fellows and predecessors, believed also that law was the measure not only of the magistrate's power but of the subject's obedience and submission.[44] "Only," he observes,

> it is very strange we should be told, at this time of day, that loyalty and slavery mean the same thing; tho' this is plainly the amount of that doctrine which some, even

42. Bradford, *Life of Dr. Mayhew*, p. 18, note; Thornton, Pulpit in the American Revolution, pp. xxxii–xxxiv. For fuller account of his work and influence see later chapters.

43. Mayhew, Sermon, 1750, in Thornton ed., pp. 81, 86, 87.

44. Mayhew, Election Sermon, 1754, p. 20.

now, have the forehead to ventilate, in order to bring a reproach upon the Revolution [1688], upon the present happy settlement of the crown, and to prepare us for the dutiful reception of an hereditary Tyrant.[45]

These and like sermons and pamphlets show clearly the continuity and strength of these political principles, how intimately they were associated with the Bible, which was interpreted to give them a divine origin and sanction, how the phrases, through long repetition and association with religion, were bitten deep into men's minds long before the outbreak of trouble with England. It becomes abundantly evident, after studying these and like words of the ministers, that Samuel Langdon, of Portsmouth, New Hampshire, was voicing a common conviction when in 1759 he said that a government which had a constitution agreeable to the laws of nature, serving the ends of society, securing the life, liberty, and property of the people, was peculiarly of God and "conformable to the perfect pattern of his supreme dominion."[46]

45. *Ibid.*, pp. 20–21. See *Sermons*, 1748, pp. 85–86, for discussion of duty of magistrates to preserve the natural rights of subjects, and Sermons, 1755, pp. 313–314, for necessity of submitting only to "rightful demands."

46. S. Langdon, Sermon at Portsmouth, 1759, pp. 9–10.

Five

Political Philosophy and Ecclesiastical Controversy before 1743

*S*omething of the close connection between religion and political theory has been brought out in the preceding chapters. To realize it more fully and to gain a better understanding of the long background and the true meaning of many of
the Revolutionary arguments, it is necessary to study in somewhat
more detail the religious and ecclesiastical controversies of the period and especially the Great Awakening which so deeply affected
men's emotions and thinking. Such a study will serve to make more
clear the interest of the New Englander in fundamental law, his belief that any violation of it by those in authority was tyranny, and
that revolt against such tyranny was legal and not only legal but a
religious duty. What civil and religious liberty, property, and equality meant to both clergy and laity at the opening of the Revolution
cannot be fully grasped without a study of the Great Awakening.
But before attempting to show how the familiar terms were thus
vitalized it is necessary to review briefly their earlier meaning.

Before 1740, we have seen, the ministers had taught that civil
liberty was a natural right. The natural man had been under no
human authority of any sort. He was free to do what he liked for
his own advantage.[1] But under civil government which he set up

1. There was before 1740 much talk of liberty as a natural right, but few
defined it as it existed in the natural state. John Wise in 1717 was among the

for his own good, restraints were imposed by compact and by law that the freedom remaining might be better secured. Therefore, liberty did not mean license. On that point the ministers were unanimous. As to how much liberty remained to men, John Wise, alone, wrote that only so much was given up as was necessary for the public good. But though not distinctly stated by others before 1740, it was implied in the emphasis upon the end of government and the office of ruler. Liberty certainly meant that those in power, chosen by the people directly or by original compact, were also limited by law and could not exert any authority over them beyond those legal limits. Most of the clergy declared that the people were under obligation to obey authority only within these limits.

Property, another natural right, was as frequently asserted and was always linked with liberty, but was less clearly defined. It evidently meant freedom from burdensome taxation, the assurance that the fruit of a man's labor would not be taken from him by arbitrary means. At times the ministers warned those in authority that people who were put to unnecessary charge were oppressed and abused and that rulers were not permitted by God or Nature to lay such burdens upon them.[2] Jared Eliot in 1738 gave some interesting details of the kind of taxes he considered just. A wise government, he said, may at times give bounties to this or that manufacture provided it be for the good of the whole, although the people might find fault thereat; it may lay import or excise duties upon such things as are superfluous or not necessary to life or upon such as may by their increase become hurtful to the commonwealth; such duties should be aimed at the common good, not private gain.[3] Just and legal taxation was not an invasion of

first to do so. Eliot in 1738, was another.

2. Stoddard, Massachusetts Election Sermon, 1703, p. 15; Hancock, Massachusetts Election Sermon, 1722, pp. 24–25. Although they did not directly say so, some of the Connecticut election sermons of the same period implied the same.

3. Eliot, Connecticut Election Sermon, 1738, p. 12. The Connecticut election sermons spoke often of the complaint of heavy taxation by the people and their belief that they were being deprived of "liberty and property." Eliot

the natural right of property, so the ministers thought. No more complete account of its origin or nature was given before 1740, so far as has been learned.

Theories concerning the natural equality of men were rarely discussed by the clergy before 1740. As will be seen in later chapters, the term, as it was used later in the eighteenth century, was applied most frequently not to society as it actually existed but to the original state of nature before the organization of civil government and seems to have meant that men in this state had an equal right to the fruit of their labors and that no man had any authority over another. It was frequently defined as meaning equal in respect to authority. John Wise seems to have been the only minister before 1740 to write of the equality of the state of nature and the right to retain that equality under civil government to the highest degree consistent "with all just distinctions."[4] This implies that a part of the original equality is preserved after civil government is organized, and the problem then would be to determine just how much and what kind should be retained.

Many of the clergy of this period were deeply concerned over what seemed to them the dangerous tendency to ignore distinctions of rank in existing society. Most of those whose discourses were published before 1740 would seem to have agreed with Pemberton, who in 1710 said:

> Sure we may be since the Apostasy, there is Absolute Necessity of Superiority and Power in some, and Inferiority and Submission as to others. He well understood the Nature of men, and of Humane Societies, that say'd, . . . That nothing is more unequal than Equality

and many others mentioned this wide-spread indebtedness of the people. He wondered that honest men and Christians should glory in cheating the people through customs dues.

4. Whether Samuel Moody, John White, and other ministers who supported Wise in his opposition to Synodical control of the churches agreed with him only in the matter of the independence of the churches or in his belief in democracy as well has not been learned.

.... Levelism is therefore an open Defiance to God, his
Wisdom and Will, as well as the Reason of Mankind.[5]

Even John Wise, democrat as he was, implied that certain distinctions between men were necessary and just. The qualities and
knowledge required of rulers, both in church and state, were such
as humble men could not easily attain.[6] The dislike of "levelism" is
apparent throughout the first half of the eighteenth century and
to some extent later. The election sermons, especially in Connecticut, lament the tendency of the people to ignore distinctions of
rank and dress, to criticize those in authority over them, and even
to wish to reduce rulers and ruled to a level. One must of course
discount these sermons to some extent. The ministers were chosen
for the occasion by either the Assembly or Council and as a rule
would naturally be those whose known opinions pleased the body
which chose them, though it is obvious that some of them indulged
in a free, bold tongue. They were usually the more prominent ministers of the colony, as were also those who published pamphlets
other than sermons. There may have been less well-known men
who disagreed but who did not publish their opinions.

It was not only in discourses on civil government that arguments were based on natural, constitutional, and Christian rights,
but in those on ecclesiastical government as well. A glance at the
ecclesiastical disputes of the seventeenth and early eighteenth centuries will throw light upon the arguments used by the clergy in
discussing the rights of laymen and in asserting that great natural and Christian liberty, freedom of conscience and of judgment.

---

5. Pemberton, Election Sermon, 1710, pp. 15–16.

6. The election sermons and many other works of the clergy emphasized
the training and learning necessary for religious and secular leaders, some clergymen believing a fair degree of wealth necesary that they might have leisure
for study. "There are men," said Edward Holyoke in 1736, "who because of their
occupations, cannot get Knowledge which fits them for public position," such a
one who "holdeth the Plough and glorieth in the Goad, that driveth Oxen and
is occupied in their Labours, and whose Talk is of Bullocks" (Massachusetts
Election Sermon, 1736, pp. 19–20).

The larger part of the Congregationalists believed in a balanced government in the church as in the state, neither democratic with power in the hands of all the members, nor aristocratic with the power in the hands of the elders, but rather what Davenport called "Aristocratico-Democratical."[7] Urian Oakes in 1673, describing the "Congregational Way," with a slight change of wording might easily be describing civil government of the balanced type:

> There is a sweet temperament in the Congregational Way; that the liberties of the people may not be overlaid and oppressed, as in the classical way, nor the rule and authority of the Elders rendered an insignificant thing, and trampled under foot as in the way of the Brownists;[8] but that there may be a reconciliation or due concurrence in the balancing of the one justly with the other.[9]

There were, however, from the beginning differences of opinion and practice. Some were accused of too great democracy, of allowing the majority to rule, even if the elders were among the minority. Some, on the other hand, were accused of giving undue weight to the power of the elders.[10]

---

7. Davenport, *The Power of the Congregational Churches*, p. 120. See also Dexter's *Congregationalism as seen in its literature*, pp. 426–27, 429; Richard Mather's *Answer to 32 Questions*, written in 1639, published in 1643, and said by Dexter to have had the general consent of Elders in the Bay.

8. ["Brownists" were named after the English Dissenter, Robert Browne (d.1633). Following his views they abandoned attempts at reform from inside the Church of England, and practiced a church polity of radical separation and independence. While Browne's early efforts fell apart (due to internal strife), his views were carried by others, most notably the Plymouth colonists of 1620. By the time of our era under discussion, some Congregationalists had developed networks, compacts, and consociations for measures of unity, order, and accountability, and radical independence was objectionable among these.—JM]

9. Oakes, Massachusetts Election Sermon, 1673, quoted from Sprague, I. 143.

10. John Cotton began a series of discussions as early as 1634. Dexter says that Cotton believed Elders were to do business and people to submit. Samuel Stone, of Hartford, called the way advocated by R. Mather "A speaking Aris-

Another subject of discussion in the seventeenth century and one involving theories of government and liberty was that of the power of the individual church. The large majority of Congregationalists and all the Baptists believed that each church was a body with all power to choose its officers and manage its affairs. The Congregationalists believed in calling Councils for advisory purposes only, allowing them no real jurisdiction. This was a point insisted upon by some of the most famous early divines and thereafter had the sanction of their names. Most of those adopting the *Cambridge Platform* of 1648 held this view, but again there was a difference of interpretation, some leaning toward Presbyterianism and some thinking little of Councils and cherishing their complete local independence.[11] These rights of the churches were held to be a part of the liberty granted by Christ. In the state men might grant away a part of their liberty if they saw fit, or might have it taken away by a potent enemy, but whatever liberties were specially granted to Christians by the great Master of the Church could not be alienated in whole or in part.[12]

tocracy in the Face of a silent Democracy." Rathband in 1644 in his *Briefe Narration*, p. 27, speaks of variety of practice in New England. See Dexter, pp. 430 ff., 460–61. Dexter thinks Goodwin and Nye referred to Plymouth when they spoke of New England churches in which the majority ruled even when the pastors were opposed.

11. J. Cotton, 1643: "No church hath power of government over another" (Dexter, *Congregationalism as seen in its literature*, pp. 424–25). H. Peter, *Answer of the Elders*, 1643, p. iv, denies Independency, but says they cannot discover that they should be "under Canon, or power of any other church; under their Councell we are. We need not tell the wise whence Tyranny grew in Churches, and how commonwealths get their pressure in the like kind" (Dexter, p. 463). See also pp. 460–61, 464, 509–11; *Result of a Synod*, 1646, p. 64; *Answer of Elders & Messengers*, 1662, pp. 79, 113–116; Davenport, Massachusetts Election Sermon, 1669, p. 13.

12. Davenport, *The Power of the Congregational Churches*, pp. 7, 123, 129–30; Massachusetts Election Sermon, 1669, pp. 13–14. See also Norton, Massachusetts Election Sermon, pp. 7, 8, 11. To some New Englanders of the seventeenth century , this meant that the civil magistrate had no power over spiritual matters. There was much discussion over this point. For a full account see Dexter, *Congregationalism as seen in its literature*; Walker, *Creeds and Platforms*. See

A natural right which was also peculiarly a Christian privilege, so the new England ministers believed, was liberty of conscience. This was fully practiced and enacted into law only in Rhode Island.[13] Yet it was preached in other parts of New England, was a part of their faith, and a fault of which they were accused by their critics. The *Confession of Faith* of the Massachusetts Churches in 1680 defined the liberty which Christ has purchased for His disciples as meaning that God alone is Lord of the conscience and has left it free from any commandment of men not contained in His word or contrary to it; that to obey such commands would betray liberty of conscience; and that to require implicit faith and absolute obedience is to destroy both liberty of conscience and reason.[14] Samuel Rutherford said of New England men of a somewhat earlier day that liberty of conscience is "their intended Idoll in the bottome of their hearte."[15] That this did not mean what we call religious toleration is too well known to need comment, but at the least it gave a starting-point from which toleration might develop. It obviously depended upon the interpretation of what was in God's word or was contrary to it.

With the eighteenth century, certain of these problems grew more acute. The attempt to establish a Synod, its failure in Massachusetts and its partial success in Connecticut, has already been mentioned. This was regarded by such ministers as John Wise, Samuel Moody, and John White, and by many of the people, as an

also Davenport, *Power of the Congregational Churches; Result of a Synod*, 1646, and other pamphlets of the day.

13. Morgan Edwards, *Materials for a History of the Baptists in Rhode Island*, 1771, pp. 318–319: "Roger Williams, (saith Gov. Hopkins, Prov. Gazette), justly claims the honor of having been the first legislator in the world that fully and effectually provided for and established a free, full and absolute liberty of conscience."

14. *Confession of Faith of Massachusetts Churches*, 1680, p. 261 in 1772 ed. See also Davenport, Massachusetts Election Sermon, 1669, p. 14.

15. Dexter, *Congregationalism as seen in its literature*, pp. 460–61 and note; Rutherford, *A Free Disputation against Pretended Liberty of Conscience*, pp. 258–59, quoted from Dexter; Robert Baillie, *Letters and Journals*, II. 179, 181, 231, 254, 271, etc.

effort to increase the power of the clergy and to take away the liberties of the people. Perhaps in answer to the satire by John Wise, *The Churches Quarrel Espoused*, published in 1713 and reprinted in 1715,[16] Increase Mather issued in 1716 a *Disquisition concerning Ecclesiastical Councils* for the purpose of proving that the lay delegates to such councils had as decisive a vote as the elders. He insisted not only upon the independence of the particular church but also upon the helpfulness and concurrence of councils in ordination and dismissal of pastors, although he allowed them no juridical power.[17] To clinch his argument he turned, as did those discussing civil government, to the Light of Nature, which, he declared, directed to the establishment of Synods as well as did holy Scripture itself. He argued that the vote of the majority, elders being reckoned as no more important than lay delegates, was decisive and that neither churches nor persons whose case called for a Council ought to have their liberties infringed. "Popery came in at this door, of Pastors assuming more to themselves than belongs to them, and the Fraternities readiness to part with what was theirs. . . ." It had been argued, he said, that this would make it possible for "Ignorant Mechanicks" to outvote their learned pastors, and he proceeded to a most interesting defence of "Mechanicks," declaring that only the "prelatists" among New England ministers were opposed to their participation in Councils. There were mechanics, he said, who though they did not excel in "Humane Learning" were

16. Cotton Mather, "Diary," *Mass. Hist. Soc. Coll.*, 7th Ser., VIII. 327, says that "a furious Man, called John Wise . . . has lately published a foolish Libel, against some of us, for presbyterianizing too much in our Care to repair some Deficiences in our Churches. And some of our People, who are not only tenacious of their Liberties, but also more suspicious than they have cause to be of a Design in their pastors to make abridgments of them; are too much led into Temptation, by such Invectives. . . ." This was in Sept. 1715. Note from Sewall's *Diary*, III. 51, says that on Aug. 2, Mather preached and censured Wise—"called it a Satanic insult twice over, and it found a Kind Reception." Again in 1717, the year of the publication of Wise's *Vindication*, Mather wonders what he can do "that the poison of Wise's cursed Libel may have an Antidote?" (p. 450.)

17. I. Mather, *A Disquisition*, pp. 4–8, believed also in concurrent power of people and elders.

yet so well versed in the Scriptures and of such excellent natural accomplishments that they might be very useful in Synods.[18]

The next year there appeared the *Vindication* of John Wise, proving also from the Light of Nature that each church was truly a proper body full of power and authority to govern itself, as were all democracies, and emphasizing the natural equality and liberty of all men and their right to judge for themselves what was most for their happiness and well-being. Thus it was an ecclesiastical controversy that occasioned the first full definition of that natural liberty which had been so long asserted, the most complete analysis of the social compact before 1763 and the first discussion of equality, natural and civil.

Although the effort to form a Synod failed in Massachusetts, the discussion continued. In 1732 William Homes, of Chilmark, published a pamphlet supporting Synodical government, in which he compared civil and ecclesiastical government. Such a government, he said,

> is no more than what the light and law of nature which is the law of God directs all large societies unto, that have the government of themselves committed to them. . . .
> So it is in Great Britain . . . for tho every freeholder has a natural right to sit in parliament yet they look upon it as more prudent to deligate. . . .[19]

---

18. *Ibid.*, pp. 15 ff. Mather refers to Hooker's *Survey of Church Discipline* and says that if Mr. Cotton "has happened to drop a notion which does not well suit with Congregational Principles, which we take to be according to the Scripture, we are not bound to write after him" (p. 26). He was troubled that so many of the ministers in New England differed from him. He seems to have been less willing to grant power to Councils and Synods than were Cotton Mather and other prominent ministers. Pemberton, Solomon Stoddard, Jonathan Dickinson, Thomas Foxcroft, Nathan Prince, Edward Wigglesworth, and Benjamin Colman were among those who favored a more Presbyterian way. Moody, White, Wise, John Checkley, and others were opposed. See Murdock, *Increase Mather*, pp. 381 ff.

19. Wm. Homes, *Proposals of Some Things . . .* , 1732, p. 11.

And again it was upon natural as well as Christian liberty that John Barnard called in his vigorous defence of the power of the individual church and of freedom of conscience before the ministerial convention in 1738. Because a church, he said, has been founded in mutual covenant, in the free consent of every member, no person, civil or ecclesiastical, has any right to impose officers upon them or divest them of any officer without their own consent or to control them in any proper action. Such a church is not in subjection to any earthly power. As it is the right of every Christian to judge for himself in what way Christ will be acceptably served by him, so in like manner it is the right of each church to judge for itself as to the mode and form of worship and the discipline most agreeable to Him.[20] As it is an invasion of Christ's authority for any to give law unto His Church, so it is "a tyrannical Usurpation upon the liberties of the Christian Church for any to attempt forcibly to reduce other churches to their Scaulting."[21] Here he quotes Hoadly, "that great Master of Reason and Thought":

> The civil Magistrate has nothing to do, to enter with his Directions and Restraints, of Temporal Laws, which are executed by Temporal Power, into these matters. A people have still an unalienable Right to make the best of their Bibles. And therefore, when the civil Powers shall take upon them, to form churches, to ascertain who shall, and who shall not, belong to this or that particular church, and who shall enjoy the full Privileges, which, as Members of that Society, they have a natural, and religious, Right to, and who not; and when Church-Men, under whatever Denomination, shall pretend to exert an Authority over other Churches, and anathematize those that will not tamely submit themselves to their Determinations; I say, if ever such Principles and Practices should obtain among us, I must have leave to

---

20. J. Barnard, Convention Sermon, 1738, pp. 7ff.
21. *Ibid.*, p. 26. "Scaulting" is "Scolding."

lament over our Churches, . . . and to write upon them *Ichabod*) the Glory of New England is departed. For whatever Cry any may make of the Platform, and Congregational Principles, it is very certain that by such Means, the very Essence of Congregational Churches will be utterly overthrown.[22]

Such a sermon as this, delivered before the annual gathering of ministers, shows that Massachusetts was far ahead of Connecticut at this time in the interpretation of Christian liberty. In Connecticut, the Saybrook platform had been adopted by a Synod composed of twelve ministers and four laymen only, eight of the ministers being trustees of Yale College, at that time just established in Saybrook. Although the Synod was in no way representative, its platform was made law by the Connecticut Assembly in 1709 under the governorship of Saltonstall, a former clergyman, and remained on the statute books until 1784.[23] By this plan there were organized in each county one or more consociations of churches with power to settle all matters of discipline and to ordain, install, and dismiss ministers. The clergy were formed into associations for licensing candidates, and a general association was held annually. Still further limiting the power of the individual church, a law was passed in 1717 which permitted a majority of the voters of a town to choose the minister, whether or not they were members of the church.[24]

---

22. *Ibid.*, pp. 26–27. This, so far as has been found, is the first use by a New England minister of the word "unalienable," soon to become so common. Barnard was of course expressing the conservative view of men who did not want to change the old way, or yield to Anglicanism.

23. Parker, "The Congregational Separates of the 18th Century in Connecticut," *New Haven Colony Hist. Soc. Papers*, VIII. 152–53, 204–08; Trumbull, *History of Connecticut*, I. 409–17; *Colonial Records of Connecticut*, V. 87. The Platform admitted of a difference of interpretation and different parts of Connecticut interpreted it differently—Fairfield County Consociation being inclined to give the Consociation as much power as a Presbytery, and New Haven County more nearly maintaining Congregationalism.

24. Parker, p. 154; *Colonial Records of Connecticut*, VI. 33–34; Palfrey, III.

This action led to disastrous quarrels among the clergy and people. The law had become the ecclesiastical constitution, as it was called, and to those in its favor as much to be obeyed as the civil constitution. To others it was an invasion of their Christian liberty and therefore null and void. Certain churches refused to accept the platform and announced their adherence to the older Cambridge Platform which made Councils advisory only.[25] It seemed to many of the people an attempt to give the ministers the sole power of church government and to destroy the privileges of the brotherhood. It was an effort of the clergy, so they thought, to "lord it over God's heritage." They spoke of "Priest-Craft," of an "Ambitious and Designing Clergy."[26] There were divisions among the clergy as well, some accusing their brethren of leading the "un-easie parties" against the government,[27] others of trying to invade the liberties of the people. It was in part this quarrel which had led the clergy to enlarge upon the meaning of lawful authority and the duty of submission on the one hand and, on the other, upon the rights and liberties of the people and the limitations upon the rulers. Perhaps owing in part to these quarrels, religion had become to many mere formalism. There were ministers who had ceased to demand a definite religious experience either of their people or of themselves and were content to preach morality and sobriety and doctrines that had lost their vitality.[28] There was now and again among the people sharp criticism of the clergy for dullness

341; Cobb, *Rise of Religious Liberty in America*, p. 258. In 1727–29, laws were passed allowing Baptists, Episcopalians, and Quakers to pay rates to their own churches, as in Massachusetts. In New Hampshire, a law of 1714 allowed free-holders of towns to employ a minister. All were taxed for his support unless conscientiously of another sect and regularly attending a different service.

25. Trumbull, *History of Connecticut*, II. 87–103. The Eccles. Papers in manuscript in Conn. State Library give many illustrations of these and similar quarrels.

26. T. Cutler, Connecticut Election Sermon, 1727, p. 55.

27. E. Adams, Connecticut Election Sermon, 1733, p. 57.

28. Trumbull, History of Connecticut, II. 3–5, 103–05; Clark, *Congregational Churches in Massachusetts*, pp. 139–44, 154.

of sermon and deadness of spirit, for interest only in getting their salaries promptly paid. There was among certain of the clergy bitter complaint of their people, their unwillingness to pay the minister's rates,[29] their absorption in material interests, their lack of respect for and interest in spiritual matters.[30] Into the middle of these disputes came the Great Awakening.

There had been signs of a stirring of the spirit here and there, notably under Jonathan Edwards at Northampton in 1734–35,[31] but it was not until the arrival of George Whitefield in New England in 1740 that the great revival swept through the land. During this first visit ministers and people welcomed him gladly and churches and colleges were freely opened to him. He charmed men by his eloquence and held them by his sincerity. "The excellent, lovely, heavenly Whitefield," he was called by the enamored Governor Belcher.[32] Mr. Cutler of Boston wrote to the Bishop of London in 1740:

> He was the subject of all our Talk, and to speak against him was neither credible nor scarce safe. . . . Indeed the bitterest Zeal about him is among the Dissenting Laity who are for him by a vast majority. The Ruling part of the Clergy are for him almost everywhere, but the Major part only in this Town-Throughout the Province, they say 3/4 tho are against Him. . . . His Journals, Sermons and Pamphlets are reprinted and eagerly bought here, and our Pulpits & Presses are never free from such Doctrines.[33]

---

29. Connecticut Election Sermons of 1724 by Woodbridge, p. 22; of 1727 by Cutler, p. 52; of 1725 by A. Mather, pp. 33, 39.

30. Blake, *The Separates of New England*, pp. 32–33; Clark, pp. 139–45; Walker, *History of Congregational Churches*, pp. 103–05, 113, 170–82, 251–53; Trumbull, II. 3–5; 103–05; Holyoke, Convention Sermon, 1741, pp. 24–25.

31. For full account see Tracy, *The Great Awakening*.

32. Belcher Papers, *Mass. Hist. Soc. Coll.*, 6th Ser. Vol. VII., Pt. II., p. 521; also pp. 538, 541.

33. Perry, *Historical Collections*, III. 347–48. For further detail see Tyerman,

Certain of Whitefield's teachings are of special significance. He believed that there were certain fundamental divine laws which a Christian subject must first obey and that he had the right to question and, if necessary, to break rules and laws that were contrary to these principles. He preached this freedom openly. When accused of breaking the church canons, he wrote to the Bishop of London:

> Your Lordship knows full well that Canons and other church laws are good and obligatory when conformable to the laws of Christ and agreeable to the liberties of a free people; but when invented and compiled by men of little hearts and bigotted principles . . . and when made use of only as ends to bind up the hands of a zealous few, they may be very legally broken.[34]

Secondly, Whitefield taught that all men, rich and poor, wise and ignorant, shared in the gospel of Christ. Consciousness of the indwelling spirit of God, the "new birth," was the one thing needful. No man, however rich, however powerful, but must share the common experience; and all men, having this experience, were equal in the fellowship of Christ. So common men, "the rabble," crowded to hear him.[35] Men here and there began to say that a learned ministry was unnecessary and they gathered about simple men who felt themselves inspired of God to preach.

In the third place, Whitefield had a tolerance, amazing in his day, of all kinds of church government and creeds, a tolerance far too broad to admit of any alliance between church and state. Many times in letters and sermons he rejoices in this freedom.[36] These

Life of the Rev. George Whitefield, 2 vols.; Whitefield, *Works*, vols. I–VI. The *Boston Weekly News Letter*, Oct. 16, 1740, reports his farewell address on the Common to a supposed 23,000 people.

34. Whitefield, *Works*, III. 163. See also IV. 25.

35. *Ibid.*, IV. 138–39; Tyerman, II. 12, 44; Perry, *Historical Collections*, IV. 83; B. Colman, *Souls Flying to Jesus Christ*, pp. 7, 9.

36. See Tyerman, I. 5–16, 438, 446, 451–52, 495, 513, II. 174; Whitefield, *Works*, I. 140; Belcher, *George Whitefield*, p. 207. Belcher says that once, from the balcony of the Philadelphia Court House, Whitefield exclaimed: "'Father

beliefs Whitefield proclaimed by means of sermons heard by thousands of people as he preached them from pulpit, common, and court-house steps. They were read by thousands more as edition after edition was published and scattered through the land.[37]

Such a man as George Whitefield could not travel through the colonies without arousing angry opposition and bitter strife, and still more his followers, who shared his earnestness but lacked his sweet and tolerant spirit. In his published journal were unflattering accounts of the ministry and the colleges. He called many of the former "unconverted" and the latter homes of darkness rather than light.[38] After Whitefield's visit, other clergymen took up the work, especially in Connecticut, and went about as itinerant preachers, among them one James Davenport, a fanatic, who came to New England in 1741, and denounced some of the ministers in their own pulpits. His excited preaching and that of other itinerants caused strange outbursts among the people—cries, faintings, and other bodily manifestations such as are often an accompaniment of great religious emotion. There arose also a spirit of questioning and of discussion, a testing of authorities by the new standards. Students began to criticize their tutors, congregations their ministers; laymen, some of whom were of the poorer classes, took it upon themselves to preach and exhort. Churches were riven in twain.

Ministers quarreled with brother ministers. Some gave their whole hearts to the cause, some believed that the awakening was so genuine and so greatly needed that they could forgive while

Abraham, who have you in heaven?"Any Episcoplians?"'No.''Any Presbyterians?' 'No.''Any Baptists?''No.''Any Methodists, Seceders, or Independents?''No, No!' 'Why who have you there?''We don't know those names here. All who are here are Christians.''Oh, is that the case? Then, God help me! and God help us all to forget party names and to become Christians in deed and truth.'"

37. See *Boston News Letter*, October 16, Nov. 6, 1740; Whitefield's *Works*, I. 274, II. 124, III. 106–08, 305–06, 310, 312, 426; Tyerman, I. 38; Perry, *Historical Collections*, III. 348. Whitefield made seven journeys to America between 1740 and 1770, in most of which he visited New England.

38. Dexter, *Documentary History of Yale University*, p. 347; Quincy, *History of Harvard University*, pp. 40–41.

regretting its excesses, but some hated it root and branch. Men were divided into "Old Lights," those who opposed the movement, and "New Lights," the most extreme of whom were known as "Separates" or "Strict Congregationalists." And there began, especially in Connecticut, a period of strife and persecution.[39]

In Connecticut some of the leading ministers were bitter enemies to the revival, as were, in general, the magistrates and chief gentlemen of the colony. They tried in all ways to suppress the movement. They attempted to confine those favoring it to their own pulpits and to refuse men of other colonies who preached reform the right to enter Connecticut. As early as May, 1741, the Association of Ministers of New Haven County had voted unanimously not to permit a man under ordinary circumstances to preach in any pulpit but his own, unless with the express approval of the regularly settled minister of the parish.[40] In October the legislature called a general consociation of churches which met in November at Guilford and took a firm stand against itinerants.[41] In May, the legislature forbade an itinerant to preach in a parish without the consent of the regular minister, under penalty of losing his salary and giving bonds for his good behavior or, if he were not a minister of Connecticut, of being expelled as a vagrant from the colony.[42] In 1743, the legislature repealed the toleration act of 1708[43] and a new act was passed which prevented

---

39. For full account, see Tracy, *Great Awakening*; Trumbull, *History of Connecticut*, II; Prince, *Christian History*, 2 vols.; Blake, *The Separates, or Strict Congregationalists of New England*; Parker, *The Congregational Separates of the Eighteenth Century in Connecticut.* Among the most conspicuous itinerants were Jonathan Parsons, of Lyme, Benjamin Pomeroy, of Hebron, Eleazar Wheelock, of Lebanon, Joseph Bellamy, of Bethlem, and John Graham, of Southbury, in Connecticut, and Jonathan Edwards in Massachusetts.

40. Dexter, *Biographical Sketches of Yale Graduates, 1701–1745*, p. 662. See also Parsons, "Elisha Williams," *New Haven Colony Hist. Soc. Papers*, VIII. 202.

41. Walker, *History of Congregational Churches*, pp. 261–62.

42. *Records of the Colony of Connecticut*, VIII. 454–57, 521; Trumbull, II. 127–31.

43. *Records of Conn.*, VIII. 522. In all the New England colonies except Rhode Island, there was little real tolerance of other sects than the Congre-

Congregationalists from forming another Congregational church without permission from the legislature.[44] Yale College was not far behind the Assembly in severity. In 1741, her trustees voted that

> if any Student of this College shall directly or indirectly say that the Rector, either of the Trustees or Tutors are Hypocrites, carnall or unconverted Men, he Shall for the first Offense make a publick Confession in the Hall, for the Second Offence be expelled.[45]

The associations of ministers in the eastern part of Connecticut petitioned the Assembly against the law of 1742, while those of Hartford and New Haven supported it.[46] Those who opposed it argued that their rights under the constitution and the Act of Toleration of William and Mary were ignored, their rights under their covenants with their churches not maintained and that they were denied the right of trial.

> We humbly conceive it infringes on our Natural & Law full Right as Subjects,—for as Such we have a Right to have our Covenants with our People fulfilled and till we are by proper Judges according to our Constitution declared guilty of Unfaithfulness to Such Covenants our People are in Justice holden by them. Yet by Said Law they Seem to be Set loose, & Such Covenants in Fact to

---

gationalists and Presbyterians. By 1729, however, Baptists, Episcopalians, and Quakers were allowed to have their own churches and pay their assessment to their own clergy and were not taxed to build Congregational churches, but they were obliged to gain release by a formal connection with some other recognized denomination. There were, however, in 1740, only a few belonging to any sect except the Congregational.

44. Records of Connecticut, VIII 521–22.

45. Dexter, *Documentary History of Yale University*, p. 351; "Thomas Clap and his Writings," *New Haven Colony Hist. Soc. Papers*, V. 254–55. See also Louise Greene, *The Development of Religious Liberty in Connecticut*, for full account of troubles in Connecticut.

46. Eccles. Papers, vol. VII., nos. 261, 262 a, 263 a, 265, 267, 268 (C. S. L.)

be dissolved, without any Ecclesiastical Process or Sentence according to our Constitution, which looks to us inconsistent with ye Rules of Common Equity.[47]

They protested against the interference of the state in religious affairs and referred to Locke and his "unanswerable Letter of Toleration, which we are glad to hear is like to have a new Edition in this Country."[48] But in spite of all protests, the authorities proceeded to enforce these laws. Boys were expelled from Yale for attending "Separate" meetings, ministers were deposed for itineracy or for ordaining "Separate" ministers, men and women were imprisoned for conscience's sake, Justices of the Peace and other officers who were "New Lights" were removed from office and "New Light" representatives were refused seats in the assembly.[49]

47. *Ibid.*, no. 263 a. See no. 262 a; VIII., no. 44 a; various others concerning violation of covenant are found in the collection. Cf. Separate Papers, I, no. 151.

48. Eccles. Papers, vol. VII., no. 261, from Association of Fairfield West. The laws were upheld by Wm. Worthington in Connecticut Election Sermon, 1744 E. Whitman, Connecticut Election Sermon, 1745; S. Hall, Connecticut Election Sermon, 1746, who said, however, that mutual covenants must be protected, liberty, property, etc., preserved. Worthington in 1744 said that they had often heard of late of the natural right to hear whom they chose. In a sense, that was right, because if men did not like a minister they could remove elsewhere, but to talk of natural right to have any minister preach in a church was absurd. It was "to tell of natural right in an affair, which is either wholly a matter of pure Institution, or meer Compact; or else a Mixture of these two and only these two; than which nothing is more absurd." Surely it could never be an infringement of natural right to punish idolatry. "But I verily believe, that if one of these old Jews had pleaded his natural Right to understand & believe for himself, and obey his own Conscience, which bid him worship an Idol, an Answer to this purpose, would have been good and seasonable, viz. We know you are wrong." Nor will it do to argue that that was a theocracy and this is not. God's word does not mean that men shall be protected in their civil rights only (pp. . 11–15). Cf. J, Todd, Connecticut Election Sermon, 1749.

49. David Brainerd and the Cleavelands were expelled from Yale. Seniors were disciplined for having Locke's *Essay on Toleration* printed. See Dexter, *Documentary History of Yale University*, pp. 368–72. Rev. Benjamin Pomeroy, of Hebron, was deposed and deprived of his salary for seven years for itinerant preaching. He openly and vehemently denounced Connecticut for the laws

In Massachusetts there was not so much difficulty. Many of the leading clergymen were Whitefield's friends and the government did not interfere. There was somewhat more opposition, however, after the publication of Whitefield's *Journals*. In 1744, Harvard College published a testimony against the evangelist, several associations of ministers declared against itineracy, bitter pamphlets were issued by Chauncey and others.[50] When Whitefield returned in 1745, the Massachusetts clergy who denied him their pulpits accused him "of a design to raze the foundations of our churches and change the religion of New England."[51] "What you have done and others who have followed your example," wrote Edward Wigglesworth, of Harvard, in a public letter,

> has had an effect more extensive and pernicious than any man could have imagined six years ago. . . . Perhaps there is not now a single town in this province, and, probably, not in Connecticut, in which there are not numbers of people whose minds are under strong prejudices against their ministers; such prejudices as almost cut off all hope of their profiting by their sacred ministrations.[52]

of 1742–43. Through seven years his people voluntarily supported him. Rev. Philemon Robbins, of Branford, was also expelled and supported by his people. Rev. Mr. Leavenworth, of Waterbury, Humphrey, of Derby, Todd, of Northbury, were suspended; lay exhorters were imprisoned. Samuel Finley, afterwards President of Princeton, was driven from the colony as a vagrant. See Robbins, *A Plaine Narrative*, 1747; Baldwin, "Branford Annals," *New Haven Colony Hist. Soc. Papers*, IV. 319–29; Tracy, *The Great Awakening*, p. 308; Parker, *The Congregational Separates in Connecticut*; Blake, *The Separates of New England*, pp. 48, 112; Trumbull, *History of Connecticut*, II. 141–46, 191.

50. Quincy, *History of Harvard University*, pp. 48–52, 61, 63–66. In 1743, a testimony against itineracy and preaching by untrained men, etc., was issued by certain Mass. ministers, but not without hot debate, and shortly thereafter a favorable report was signed by 68 members of a new convention and by 56 others whose names were sent by letter. Similar attestations were made in Conn. See Tracy, pp. 287–91, 294–302; *The Testimony and Advice of an Assembly of Pastors of Churches in New England*, pp. 6–15, 49–51. See also Trumbull, II. 198–205.

51. Tyerman, II. 137.

52. *Ibid.*, p. 135–36. Not always was it due to the people's wishing to hear

The "fruits the times had tasted" were

> children teaching their parents or ministers; low-bred,
> illiterate persons settling difficult points of divinity bet-
> ter than the most learned divines; a learned ministry de-
> spised; seminaries of learning spoken against as injuri-
> ous to religion . . . churches full of contentions."[53]

A spirit of revolt against constituted authority was abroad in the
land.

Persecution could not stop the movement toward freedom
and greater independence of thought and action. In all probabil-
ity it was strengthened by the very effort to destroy it. The majority of the "New Light" clergy and people did not leave their
church but gradually won greater tolerance and harmony; some
joined the Presbyterians; more the Baptists, and so gained relief;
but some formed "Separate" or "Strict Congregational" churches
of their own in spite of the law.[54] In certain churches where the

---

Whitefield and the pastor's opposing; sometimes it was the reverse. See T. F. Waters, *Ipswich in the Massachusetts Bay Colony*, II. 459; Thos. Smith, *Journal*, pp.
115–16 and note; Sylvester Judd, *History of Hadley*, p. 330; Sprague, I. 423–24.

53. Quincy, p. 61. See Whitefield, *Works*, IV. 85.

54. In 1752, Massachusetts passed a law that if individual or church wished
to escape taxes for Congregational church by becoming Baptist they must be
certified to be Baptists in good and regular standing. See *Colonial Laws*, p. 527;
Palfrey, IV. 78–100. This was not easy, and then and later caused much trouble
and injustice. The number of "Separate" churches is hard to determine. Tracy
says there were some ten or twelve in Connecticut; Sprague, VI. 29, some thirty; Bates in his *List of Congregational Ecclesiastical Societies established in Connecticut before 1818*, p. 4, says they were numerous, for the most part without
legal existence; Clarke, in his *Historical Sketch of the Congregational Churches in
Massachusetts*, p. 169, says there were some twenty "Separate" churches founded between 1740 and 1750 in Massachusetts, but that most became Baptist.
There were a few in Rhode Island and New Hampshire, as is shown by the
town histories and town and state papers. For further details, see Parker, *op.
cit.*; Stiles, *Itineraries*, pp. 265– 67; Learned, *Contributions to the Ecclesiastical
History of Connecticut*, 1861; Cobb, *Rise of Religious Liberty in America*; Green,
Development of Religious Liberty in Connecticut.

pastor and people were "New Light," but moderate, and a group
of the people wished greater enthusiasm, the "New Lights" became as averse to separation as ever the "Old Lights" had been
and the pastors refused to ordain the unlearned men whom the
people wished as pastors. These churches then made a covenant
together and their pastor was ordained by another "Separate" but
was often refused recognition and fellowship by the more regular
churches.[55] The "New Lights" were strongest in Connecticut in
the eastern section, in Fairfield East, Windham, and New London counties, though after its formation in 1751 Litchfield County also was largely "New Light." The Associations of Windham
and Fairfield East were the strongest and here too was the center
of the Separates.[56] Many, however, became "New Lights" who op-

55. E. Stiles, *Itineraries*, pp. 233–34.

56. Trumbull, II. 217; *Historical sketches of Fairfield East Association; Hundred and Fiftieth Anniversary of Fairfield County Consociation; Prince, Christian
History*, I. 157–95, 199–210. The leading "New Light" ministers in Conn. were
Jedediah Mills, of Ripton, Nathaniel Hunn, of Reading, Hezekiah Gold, of Stratford, Samuel Cooke, of Stratfield, Anthony Stoddard, of Woodbury, John Graham, of Southbury, Jonathan Todd, of East Guilford, Joseph Bellamy, of Bethlem, James Lockwood, of Wethersfield, Jonathan Parsons and Stephen Johnson,
of Lyme, Solomon Williams and Eleazar Wheelock, of Lebanon, Benj. Pome-
roy, of Hebron, Philemon Robbins, of Branford, Ebenezer White, of Danbury,
Daniel Humphreys, of Derby, Joseph Meacham, of Coventry, and many others.
Nathaniel Eells, Samuel Whittelsey, of Wallingford, Isaac Stiles, of New Haven,
William Worthington, of Saybrook, Nathaniel Chauncey, of Durham, Elnathan
Whitman, of Hartford, and Samuel Hall, of New Cheshire, and others were "Old
Lights." Some of the best known "Separates" were Solomon and Elisha Paine, of
Canterbury, Samuel Bird, of New Haven, Isaac Foster, of Stafford, Eben. Froth-
ingham, of Middletown, John Hovey, of Mansfield, Jedediah Hide, of Norwich.
Some of the churches surviving were those in Windham, Lyme, Wethersfield
(which removed to Middletown), Milford, Danbury, Killingly. See Bates, *List of
Congregational Ecclesiastical Societies established in Connecticut before 1818*, and for
names of "Separates," Eccles. Papers (C. S. L.).
     Among the best known "New Light" ministers in Mass. were Thos. Foxcroft,
Wm. Cooper, Joseph Sewall, Thos. Prince, Joshua Gee, of Boston, Samuel Moody,
of York, Thos. Smith, of Falmouth, Joseph Emerson, of Malden, John White, of
Gloucester, Joseph Adams, of Newington, N. H., Peter Thacher, of Middleborough, Thaddeus Maccarty, of Kingston, and many others. Benj. Colman was

posed Separation but who believed the laws of 1742–43 violated the liberties of the subject.

The persecution was at its height in Connecticut from 1742 to 1750. By the latter date the laws were somewhat modified and the Assembly began to sanction the formation of "Separate" churches. The more moderate "New Lights" were growing more numerous and more powerful. By 1748 some of the "New Light" Justices of the Peace were restored to office, by 1775 "New Light" representatives were again elected and were now allowed to take their seats, the ministers' association restored "New Light" clergy to fellowship, by 1758 the "New Lights" had won control in Connecticut and in western Massachusetts.[57]

But this did not bring peace. One of the results of the Great Awakening was a doctrinal controversy which had had its beginnings before 1740 and which was doubtless in part the reflection of European rationalism. The "New Lights" were for the most part strict Calvinists and opposed Arminianism, with which they believed their opponents tainted. In Connecticut the "New Lights," as they gained power, tried in certain cases to force their beliefs by law.[58] This roused violent opposition among both ministers and laymen and its repercussion was felt in other colonies. The more liberal Arminians now united to gain the liberty which earlier they had denied to others.[59]

---

one of Whitefield's best friends but took a somewhat neutral stand. Some of the ministers became estranged later because of separations, etc. Nathaniel Appleton, Chas. Chauncey, Ed. Wigglesworth, Eben. Gay, and others opposed him.

57. J. H. Trumbull, *Sons of Liberty in Connecticut*, p. 305, says that the "New Lights" had a majority in the Assembly when Wolcott became governor in 1750. See also Cobb, p. 279; Parker, p. 161; Tracy, p. 308; Trumbull, *History of Connecticut*, II. 191; Hodges, "Yale Graduates in Western Massachusetts," *New Haven Colony Hist. Soc. Papers*, IV. 258–59, 272, 279, 282ff. Many of the graduates of Yale and some from Harvard who had been strongly influenced by Whitefield went to the western frontier in Berkshire. Yale graduates predominated in the old Hampshire Co. Some had studied theology with "New Light" ministers such as Pomeroy and Bellamy. See Reynolds, *Two Centuries of Christian Activity at Yale.*

58. See next chapter.

59. Trumbull, *Songs of Liberty in 1755*, pp. 305–06. Benjamin Gale, son-in-

It has seemed necessary to summarize in this brief fashion the essential facts of the Great Awakening in order to present clearly its bearing upon the development of political theory. The controversies arising directly or indirectly out of this movement were many. Clergy and laymen were involved and many arguments were used which had a direct bearing upon the later theories of the Revolution. During these years the New Englanders were engaged among themselves in excited disputes over the very kind of things they later disputed with England. The definition of natural and constitutional rights became clearer and more inclusive.

---

law of Rev. Jared Eliot, both of whom were ardent believers in religious freedom, Ingersoll, Thos. Darling, perhaps Col. John Hubbard, friend and relative of Ezra Stiles, and others are said by Trumbull to have formed a society to further civil and religious liberty and to have been called, in derision, "sons of liberty." In 1765 these men believed there was no way but to yield to Parliament, unless Parliament itself repealed its acts. On the contrary, the Rev. Stephen Johnson, of Lyme, Wm. Williams, Trumbull, of Lebanon, and the eastern faction in general were ardent leaders of the American cause (*ibid.*, pp. 306–12). In 1767 they defeated Hubbard for the Assembly. See also Gipson, *Jared Ingersoll.*

Six

Political Philosophy and
Ecclesiastical Controversy: 1743–1763

*T*he years from 1743 to 1763 were prolific in sermons, pamphlets, and petitions in which constitutional rights, civil and religious liberty, the right to resistance, etc., were more clearly defined and more positively asserted than ever before. Laymen as well as clergy, poor and unlearned as well as those of higher estate, expressed their conviction in no uncertain terms, and again the Bible, natural law, the rights of Englishmen, covenants, charters, and statutes were drawn upon for arguments. To the conservative, the law and the constitution must be enforced and government and discipline maintained. God commanded it.[1] To the liberals, the restrictive laws violated the rights and liberties which they possessed as men, Christians, and Englishmen and were therefore unconstitutional and to be disregarded. The phrase "unalienable right" grew more common and the references to Locke, Sydney, and other radical theorists more frequent.[2]

1. For illustrations of the conservative position see the Convention Sermons of E. Holyoke, 1741; of Appleton, 1743; of C. Chauncey, 1744; of Clark, 1745; the Connecticut Election Sermons of Isaac Stiles, 1742; of Wm. Worthington, 1744; of Whitman, 1745; of Woodbridge, 1752; *Extracts from Records of Convention of Ministers in New Hampshire, 1747–1774,* from More's and Farmer's *Collections, Topographical, Historical, and Biographical,* pp. 264–65.

2. That Locke was frequently read before 1742 seems evident from the following reference in a sermon of Thos. Foxcroft in Boston, 1740. On the title

One of the most interesting of the pleas for religious liberty was a pamphlet issued in 1744, called The Essential Rights and Liberties of Protestants, a Seasonable Plea for Liberty of Conscience and the Right of Private Judgment in matters of Religion, without any control from Human Authority. This pamphlet, signed Philalethes, is attributed by Tracy to Elisha Williams,[3] a follower of Whitefield, and is the fullest discussion of equality and liberty since the time of John Wise. Like Wise's pamphlets it was called forth by religious and ecclesiastical difficulties, and like his Vindication, it deserves a somewhat careful study.

The author defines natural liberty as freedom from any superior earthly power, as subjection only to the law of nature, which he declares to be the law of God. He then gives the clearest and fullest explanation of the so-called natural right to property to be found among any of the clerical writings of the eighteenth century:

> As Reason tells us, all are born thus naturally equal, i.e. with an equal Right to their Persons; so also with an equal Right to their Preservation; and therefore to such Things as Nature affords for their Subsistence. . . . And altho' no one has originally a private Dominion exclusive of the rest of Mankind in the Earth or its Products, as they are consider'd in this their natural State; Yet since God has given these Things for the Use of Men and given them Reason also to make use thereof to the best Advantage of Life; there must be of Necessity a Means to appropriate them some Way or other, before they can

page, quoted from Dr. Watt's Humble Attempt, is the following: "You are not to stand up here (in the Pulpit) as a Professor of ancient or modern philosophy, nor an Usher in the school of Plato, or Seneca, or Mr. Lock . . ."

3. Tracy, p. 308, note; Parsons, in *New Haven Colony Hist. Soc. Papers*, VII. 202–03. Clark ascribes it to Thos. Cushing; Wm. Cushing in his *Anonyms*, p. 223, ascribes it to Rev. Ebenezer Williams of Pomfret. The copy in the Kingsley Collection, Yale College Library, was given in 1774 by John Potwine, of Hartford, to "Benj. Pomeroy," probably Rev. Benj. Pomeroy, of Hebron, the famous "New Light."

be of any Use to any Particular Person. And every Man
having a Property in his own Person, the Labour of his
Body and the Work of his Hands are properly his own,
to which no one has Right but himself; it will therefore
follow that when he removes any Thing out of the State
that Nature has provided and left it in, he has mixed
his Labour with it and joined something to it that is his
own, and thereby makes it his Property. . . . Thus every
Man having a natural Right to (or being Proprietor of)
his own Person and his own Actions and Labour, which
we call Property; it certainly follows, that no Man can
have a Right to the Person or Property of another: And
if every Man has a Right to his Person and Property; he
has also a Right to defend them, and a Right to all the
necessary Means of Defence, and so has a Right of pun-
ishing all Insults upon his Person and Property.[4]

There follows a summary of Locke's theories concerning the
origin and purpose of society and government and the consequent
power of the people.[5] The author believed that one could tell what
natural rights had been given up by considering the ends for which
they had been yielded.[6] Evidently there had been certain criticism
of those who read Locke, for he rather defiantly declares that man
"in a State of Nature . . . had a right to read Milton or Locke for
their Instruction or Amusement and why do they not retain this
Liberty under a Government that is instituted for the Preservation

---

4. E. Williams, *A Seasonable Plea*, pp. 2–3.

5. *Ibid.*, pp. 3–6. He says he has given "a short sketch of what the celebrated Mr. Locke in his *Treatice of Government* has largely demonstrated; and in
which it is justly to be presumed all are agreed who understand the natural
Rights of Mankind."

6. "This I rest on as certain, that no more natural Liberty or Power is given
up than is necessary for the Preservation of Person and Property." One liberty
that all members of a free state and especially Englishmen hold dear is the right
to speak their sentiments openly concerning such matters as affect the good of
the whole (p. 7).

of their Persons and Properties, is inconceivable."[7] With equal clarity and decision he asserts that there is "no binding Force in a Law where a rightful Authority to make the same is wanting."[8] He then turns to the natural and unalienable right of men to judge for themselves in matters of religion, which they also retain in a civil state.[9] This could not be given up even if men were so weak as to offer it, for the rights of conscience are "sacred, equal in all, and strictly speaking unalienable."[10] No power over religious matters was or could be vested in the civil Magistrate by the people "by any original Compact which is truly supposed the Foundation of all civil Government."[11] Men must keep in mind that there are two kinds of powers, those that are and those that are not.

> For instance; the Powers that be in Great Britain are the Government therein according to its own Constitution:—If then the higher Powers for the Administration rule not according to that Constitution, or if any King thereof shall rule so, as to change the Government from legal to arbitrary; the Power from God fails them, it is then a Power not in the text, and so no Subjection due to it from the Text . . . [the powers that be are of God] . . . their Power is a limited one: and therefore the Obedience due is a limited Obedience. . . . If civil Rulers should take it into their Heads to make a Law, that no Man

---

7. *Ibid.*, p. 7.

8. *Ibid.*

9. He argues that in religious matters every group has the right of withdrawal; the majority can elect, but the minority can withdraw. "It is not here, as in the civil Societies where the Right of each Individual is subjected to the Body, or so transferred to the Society as that the Act of the Majority is legally to be considered as the Act of the Whole, and binding to each Individual" (pp. 48–49). Every Christian is bound to search the Scriptures and so "has an unalienable Right to judge of the Sense and Meaning of it, and to follow his Judgment wherever it leads him; even an equal Right with any Rulers be they Civil or Ecclesiastical" (p. 8).

10. *Ibid.*

11. *Ibid.*, p. 63

shall have Luther's Table-Talk in his House, that every Man shall turn round upon his right Heel at twelve of the Clock every Day, (Sundays excepted) or any such like wise Law (Thousands of which might be invented by a wise Tyrant,) By this Rule these Laws are to be strictly obeyed, a higher Law to the contrary not being found. And yet I think it may be presumed, a free-born People can never become so servile as to regard them, while they have Eyes to see that such Rulers have gone out of the Line of their Power, . . . There is no Reason they should be Fools because their Rulers are so. . . .[12]

As to what people must do to free themselves from tyranny, the author refers again to Locke. Here is a minister in 1744 using the very arguments of 1775, declaring that subjects and rulers are bound by the constitution and that a law violating natural and constitutional rights is no law and requires no obedience. Here is clear evidence of the transmission through the clergy of the theories of Locke. The importance of this and like pamphlets is this: they show how the thinking and the theory that came out in the Revolutionary period were uttered not alone in theoretical election sermons but in practical disputes and controversies over church and individual rights long before the trouble with England arose.

There was an increasing number of sermons and pamphlets breathing the spirit of liberty and constitutional rights.[13] Nathaniel

---

12. *Ibid.*, pp. 26–27. For fuller quotation, see Appendix A.

13. "I have heard it cast as a Reproach upon the Clergy, that they have been the foremost in propagating the Principles of Sedition, and Disobedience to Authority. I am persuaded the Charge is unjust: And hope, the Instances are but few, of those that have given Occasion for such a Charge. . . . I suppose some ministers under the power of enthusiasm representing the Leaders & Rulers of this People, as unconverted & Opposers of the Work of God, and usurping an Authority that did not belong to them, was the Occasion of this Charge, And I make no doubt hut it had an unhappy Influence upon the People, and encouraged many to despise Government, and to speak Evil of Dignities. But yet it is unfair to Object this to the Clergy in general" (J. Todd, Connecticut Election Sermon, 1749, p. 74; and note pp. 74–75).

Hunn, a "New Light," preached the Connecticut Election Sermon
in 1747 on the subject, "The Welfare of a Government considered,"
in which he extolled liberty, defining it as a free and secure enjoyment of a people's just rights, natural, civil, and religious, free on
the one hand from oppression and tyranny and on the other from
popular tumults and disorders, free from heavy and unreasonable
taxes, from having the fruits of their labor snatched untimely from
their hands, their religious immunities at the mercy of tyrants.[14]
Moses Dickinson, of Norwalk, in 1755 defended the ecclesiastical constitution of Connecticut as a whole and asserted that law
must be upheld else there would be no civil liberty, yet declared
that persecution for religion was a violation of the law of nature
and the law of Christ.[15] William Rand, of Kingston, in his Massachusetts Convention Sermon of 1757, asserted the right of private
judgment, saying that Christ has not made any particular person
or persons infallible interpreters of the Bible; therefore every individual must interpret for himself what he finds in the sacred Scripture.[16] The same ideas may be found in the Convention Sermon
of William Balch in 1760. Religious sincerity includes, he said, a
"universal Love of Truth, and a free impartial entire Submission
to its Empire . . . as the Force of Evidence has obliged us to believe, so much we speak."[17] And again in 1760, Joseph Fish in his

Some of the Massachusetts election sermons as well as some of those of
Connecticut during this period show a recognition of arbitrary dealings by the
colonial governments. John Cotton, of Newton, Mass., in 1753 says that the
"Cry of Unrighteousness, Oppression and Extortion" is heard in the land, and
in 1762 Abraham Williams speaks of "all men being naturally equal" and of "Attempts of domestic Traitors, arbitrary bigotted Tyrants." Swift, "Massachusetts
Election Sermons," *Mass. Col. Soc. Pub.* I. 419, 421.

14. Hunn, pp. 14–25. The whole sermon is on this subject.

15. M. Dickinson, Connecticut Election Sermon, 1755, pp. 7, 11–12, 24,
33, etc., argues in favor of war of resistance in defence of lives, liberties, and
properties.

16. Wm. Rand, Convention Sermon, 1757, pp. 14–23.

17. Wm. Balch, Convention Sermon, 1760, pp. 14–16. The Massachusetts
sermons of the period are as a whole more insistent on liberty than those of
Connecticut. See Stevens, Massachusetts Election Sermon, 1761, Thos. Bar-

Connecticut Election Sermon said, "Every Man has a natural, unalienable Right to think and see for himself."[18]

Perhaps the two most famous exponents of religious liberty in New England during these years whose works were most widely circulated in the colonies and in England were Jonathan Mayhew, of Massachusetts, and Ezra Stiles, of Rhode Island. As early as 1748 Mayhew taught the separation of church and state and freedom of judgment in religious matters. This right to judge and act for oneself, he said, is "absolutely unalienable in its own nature."[19] Some of Mayhew's sermons and pamphlets were caused by the fear of an American Episcopate which seems to have been in the minds of many Congregationalist and Presbyterian ministers throughout the colonies and to have given rise to heated arguments. This grew more serious after 1763 and doubtless was one reason for some of the earlier discussions of government and religious liberty. In the confusion of the Great Awakening the Episcopal church in New England had won new members, and to the missionaries of the Society for the Propagation of the Gospel it seemed a propitious time to strengthen their hold.[20] Certainly Mayhew's sermon of 1750, referred to in an earlier chapter, was caused by his dislike and dread of the Anglican Church and the doctrines upon which he believed it to be founded. Probably, also, his own experience in finding certain of his fellow-ministers cold

nard, Massachusetts Election Sermon, 1763, and many others. The French and Indian War helped to interest clergy and people in freedom and constitutional government. See Chap. 7.

18. J. Fish, Connecticut Election Sermon, 1760, pp. 13–14, 45–46.

19. Mayhew, *Sermons*, 1748, p. 88. We must use reason only, weigh evidence, and cheerfully accept truth, wherever found. This was the method of Jesus and the Apostles (pp. 38–79); and we must give the same liberty to others. "Nothing is more incongruous than for an advocate of liberty to tyrannize over his neighbors" (p. 89). In his Election Sermon of 1754 he questions whether there are not some laws in force not reconcilable with the religious libert'y which they profess and which is guaranteed by the Royal Charter, and whether these laws are sufficiently abhorrent of the persecuting spirit found in Connecticut (p. 28).

20. A. L. Cross, *The Anglican Episcopate and the American Colonies* (a full treatment of the subject); Pascoe, *Two Hundred Years of the S. P. G.*, p. 45.

to him because of his liberal doctrines helped to make him so outspoken a friend of liberty.

Ezra Stiles' *Discourse on Christian Union*, published in 1760, had also wide influence. Stiles was in correspondence with men in all the colonies and in England and travelled widely in New England. Of this sermon he said that Chauncey had it printed for him in Boston in 1761 and sent extra copies to Connecticut, believing it especially adapted to serve that colony. In 1766 his printer told him that seven to eight hundred copies had been sold, that more had been made out of it than was ever made by any one sermon in Boston, and that it might be readily printed again.[21] As did Mayhew and others, so Stiles wrote in behalf of the unalienable right to private judgment and liberty, especially in religion, and also in behalf of the local rights and privileges of churches.

Such were the arguments used by the regularly ordained ministers in their sermons in behalf of religious freedom. But it is not only here that such discussions can be found. In every ecclesiastical controversy which brought out letters and pamphlets one runs across them. When in 1753 President Clap, fearing that the students might imbibe heretical doctrine, organized at Yale a separate church, he alienated the "Old Lights."[22] And when shortly thereafter he required a public acceptance of the Saybrook creed and confession from the fellows and professors and published in 1755 a pamphlet urging a careful examination of the candidates to the ministry by the Association to ensure their orthodox Calvinism, he roused a storm of protest.[23] He answered the assertion of reli-

---

21. Ezra Stiles, *Itineraries*, pp. 440–41; 440, note.

22. Thos. Dexter, "Thomas Clap and his Writings," *New Haven Colony Hist. Soc. Papers*, V. 257, 260. He was never liked by the "New Lights," but because of his interest in politics was dubbed a "political New Light." Stephen White, Connecticut Election Sermon, 1763, p. 32, speaks of general dissatisfaction concerning the college.

23. Thos. Clap, *A Brief History and Vindication of the Doctrines . . .* , 1755, p. 25, reprinted in 1757. See Wm. Hart, *A Letter to a Friend wherein some free Thoughts are offered*, pp. 14–17 (Hart believed that the move was political); Noah Hobart, *A Congratulatory Letter From a Gentleman in the West*, 1755

gious freedom by saying that although men had a right to judge for themselves, they had not the right to judge wrongly. He declared that the Saybrook Confession was established by law and as such must be enforced. Laymen took up the challenge, lamenting the growing lust for power among the clergy and their constant ambition to interest themselves in affairs of state.[24] One lay pamphleteer said that the people would not accept standards of faith set up by Council or Ministers. In bold and vivid phrase he asserted the freedom of Americans.

> These things will never go down in a free State, where People are bred in, and breathe a free Air, and are formed upon Principles of Liberty; they might Answer in a Popish Country, or in Turkey, where the common People are sunk and degraded almost to the State of Brutes, by Poverty, Chains and absolute Tyranny, and have no more Sense of Liberty and Property, than so many Jack-Asses: But in a free State they will be eternally ridiculed and abhorred. . . . 'Tis too late in the Day for these Things, these Gentlemen should have lived 12 or 13 Hundred Years ago, or they should have been born in a Popish Country, then they would have had something to do: But as to Us in this Country, we are Freeborn, and have the keenest Sense of Liberty, and han't the least Notion of pampering and making a Few great, at the Expense of our own Liberty and Property.[25]

About the same time an affair occurred which again split the clergy of Connecticut into opposing parties and struck further

---

(satirical); Clap, *The Answer of the Friend in the West, To a Letter From a Gentleman in the East,* 1755.

24. Catholicus, *A Letter to A Clergyman in the Colony of Connecticut from his Friend,* 1757; *Some Remarks on Mr. President Clap's History,* pp. 3–4, 43, 59. The sanction of Fathers and Councils in matters of the Faith "is as impertinent, as a Man's pretending to give a Sanction to the Constitutions of the Great God."

25. *Some Remarks,* pp. 109–10.

blows at the ecclesiastical constitution. It brought out unusually interesting and significant discussions of constitutional rights from minister and layman. A Mr. Dana was desired by the majority of the church at Wallingford as their pastor and was ordained by a group of neighboring ministers without the approbation of the Consociation of New Haven, to which the Church belonged. Both the New Haven and the Hartford Consociation disapproved of Dana's doctrines. The New Haven Consociation thereupon declared the ordination illegal and void. The affair aroused very general concern and interest which lasted over several years and extended into other colonies. Some thought it so serious as to affect the government and even the state. Some believed it was being used by those who would attack both. People began to inquire into the nature of ecclesiastical councils and the whole ecclesiastical constitution was felt to be at stake.[26]

The issues were the right of a church to choose and ordain its pastor without yielding to the authority of the Consociation, the rights of the majority in a church election, and the relation of the Consociations to the Ecclesiastical Constitution; here was a question of constitutionality. Edward Eells, in support of the action of the Consociation, said,

> I suppose it is a settled rule, and common law, that when anything is done contrary to law, or constitution, that such a doing is either absolutely void, or voidable; if it be so absolutely void, then it requires no court to judge it so; if only voidable, then it is voided, or nullified, by the sentence of a proper court. Now, Mr. Dana's ordination, . . . being carried on contrary to constitution, was voidable and was justly declared void, by the united council; and so none, adhering to the constitution, can be holden to be subject to him as their pastor . . . ."[27]

---

26. N. Hobart, *The Principles of Congregational Churches*, p. 3; Layman, *A letter to a Friend*.

27. Eells, *Some Serious Remarks*, p. 50. The most prominent writers on the

Hobart said that those upholding Wallingford were making "tragical outcries of tyranny and oppression,"[28] but that nothing had been done but to uphold the constitution. The opposition, however, claimed that the authority of the Consociation was derived wholly from the constitution and was absolutely limited by it, for they owed their very being to it. They had, therefore, no right or authority to intermeddle in any matters or cases that were not put into their hands by the constitution itself. Nor could they extend their power or authority beyond the limits of the consociated churches nor claim a right of jurisdiction over any person who was not a member of that body or in any case that was not made cognizable by them by the constitution itself.[29] This seems to have been an early case of strict interpretation.

side of the Consociation were Rev. Noah Hobart, of Fairfield, Rev. Edward Eells, of Middletown, Rev. Moses Dickinson, of Norwalk. Hobart, Dickinson and several others on this side had been among those protesting against the laws of 1742 and 1743 as taking away the constitutional rights of the ministers. Among those opposing the Consociation were Rev. Wm. Hart, of Saybrook, Rev. Jonathan Todd, of East Guilford, an unknown layman, and Mr. R. Wolcott.

28. Hobart, *The Principles of Congregational Churches*, pp. 4, 14. See the whole pamphlet; also, *An Attempt to illustrate . . .* , pp. 25–26, 38–40, 43–44. "The essential Laws or fundamental Principles of Society are ratified and confirmed by the Gospel. Christ came not to destroy the Law of Nature . . . on the contrary, he confirmed these relations." Hobart believed that one of the duties following from these relations and strongly supported by Christ and the Apostles was submission to magistrates. He declared it absurd to argue that the Saybrook Platform as interpreted by his side was inconsistent with Christian liberty. "The great Difficulty in civil and ecclesiastical Policy, is to fix the Ballance between Authority and Liberty. Authority is apt to degenerate into Tyranny and Liberty into Licentiousness and confusion . . . The constitution of the consociated churches in Connecticut is in my opinion the true medium between these Extreams." This was published in 1765 while the controversy was still raging. He hoped to show that the constitution agreed with the Scriptures, with itself, the rights of churches and the liberties of men and Christians (p. 12).

29. Hart, *Remarks on a late Pamphlet*, pp. 17–18, 47, 52, defends the act of ordination as strictly constitutional, defines tyranny, and compares civil and religious tyranny.

The general offence at the action of the Consociation seems not to have been because of the doctrines involved but because unconstitutional and arbitrary measures were taken to uphold them and because it was feared that this was but a step to extend the Consociation's power over all the churches. Hart in opposing the Consociation thought of himself only as defending the cause of liberty and the constitution. He defined tyranny as

> the exercise of a power or government over another, under pretence of authority, but really without right and warrant of law. The same action may be either authoritative or tyrannical, according as it is warranted by law and right, or not. If a magistrate, vested with just authority therefor, imprisons my body or takes away my goods, in a legal way, this is a just act of power. But if this same magistrate, without authority, without, or contrary to law, does the same action, under pretense of authority, his conduct is tyrannical.[30]

It was on this side of the case that the laymen argued. They discussed again natural and unalienable rights, and voiced the resentment of many that the ministers of late seemed determined to increase their power.[31] The whole case, so they thought, would tend to make men sick of the ecclesiastical constitution.[32] The

---

30. *Ibid.*, pp. 55–56. See also J. Todd, *A Faithful Narrative*, pp. 59, 78, note, 80–81. Another minister supporting Wallingford quoted Hoadly and the liberty of English subjects. Todd maintained the right of the majority to decide an election, p. 53, See also *A Reply to the Reverend Mr. Eells*; Hart, *An Answer to the Rev'd Mr. Hobart's Principles*; *An Answer to a Letter From an Aged Layman by an Aged Minister*.

31. *Aged Layman of Connecticut, A Letter to the Clergy of the Colony of Connecticut*, 1760.

32. Layman, *Letter to a Friend*, 1760, pp. 14–16. Cf. also R. Wolcott, *Letter to Reverend Mr. Hobart*, 1761, pp. 17–18. This letter, which advocated the rights of the laity, the Cambridge platform, and the right of the majority in both civil and religious affairs, is one of the most significant of their pamphlets. A body politic, he said, might oppress a single man or many men, considering

significance of this case for the present study is in the close arguments on constitutionality which it produced. Since the controversy excited much interest, these arguments must have been carefully pondered by many in the New England colonies. It served,
by applying them to a definite case of wide interest, to vivify and
define arguments which were to many, perhaps, general principles
rather vaguely appreciated.

The significance of religious and ecclesiastical controversy in
developing and spreading abroad political theory might be illustrated by reference to the present situation in America.[33] The recent injection of religious questions into political campaigns and
the attempt to limit by legislative action freedom of thought and
teaching in matters concerning the Bible and religion have caused
a wide interest in the political theories which underlie the separation of church and state and the relative rights and powers of the
state and the individual. One even hears discussions concerning
the natural rights of men. In the eighteenth century, when men's
attention was less scattered by a multiplicity of interests, and their
relation to the church was far closer than today, the influence of
such discussions and conflicts was undoubtedly greater. As a result, the more or less abstract theories of the election and other
political sermons became concrete and practical.

Thus far the arguments considered have been those of the
regularly ordained ministers and a few laymen in behalf of

the oppressed as individuals, but a major part in such a body could not oppress a minor part by over-ruling them by their votes. The main issue was really
the interpretation of the Saybrook Platform (pp. 19–20). He insisted that the
Congregational Church had from the beginning stood for the right of private
judgment by the laity and that it was the greatest privilege man can enjoy and so
to be cherished (pp. 22–23).

33. [Keep in mind, this book was originally published in 1928. Dr. Baldwin
most likely had in mind the lead-up to the 1928 Presidential election, in which
the Democrat candidate Al Smith, a Roman Catholic, drew wide denunciation
from Protestant churches and denominations. Catholicism was almost uni-
versally rejected in America at the time as un-American and an "alien culture,"
and even prompted a resurgence of the dwindling KKK. Smith lost to Herbert
Hoover in one of the largest electoral landslides in American history.—JM]

constitutional government and civil and religious freedom. Did they pass over the heads of the great mass of people or did they make a permanent impression and become a part of their mental possessions? The extent of their influence is hard to determine, but that some of these same arguments were used upon occasion by humble men is certain. It seems fair to suppose that at least one source of their convictions was the constantly reiterated arguments of the ministers. The numerous petitions, confessions of faith, and other documents presented to the assemblies by the "Separates" during these trying years show clearly that many of their members were of the poorer classes. The laws of Massachusetts, New Hampshire, and Connecticut, all of which required citizens to pay taxes to a recognized church and which in Connecticut especially made the establishment of a "Separate" Congregational church almost impossible, fell upon these men and women with special severity. Some no doubt fought the law simply to escape taxation, but some fought for principles for which they were willing to suffer, and they fought well.

Again it is only by quotations that one can get the flavor of the olden days and the exact meaning and force of the familiar phrases. One of the leaders of the common people in Connecticut was Solomon Paine, of Canterbury, who published in 1752 a pamphlet on the "Separates."[34]

> The Word of the Lord was like a Fire shut up in my
> Bones, and the Cry of the poor Innocents, who are some
> of them shut up in Prisons, and others with their little
> Children crying for Milk, and could get none, for the
> Collector had taken their Cow for the Minister; and the

---

34. *A Short View of the Difference between the Churches of Christ, and the established Churches*, 1752. Paine speaks of "New Lights" who first encouraged them and then joined with others to make up the differences between the "New Lights" and the standing churches (pp. 32–33). See *The Result of a Council of The Consociated Churches of the County of Windham*, 1747; Many "New Light'" clergy refused to recognize the "Separate" Churches, declaring they had set up absolute independency (pp. 16–17).

very grey-headed stript of their necessary Housh old-
stuff; And poor weakly Women, their's taken away, even
to their Warming-Pan. Men's Oxen taken out of their
Teams; Horses stript of their Tackling; All the Meat
taken away from some, just at the setting-in of Winter,
when the poor Menhad nothing in the List, but their
Head and one Creature : And when they have nothing
but a Family of small Children, to prison with the Head
of the Family, and all to support the Minister .... I had
a secret Conviction, that it was best to publish by the
Press, the Light that God had given men, to discover
the destructive and damning Nature of the Established
Constitution of Religion in this Colony .... Again I put
it off under the following Excuses: That I had not the
Gift that some had, like a great Eagle, &c. to take off the
Top of the tall cedars; but this Excuse was taken off, by
a Conviction, that I am a Worm which God hath prepared at the Root of this Gourd ... and in Love and Pity
to my dear Country People, I yielded to the Conviction
to give them one public Warning more.[35]

What sincerity, simplicity, and tender sympathy this man had
in his heart! Paine argued that the ecclesiastical constitution was
against the charter and the Act of Toleration of William and Mary,
that to uphold it meant breaking God's law, that to take away men's
estates without their leave was a sin which God "has threatned
with publick Judgments."[36] He declared they had rather die than
lie to get liberty.[37]

Petitions from individuals and communities also give vivid
pictures of conditions. Daniel Hovey, of Mansfield, was imprisoned for refusal to pay the church tax and in 1747 petitioned the

35. Paine, pp. 4–13. A like statement of suffering is given by Blake, p. 117.
36. *Ibid.*, pp. 25, 35.
37. *Ibid.*, p. 36. Everything religious is governed by God "without any
Dependence upon Human Laws, Decrees of Council, Votes of Towns or Societies" (p. 5).

Assembly for relief. He held liberty of conscience in matters of religion "to be ye unalienable Right of Every rational Creature, which no Authority under Heaven can deny without assuming ye Seat of God . . . ."[38] His conviction and the denial of the right of appeal he declared "not only Contrary to ye Law of God & ye nation, but to ye Laws of this Government & the Law of nature, too." He conceived it contrary to the law of reason that a man should be forced to help to maintain that form of religion which he believed to be contrary to the Gospel and that there was no foundation for such practice in the charter of the colony. If not relieved, he must continue to obey God, though he should be stripped of all his worldly goods.[39] Another petition of like sort was made by some of the "Separates" in Canterbury. They acknowledged themselves bound to obey the government "in its proper place where God hath Set it (viz) in ye Kingdom of providence for ye Defence of everyone in ye free enjoyment & improvement of Life, Liberty & propriety from ye force, violence & fraud of others; their diferent opinions in ecliseasticle affairs notwithstanding."[40] But to invade the civil rights and worldly goods of men upon pretence of religion was "Directly Contrary to ye Law of God, & ye act of toleration made in ye Raign of King William and maintained by our gracious King George."[41] Nevertheless, their estates had been seized and sold, even the meat being taken when none was left for the children.[42]

In all these petitions there should be noted the close alliance of the laws of God with those of nature and of Great Britain. A badly spelled manuscript left by some of the Canterbury "Separates" is an amazing document. These poor men insisted on granting to

---

38. Eccles. Papers, X. no. 21 (C. S. L.).

39. *Ibid.*

40. Eccles. Papers, X, no. 58, (C. S. L.). Made in 1747 but negatived, as were most of these petitions. [Original spellings retained.—JM]

41. Blake gives various quotations from other documents of like nature, and others are to be found in the Eccles. Papers. [Original spellings retained.—JM]

42. I. Backus, *Letter to the Reverend Mr. Benj. Lord of Norwich*, 1764, p. 34. Thos. Marsh in 1746, deacon of the church in Windham, was imprisoned from January to June for preaching without license.

others the freedom they claimed for themselves. They were attempting to live as they conceived Christians should. One "Joseph
Marshl," a "Separate" pastor, wrote to "Brother Morss" in 1763:

> Now there is Parte of Said in habitants That Like Siad
> Constitution & Chuse to be undere it & Part that Dount
> But Chuse to be at free Liberty to maintain the Gospel
> a thay thinke best the question being Put to the wholle
> whether they all are agree and are willing Said Disat-
> tisfied bretherin Should be Releast and wee all Say in
> the affermitive—as wee thinke they have a nateral Right
> to act for thamselves. . . . And agane you Objact aganst
> our accepting of freedom by Name So that the Society
> Can Assess there members without us . . . to which we
> answ a Say that they have as Good natrel Right to act
> for thamself as we have therefore for us to Say that wee
> wont have freedom unless they Destroy that they Jdgue
> to be agrebl to the word of God thoe wee Do not, we
> thike Conterary to natrel Rght and Christone Libbert,
> for us to Say that they hant Libberty to act for themselfe
> Ceme to Contredect what wee have Bene Contending
> for to wet that we have unalienable Right to Judge in
> matters of Faith and Practices for our Selves.[43]

These simple men could easily have given lessons in toleration to
their betters.

43. Separate Papers, I, no. 184 (C. H. S.). For other petitions see Eccles.
Papers. X, no. 61 (C. S. L.). A petition by "Separate" Churches in Mansfield,
Windham, Colchester, Plainfield, Canaan, Stonington, Canterbury, Voluntown, Killingly, 1753, was negatived, but in 1755 those in Killingly were exempted. "We . . . Value Our-Selves Highly On the Privilege of an English Constitution and the Civil Government of this Colony." It says also that the word of
God forbids such treatment. No. 20 is a petition of 1748 with 38 signers from
Mansfield, Windham, Tolland & Coventry. Nos. 36, 37, 39–57 give examples
of goods sold and men imprisoned in Voluntown, Plainfield, and Killingly. According to Separate Papers, XI, no. 247, in 1760, the First Society of Canterbury was exempted.

There are also such petitions to be found in Massachusetts and New Hampshire in which natural, Christian, and constitutional rights were asserted.[44] Now and again among published pamphlets and unpublished manuscripts there is an amusing bit that makes the writer's personality stand out vividly. One such is a manuscript book written largely by Nathan Cole, of Kensington, Connecticut, who in 1741 had heard Whitefield and after two years' storm of soul had become a "Separate." For years he was compelled to pay taxes to support the church in Kensington. Several times he petitioned for freedom from these taxes. All this he tells in his manuscript. In one of his petitions he says he rejected the Saybrook constitution because he could not make it agree with God's word and is bound in conscience to obey God rather than men when he cannot make them agree. He says,

> Now see, we are free born as much as you be & have as
> good a right to liberty as you have every way from God
> himself & now see what a heavy curs & dredfull judgment God has pronounced against them that will not

---

44. Eccles. Papers, vol. XII, nos. 626–628 a, 680, 721, 725, and others (M. S. L.). A petition in 1749 from the "Separates" of Rehoboth, Attleborough, Norton, Bridgewater, Mendon, Grafton, Upton, Billingham, Hopkinton, Uxbridge, Athol, Chatham, Easton, Harwich, Middleborough, Raynham, Sutton, Yarmouth, and Roxbury reads: "God hath given to every Man an Unalienable Right in Matters of His Worship to Judge for himself as his Conscience reserves yᵉ Rule from God." It speaks of their forefathers, the charter, etc., and claims they have been put in the stocks, imprisoned, had goods taken, etc. The petition was disallowed. John Cotton, *A Narrative of the Transactions at Middleborough*, 1746, speaks of rights of mankind, both natural and Christian (pp. 12, 21, 23). See *New Hampshire Town Papers*, IX. 282–97, on trouble in Exeter, 1743–44: "Is not Liberty Equally every mans right who has not forfeited it?"; it asserts the right to judge for oneself, the right to separate, the right to be freed from taxes for other churches; in 1755 they petitioned again; their opponents urged that sacred covenants must be maintained (pp. 364–73). There are petitions from Hampton Falls and other places in volumes XII and XIII, but there is not so frequent use of these arguments as in Connecticut. In Exeter, a "Separate" minister, Daniel Rogers, was converted by Whitefield. See C. H. Bell, *History of the Town of Exeter*, p. 196.

give their brethren & fellow servants the same liberty as they take themselves . . . altho we are English men & free born as any one. . . .[45]

A humorous fellow he must have been as well as an earnest.

Ye civel rulers have no liberty to come & git in Aarons seat & make or mend laws about religion or conscience nor never had in all ye whole bible. . . . Now men have been at work to hew down this Constitution tree of Connecticut & i am quit willing to doo my part & it seemeth allmost as if I see people very desireous to have this constitution tree cut down . . . & as it were see me a comeing with a battel ax or eternal truth to help to hew down this tree say to those about them pointing at me

> 1   Oh he was once a lump of sin
>   but now he's just a enter'g in
>   & here he comes a willing soul
>   I say to you make room for Cole
>
> 2   See now Paine Frothingham & Cole
>   have labour'd with a willing soul
>   our harts unite & all agree
>   to help in hewing down this tree.[46]

It was then a gallant band of men, mostly poor, who struck such sturdy blows at this constitution tree. They believed in complete democracy in religious matters, in entire separation of church and state; that liberty of conscience in questions of religion is an inalienable right; that only the call of the Spirit is necessary to one who wishes to preach the Gospel; that, though convenient and profitable, the knowledge of tongues and liberal sciences is not absolutely essential to such a one; that it was contrary to the laws of God, of nature, and of the English people to tax them to support

45. Nathan Cole, MS. in C. H. S.
46. *Ibid.*

a church not their own; that, in such case, God, not man, must be obeyed.[47] These doctrines were in essence revolutionary, yet here, as in the protests of the ministers, the "Separates" believed they were the ones who were upholding the fundamental law and the rights of English men and Christians, and that the legislatures in passing the laws against them were in reality law-breakers.[48]

The Great Awakening with its consequent confusions, political strife, and doctrinal discussions had stimulated men to new and lively thinking in religious and civil affairs. It had brought with it much intolerance, yet out of it had grown a passionate conviction in man's right to freedom of conscience and a struggle, partially successful, to obtain it. It had brought independent judgment and a revulsion against undemocratic methods of ecclesiastical control and state interference and a more determined devotion to the old Congregational way of local self-government in religious affairs. It had sent men to their Bibles, to Sydney, Locke, Milton, Hoadly, and other writers to find arguments to support their

47. See Trumbull, II. 191: petition of S. Paine and 300 other "Separates" to the Connecticut legislature in 1748. See also Blake, pp. 60, 62, 68, 80, 81, 117–21, with many quotations from original documents.

48. After 1763 there were still petitions such as those given. The same arguments were used, and sometimes reference was made to the situation in the colonies. In such a request from the Connecticut towns of Middletown, Haddam, Wethersfield, Gassenbury, Hartford, Windsor, Symbury, and Farmington in 1767 they said that they considered their request altogether reasonable. "The Cry has gone through this North America like lightning, (as it was) Liberty and Property, the Attention Labour and Measures, that this Colony and North America has ben at and taken to secure their natural and Civil Rights, Argues Strongly in our favour, that we shall Prevail . . . and in Proportion, may we be Incouraged, as our Sacred rights, are of more Importance than our Civil." But this and a similar petition in 1770 were disallowed (Eccles. Papers, XV, nos. 225, 232, C. S. L.). See no. 249, a petition in 1768 of "Separates" in Colchester, which speaks of taxation without representation as one reason their ancestors left England; also nos. 184, 213, 214 a, 239, 240. Parker, in *The Congregational Separates of the Eighteenth Century in Connecticut*, p. 161, says that he believes "it was in a large measure due to the Separates that the revision of the laws in 1750 omitted much previous harsh legislation, and that in 1784 the legal establishment of the Saybrook Platform was abrogated."

cause. Clergy and laity, cultured and ignorant had argued for their legal, constitutional rights and, whatever the side to which they belonged, believed they were contending for the fundamental law and constitution.

In certain sections, notably eastern Connecticut, it had stirred common men to an assertion of their rights and a willingness to suffer for them. It had made them peculiarly sensitive to what they considered unjust taxation. When, therefore, the trouble with England began there were many ministers who in colleges and parishes had shared in this religious conflict, some who had suffered because of their beliefs. There were laymen who had striven for their "inalienable rights" and had endured imprisonment and loss of property rather than pay taxes they deemed unjustly levied. In all these struggles men had founded their claims upon great principles of government and upon the support given to these principles, as they believed, by the Bible. There were many men unaffected by such contentions, many of those concerned in them whose purposes, doubtless, were political or economic rather than religious, but there is no doubt that men of all classes not only had become more familiar with the arguments which they were so soon to apply to the new emergency, but had given them deeper meaning and greater urgency.

Seven

Loyalty and Resistance to England: 1754–1766

*I*n the foregoing chapters it has been shown that the New England clergy had built up from the Bible, from ancient and more modern writers, and from their own thinking and experience, a political philosophy in which they had implicit faith and which they had through many years taught to their people. It was a philosophy by which they justified resistance to any invasion of their natural and contractual rights, whether the attempted invasion was made by those in authority, by a foreign enemy, or by the mob.

At one time or another before 1763 the ministers had included in these natural rights many things which they cherished. They had declared the following rights natural and inalienable—in religious affairs, the right of a church to choose its own ministers; the right of having the various kinds of religious covenants preserved, unless by proper judges one party had been found guilty of breaking them;[1] the right to read and interpret the Bible for oneself and the right to complete freedom of conscience;[2] in civil

---

1. Some had argued that in religious matters, though not in civil, the minority had the right of withdrawal from the union made by covenant.

2. Some interpreted this to mean freedom from all taxation to support the clergy, but the majority believed that it did not imply that a man was not bound to pay a tax to support his own pastor at least and in some cases the pastor

affairs, the right to freedom of reading and of speech, to the sacredness of compacts, to the choice of officials, to the right of trial
and appeal, to the fruits of a man's labor, unless given up with his
own consent, to taxation for the good of the whole levied by the
people themselves, to all the rights of Magna Charta and, implied
in all these, the right to resist any encroachment upon these rights
and, as a consequence, the right to all necessary means of defence.
Not all these had been included by each minister who discussed
the natural rights of men, but these and others had been at divers
times asserted as natural, and as protected by God and the English
government, in whose fundamental constitution they lay imbed-
ded. Laws in contradiction of such rights they believed were null
and void. When Jonathan Mayhew, in 1763, said that true religion
comprised the love of liberty and of one's country and the hatred
of all tyranny and oppression, he was expressing the common conviction of the New England ministry that the civil liberty which
they cherished so dearly received its chief sanction from their religious faith.[3]

 To the New England ministers the government of Great Britain after 1688 and of their own colonies came nearest to their ideal
of what government should be. They had come to the very brink
of losing all they held dear under the Stuarts, that "set of degenerate men," that "infamous race" of "sceptred tyrants."[4] The Glorious

chosen by the majority of the parish.

 3. Mayhew, *Sermons to Young Men*, 1763, p. ix.

 4. Mayhew, *Sermons*, 1758, p. 48; *Observations*, p. 154. Caner in *A Candid Examination*, 1763, pp. 23, 70–72, quotes these and other like phrases used by Mayhew and criticises him for their use. There were many such references to the Stuarts by the Congregational ministers and to their salvation from "popery and slavery." Lockwood, in his Connecticut Election Sermon of 1759, p. 12, says: "When King Charles the first attempted to introduce arbitrary Government, it blew up a Civil War, which ended in the Loss of his Head; and when his Son King James the Second, took large strides toward arbitrary Rule, the Nation jealous of their Liberties, invited over the Prince of Orange." See especially the Connecticut Election Sermon of 1728 by Buckingham, pp. 35–36; the Massachusetts Election Sermons of 1728, by Breck, pp. 36–37; of 1746 by Foxcroft, pp. 70–71; of 1747, by Chauncey, p. 34.

Revolution was founded on the very principles of government which the ministers so continually expounded and upon them was based also the Hanoverian succession.[5] Under William III and the Georges the English government was, they thanked God, not arbitrary but legal, a mixed government in which the prerogatives of sovereign and people mutually supported each other, a government with the best constitution in the world, formed on common reason, common consent, and common good, by which the rights and liberties of the people were carefully guarded and the rulers were bound by law. "The grand northern Hive . . . has been stil'd the Shop of the nations; and might . . . have been called . . . the Shop of Liberty," said Thomas Frink.[6]

All that they valued depended, so they thought, on the Hanoverian succession. The attempts to restore the Stuarts and the wars with France kept alive their fears and occasioned many of their discourses. They never tired of praising William III and the Georges whose glory it was never to have violated the constitution nor invaded the rights of the people.[7] In his famous sermon of 1760 on *Christian Union*, Ezra Stiles said, "All the New England sects are loyal, but the principles of loyalty to the illustrious house of Hanover are inculcated on the people by the congregational clergy with peculiar sincerity, faithfulness and constancy."[8] It was partly no doubt their own position and power which the clergy

5. Frink, Massachusetts Election Sermon, 1758, p. 82: "The happy Revolution ought never to be forgotten by Protestants, Britons, and Transmarine English." The whole sermon is ecstatic on English government. Lockwood, in his Connecticut Election Sermon of 1759, p. 13, says, "There is no Nation now in Europe, on the Earth, whose Civil Government is like that of Great Britain . . . none that exceeds, perhaps none, that, in all Respects, equals it in Excellency." Haven in a sermon at Portsmouth, 1761, p. 18, says, "The Balance of our Government is hung indeed in the nicest manner imaginable; a single Hair will turn it."

6. Frink, p. 76, note.

7. *Ibid.*, p. 57. See also Cotton Mather, Sermon on Christian Loyalty, 1727, p. 17, and the Election Sermons of Breck, 1728; Wise, 1729; Webb, 1738, who praises George II for filling the appointive offices in Massachusetts with colonials (p. 24); Eliot, 1738; Phillips, 1750; and many others.

8. Stiles, Discours,e on Christian Union, 1760, p. 128.

were consciously or unconsciously protecting. It was in large part a devotion to the religion and worship which they had received from their ancestors and which they guarded so jealously from any threatened attack. In the election sermons it was a matter of tradition and of policy to praise the government of Great Britain. But the ministers seem also to have had a deep-seated conviction of certain principles of government which they believed were tenderly guarded by the Hanoverians.

Not only did the ministers laud the British government, but they also grew eloquent over their own. In Massachusetts they talked of the precious, invaluable privileges secured to them by the charter of 1691 and urged the legislatures and the governors to be very tender of them. All the rights of natural-born Englishmen had been confirmed to them and in addition the blessing of choosing their own councillors, so valuable a privilege that for it alone the charter must never be parted with. By great expenditure of hardship, blood, and treasure had these dear-bought liberties been gained, and they must be preserved against both domestic oppression and foreign slavery.[9] Occasionally a minister attacked some colonial measure which seemed to him dangerous to the people's liberty. For example, an anonymous pamphlet of 1754 which attacked a proposed Excise Bill is attributed to the Rev. Samuel Cooper, of Boston. The author forcibly presents many of the Revolutionary arguments. Such a bill would, he said, deprive the people of a part of their reserved rights. It was "inconsistent with the Natural Rights of every private Family in the Community," and was an

---

9. Appleton, Sermon, 1742, pp. 41–42. Swift, in his "Massachusetts Election Sermons," Mass. Col. Soc. Pub. I. 418, speaks of the "old and well-worn themes as the inviolability of Charter rights," and thinks that mention of them in so many sermons for a few years after 1738 seems to show that there was at the time some special danger apprehended or that possibly it was due to the slow advance of Episcopacy. For the politics of the period see J. T. Adams, Revolutionary New England. Typical references are: Breck, 1728, p. 36; Barnard, 1734, pp. 2, 54; Webb, 1738, p. 24; Dexter, Sermon in Dedham, 1738, pp. 261–62; Allen, 1744. pp. 8, 47–48; Chauncey, 1747, p. 54; Phillips, 1750, p. 32; Parsons, 1759, pp. 28–29. For further details see Bibliography.

"Entering Wedge into the Constitution." He pictured the possible loss of liberty and the bloody war which would either restore the constitution or fix the people in "irretrievable Slavery" and urged the people to a man to unite in instructing their representatives "to cherish Liberty and Property." A friend to the constitution, he declared, was a friend of God.[10]

The Connecticut clergy were no whit behind those of Massachusetts. By charter they had been made a body politic with all the rights of a free people, free to make their own laws, to elect their own rulers, a specially valuable privilege, to levy their own taxes.[11] These liberties were inconceivably valuable, envied by other governments and, so said some, lacking appreciation only in Connecticut. Nathaniel Hunn, in 1747, in a sermon urging the value of liberty upon the legislature and giving a vivid picture of a people

---

10. The Crisis, June, 1754, pp. 4–15. The proposed bill was to lay an excise in order to pay for erecting a fort on the frontier, and was vetoed by the Governor. Sabin, IV. 515, says: "this pamphlet was reprinted in London in 1766 under the title, The Crisis or a Full Defence of the Colonies, in which it is incontestably proved that the British Constitution has been flagrantly violated in the late Stamp Act, and rendered indisputably evident that the Mother Country cannot lay any Arbitrary Tax upon the Americans without destroying the Essence of her own Liberties." The two pamphlets seem to have been much alike or to have been confused by various authors. The author says: "It is a great misfortune that the Promoters of the B—ll were so unacquainted with the British Constitution and the patriotick Struggles to preserve it from this destroying Corroder in 1753."

11. Lockwood, Connecticut Election Sermon, 1759, pp. 13–14, 16–17. By the charter, "this colony was made and constituted a Body Corporate or Politick, with all the Rights and Immunities of a Free People." To the legislature belongs the right "to levy and raise such Taxes upon the Community, and impose such Customs and Duties, as may be needful for the Security of the People in their Lives, Property and Rights, for the Support of Government, & the Peace and Welfare of the State . . . The Laws we are under . . . are not the Sovereign Injunctions of an arbitrary Ruler, but they are all Laws of our own making . . . Our Lives and Limbs, our Property and Estates, our Rights and Liberties, our Characters and good Names lie at no Man's Mercy." See also Bulkley, 1713, p. 68; Mather, 1725, pp. 19–20; Buckingham, 1728, pp. 40–41; and many later sermons.

oppressed -and heavily burdened, exclaimed:

> I know this is unintelligible Language to the greater Part
> of New English People. Happy are you, Sons of New-
> England, that you know it not by your own Experience.
> . . . When I look over a numerous Assembly of New-
> English People, I can but bless God, and congratulate
> my Country, at the Sight of so many free People, who
> carry Liberty in their very Faces, whose Countenances
> shew that they are not galled, & born down by the igno-
> ble Yoke of Tyranny & Oppression; but are contented &
> happy in Liberty & Plenty . . . Liberty is New England's
> Property and Glory. Let us bless God for it, and prize &
> improve it. . . .[12]

With the French and Indian War there came an outburst
of enthusiasm among the clergy. Dennys de Berdt, writing from
London to his friend the Rev. Eleazar Wheelock, said: "While our
ministers of state are nicely choosing out men to fight Amalek lett
the ministers of Christ be much in the Mount."[13] And assuredly
the ministers had their goodly share in the success of the English
cause. Some served as chaplains; many preached inspiriting sermons to the troops; then, as in the Revolution, they revived flag-
ging spirits and won recruits by their fiery addresses; and always
they contrasted the free English government where law ruled with
the arbitrary government of France where the will of the King was
the law of the subject. "Would you see an End to Law, and everything depend upon the Will of him that had the Power over
you? Is not Slavery in these Respects a terrible Thing?" asked John
Lowell of Newbury in 1755, urging the people to action against

---

12. Hunn, Connecticut Election Sermon, 1747, pp. 17–18. Hunn implies
that some at least of the Connecticut people were suffering the oppression he
pictures. Connecticut was in the midst of the "New Light" and "Separate" troubles at this time. See Welsteed, Massachusetts Election Sermon, 1751, p. 33;
Phillips, Massachusetts Election Sermon, 1750, p. 33.
13. "Letters of Dennys de Berdt," in :Mass. Col. Soc. Pub., XIII. 412.

the enemy.[14] This was the key-note to all the sermons.

> And are we willing to give up our civil Rights and Privi-
> leges, and become subjected to Tyranny and arbitrary
> Government? And are we willing to give up our Reli-
> gion? O! for God's sake, let us think of our Danger, and
> labour to prevent our Ruin . . . Your All lays at Stake.

So exclaimed Isaac Morrill, in 1755, to a company of soldiers.[15]

This danger caused the ministers to explain anew the nature
and value of a constitutional government and of liberty, and not
only the right but the duty to fight if men's lives, liberties, properties, and religion were threatened.[16] They besought the people to
realize the urgency of the cause, to contribute freely, and not to
grumble and think themselves oppressed if the taxes were heavy.
We can imagine that there was a larger attendance than usual
on the ministration of the clergy during these anxious years and
a closer attention paid to their words. How the ministers played
upon the affections and fears of the people! How warmly they

---

14. John Lowell, Sermon, May 22, 1755, p. 21.

15. Isaac Morrill, Sermon at Wilmington, April 3, 1755, to the company
under Capt. Phinehas Osgood, pp. 21–22.

16. Dickinson, Connecticut Election Sermon, 1755; Beckwith, Connecticut
Election Sermon, 1756, pp. 7, 63; Pemberton, Artillery Sermon, 1756; Cogswell, Sermon in Pomfret to Co. under command of Capt. Israel Putnam, April
13, 1757: "There is a Principle of Self-Defence and Preservation, implanted in
our very Natures, which is necessary to us almost as our Beings, and which no
positive Law of God ever yet contradicted. . . . When our Liberty is invaded and
struck at, 'tis sufficient Reason for our making War for the Defence or Recovery
of it. Liberty is one of the most sacred and inviolable Privileges Mankind enjoy;
. . . what Comfort can a Man take in Life when at the Disposal of a despotic
and arbitrary Tyrant, who has no other law but his Will: . . . To live is to be free:
Therefore when our Liberty is attacked, and clandestine, underhand Machina-
tions, or open Violence threaten us with the loss of so dear a Blessing, 'tis Time
to rouze, and defend our undoubted and invaluable Privileges . . . When our
Religion is in danger . . . it will warrant our Engaging in War. . . . Religion is a
treasure never to be parted with . . . we fight for our Properties, our Liberties,
our Religion, our Lives" (pp. 10–12, 24).

besought them to give generously, to fight and fight again for all they held dear! One can imagine the ardent Mayhew as he cried:

> And what horrid scene is this, which restless, roving fancy, or something of an higher nature, presents to me, and so chills my blood! Do I behold these territories of freedom, become the prey of arbitrary power? . . . Do I see the slaves of Lewis with their Indian allies, dispossessing the free-born subjects of King George, of the inheritance received from their forefathers, and purchased by them at the expense of their ease, their treasure, their blood! . . . Do I see a protestant, there, stealing a look at his bible, and being taking [sic] in the fact, punished like a felon! . . . Do I see all liberty, property, religion, happiness, changed, or rather transsubstantiated, into slavery, poverty, superstition, wretchedness !.[17]

17. Mayhew, Election Sermon, 1754, pp. 37–38. Lockwood in his Election Sermon, 1759, pp. 18, 24, says: "we ought I think, in all Reason, to take some Pains to bring Ourselves acquainted with the Liberties & Privileges we enjoy; how they differ from, and exceed in Excellency those, of almost all other Countries and Civil Commonwealths on Earth . . . their vast Importance and unspeakable Value . . . we . . . are called to Freedom and Liberty. Liberty! . . . May we never know it's worth and inestimable Value by being strip't and depriv'd of it." He lamented the disposition in Conn. to complain of the government and the heavy taxes, to imagine they were being chained and shackled and deprived of their liberty by the legislative body. "The Temper & Conduct now hinted at, I am persuaded, is a great and heinous Sin" (pp. 16–17). See also S. Bird, Sermon in New Haven, 1759, to Co. of Col. David Wooster; N. Potter, Discourse at Brookline, 1758, p. 21; Throop, Election Sermon, 1758, p. 24.

A sermon which apparently had much influence in New England, as well as in other colonies, was one preached in 1758 by Samuel Davies, a "New Light" Presbyterian of Hanover County, Virginia, to the militia. It won at once more volunteers than could be used, whereas before it had been almost impossible to get recruits. Davies sent it to Dennys de Berdt, the friend of Whitefield and of many "New Light" clergy in the colonies. De Berdt had it printed in London and sent copies to Eleazar Wheelock and to others. De Berdt says in his preface that the discourse had, he believed, a "Direct Tendency to raise a Noble Spirit among the Inhabitants of the Western World," and he wrote later to Wheelock that he was glad it had been so profitable. See McIlwaine, *Religious Toleration in*

Better to die than be enslaved by the arbitrary rule of France.[18] Death would be infinitely more desirable to those who had relished the "Sweets of Liberty and Property, Englishmen's Darlings,"[19] than to suffer the unutterably dreadful consequences of the French becoming their masters.

When the victory was gained, once again the ministers gloried in the liberties they enjoyed under the British constitution and the Hanoverian house which had so well asserted and defended the natural rights of Englishmen and breathed so free a spirit of liberty over Europe. One at least, Ezra Stiles, of Providence, looked forward to a time when there would be formed a "Provincial Confederacy, and a Common Council, standing on free provincial suffrage"; which might in time "terminate in an Imperial Diet, when the imperial dominion will subsist, as it ought, in election!"[20] But the majority contented themselves with praising the existing constitution and looking forward to an era of peace and prosperity.

Virginia, p. 232; Writings of Washington, Sparks ed. II. 89; "Letters of Dennys de Berdt," Mass. Col. Soc. Pub., XIII. 297, 413–19. The sermon was published also in Phila. It has the same theories of government and natural rights and the same martial spirit as those of New England, also the same appreciation of William III. "We fight for our People; . . . Our Liberty, our Estates, our Lives! . . . shall we tamely submit to Idolatry, and religious Tyranny? No, God forbid: Let us play the Men, since we take up Arms for our People, and the cities of our God . . . to secure the Liberties conveyed to you by your brave Forefathers, and bought with their Blood" (pp. 18–20). This is the sermon in which Davies speaks of Washington as an instance of the kindling of martial fire in the country. "As a remarkable instance of this, I may point out to the Public that heroic Youth Col. Washington, whom I cannot but hope Providence has hitherto preserved in so signal a Manner, for some important Service to his Country" (note to p. 12).

18. [The rule of France would have been considered "arbitrary" because of its legal system based in Roman Catholicism which did not afford the same rights and protections as English Common Law. It was viewed with horror by Protestants who detested not only Roman Catholic religious practice, but also the legal systems of tyranny which followed it.—JM]

19. Bird, Sermon, 1758, pp. 5, 16.

20. Stiles, Discourse on Christian Union, 1760, quoted from Sprague's Annals, I. 475. See also Haven, Sermon at Portsmouth, 1761, p. 17; Wm. Adams, Thanksgiving Sermon, 1760, p. 18; Barnard, Election Sermon, 1763, pp. 33–43.

It seems a most significant fact, and one never sufficiently realized by historians, that for the seven years before the beginning of the trouble with England the people had heard continually from the pulpit such ringing words upon the unspeakable value of their chartered privileges and their rights as Englishmen; of law and constitution as contrasted with tyranny and arbitrary government; of the danger of becoming slaves and losing all their freedom, civil and religious, under such a government; of the justification of war in defense of their cherished rights and liberties. The English constitution was to be defended at any cost because it assured a government of law, because it was so nicely balanced, each part with its own carefully defined rights and limitations, because it guarded so jealously the natural and legal rights of the subjects. Were taxes heavy? None could be too heavy to preserve such cherished rights. Were recruits lacking? No sacrifice could be too great to defend such dear liberties.

It is true that hardly any idea in any sermon had not been presented through an unbroken continuity of nearly a hundred years, but rarely with such zeal and fire. Whatever the more practical economic reasons for fighting, the clergy had given them the color and warmth of idealism. The familiar old themes had suddenly roused to glowing life. The war[21] associated them with danger and sacrifice and loss and at last with victory. If then, when the after-war pressure was upon them and the after-war disorder and irritability were at their height, the Mother Country in her turn became exacting, in her turn threatened the sensitive western liberty, was it not inevitable that the same arguments should spring naturally to their lips? Were they not defending the British constitution itself from a more sinister attack than that by the French? The needed arguments and even the very phrases were ready to their hand and had behind them the sanctions of tradition and of religion.

When the controversy with England began it would be but natural, provided these convictions were sufficiently deep and sincere, that the ministers should enter the contest in support of what

21. [The French and Indian War (p. 109 above).—JM]

they believed their legal rights. So great a proportion entered it early, and defended the American cause so heartily and so steadfastly that they were given by their opponents the credit of being peculiarly responsible. It will then be of especial interest to study the development and application of their theory and to follow their activities through the Revolution.

It was in March, 1765, that the Stamp Act was passed and on May the twenty-ninth that Patrick Henry introduced his famous resolutions into the Virginia House of Burgesses. On that same day the Rev. Andrew Eliot of the New North Church in Boston preached before the Governor and General Court the annual election sermon. Well read in Sydney, Locke, and other writers on government, Eliot gave an address which, full of expressions of loyalty to the English government, was yet a forthright discussion of the fundamental constitution of Great Britain, of government as a compact and of the right of resistance. In this sermon, loyal as it was, he foreshadowed the main lines of argument against England by the colonists. He spoke of the Massachusetts Charter as an especially sacred contract between the King and their ancestors, of the constitution as the foundation of the state, a kind of fundamental law the violation of which might well end in overturning the state, of the grave danger of touching the liberties of a free people and greatly altering a long established government. "When a humour of changing once begins," he said, "no mortal can tell where it will end." Hard it might be to tell where lawful resistance should begin, but submission to tyrannical perversion of power was a crime, an offense against the state, against mankind, and against God. He attributed the lamented difficulties which had arisen and which had so alarmed all orders of men throughout the colonies to mistakes and misapprehensions and declared that perhaps not a man among them desired independence of the mother-country. [22]

22. Eliot, Election Sermon, 1765, pp. 41, 42, 45. See also p. 13. "All power has its foundation in compact and mutual consent, or else it proceeds from fraud or violence: . . . When government is founded in mutual consent, it is the

Andrew Eliot was one of a group of influential ministers in Boston and the towns nearby who were leaders in the revolt against the Stamp Act. Better known than he were Charles Chauncey of the First Church, Samuel Cooper of Brattle Square, and Jonathan Mayhew of the West Church. They were friends of Otis, Samuel and John Adams, John Hancock, and other leaders, and had doubtless already discussed the Writs of Assistance and similar signs of encroachment, as they believed, on the part of England.[23] Moreover, Mayhew had begun as early as 1763 an attack on the activities of the Society for the Propagation of the Gospel and what he deemed the danger of the establishment of an Anglican Episcopate in America. This possibility had haunted the New England clergy for some years and between 1763 and 1775 seems to have caused fear not only among clergy but among laymen as well.[24] Nor was this fear confined to New-England. From 1766 to 1775 the consociated churches of Connecticut frequently met with the Synod of New York and Philadelphia to discuss the danger and to devise measures to combat it.[25] Mayhew and Chauncey

undoubted right of the community to say who shall govern them; and to make what limitations or conditions they think proper." He emphasized the great privilege of electing the councillors and exclaimed: "God grant that the privilege may never be wrested from us!" (p. 4). Cf. also pp. 16, 34–38.

23. Hollis Papers, no. 50, 1765. Hollis sent through Mayhew two books to Otis and said he had read the latter's *Rights of the British Colonies*. From 1759 Hollis sent books on government to Mayhew and through him to others and received from Mayhew sermons, pamphlets, etc. See Chap. 1.

24. Hollis Papers, 1759–1771. Beginning 1762 Mayhew wrote of this scheme. See A. L. Cross, *The Anglican Episcopate and the American Colonies*, for full discussion.

25. *Records of the Presbyterian Church; Minutes of the General Consociation.* A study of the minutes reveals a determined opposition to an American Bishopric. J. Adams, *Life and Works*, X. 185, says this apprehension of Episcopacy contributed "as much as any other cause, to arouse the attention, not only of the inquiring mind, but of the common people, and urge them to close thinking on the constitutional authority of parliament over the colonies." When Mayhew's pamphlets appeared, says Adams, "The controversy soon interested all men, spread through America and in Europe ... All denominations in America became interested in it, and began to think of the secret, latent principle upon

were the most prominent opponents of the scheme, and the Rev. East Apthorp, the Episcopal missionary in Cambridge, and Dr. Chandler of New York perhaps its most prominent supporters. The pamphlets written by these and other men were widely read both in England and America.

This controversy was without doubt one of the reasons for the almost unanimous and persistent critical attitude of the Congregational and Presbyterian ministers toward the British imperial policy and had already roused many of them to watchfulness before the passage of the Stamp Act. It was the logical result of this fray, as well as of their friendship for Otis and other leaders and their long familiarity with political and constitutional theory, that the Boston ministers should share and at times lead the movement against the Stamp Act.[26] Mayhew had long been writing in support of liberty, both civil and religious, and was known all over America and in England for his bold attacks on arbitrary power and for his arguments in behalf of the right of resistance and against the doctrine of passive obedience. His correspondence also was unusually large. Regarding the Stamp Act he declared himself to have been "penetrated with the most sensible grief" and he expressed his sentiments boldly in pulpit and press.[27] His sermon on the repeal of the Stamp Act, which Eliot thought the best published on this occasion, came out in Boston within six days of its delivery, went through a second edition the next year and shortly afterwards was published in England also. This sermon, and those of Chauncey and other ministers, asserted

---

which all encroachments upon us must be founded, the power of parliament. The nature and extent of the authority of parliament over the colonies was discussed everywhere, till it was discovered that it had none at all" (pp. 187–88).

26. Gordon, *History of The . . . Independence of . . . America*, I. 102, tells of the story that Whitefield in April of 1764 told Dr. Langdon and the Rev. Jason Haven of a secret plot against the civil and religious liberties of New England which he had learned from the best authorities in Great Britain. Dr. Langdon is said to have told of this in private to the convention of ministers.

27. Hollis Papers, No. 80. Mayhew wrote on June 19, 1766, of the great wisdom of having secured an influence over "the Public Prints, which influence evidently had been of highest Utility on both sides the water & may & will & must be again." Bradford's *Life of Mayhew* gives many letters and other documents.

that the Stamp Act could never be enforced without bloodshed.[28] It was Mayhew who suggested to Otis in 1766 the idea of circular letters to build up a "communion of colonies."[29] Friend and foe alike gave tribute to his great influence, and his death in 1766 was deeply lamented by all lovers of liberty.[30]

Dr. Charles Chauncey was another minister credited by John Adams and others as being one of the leaders in Massachusetts.[31] Less tolerant than Mayhew in religious and ecclesiastical matters, he was at one with him in antagonism to the project of an Episcopate and in his quick reaction to the Stamp Act. He also by newspaper articles, sermons, and pamphlets urged opposition and established its grounds. In his sermon on the repeal of the Stamp Act he spoke of trial by their equals and making grants to government either in person or through representatives chosen by themselves as being inalienable and constitutional rights to which the people believed themselves natural heirs and the defence of which could not be regarded as either a lack of loyalty to the King or lack of due regard to the British Parliament.[32]

---

28. J. Mayhew, *The Snare broken* (2nd ed. printed in Boston, 1766). See *Boston News Letter*, May 22, May 29, 1766, May 7, 1767, quoting notes on sermon from London, in *Critical Review of January*. J. Adams, *Life and Works*, X. 191; Hollis Papers, no. 63, Aug. 8, 1765. Mayhew wrote that people were far from wishing independence, but that the Stamp Act would not be carried into effect without much bloodshed. Mayhew was accused of having by a sermon incited the mob to attack Hutchinson's house, but denied it and was much hurt by the story. Eliot told Hollis that Mayhew had preached on Liberty but said not a word of any attack,—questioned whether any of the rioters had ever heard of Mayhew's sermon. Next Sunday Mayhew preached against abusing Liberty (Hollis Papers, nos. 26–78, 115. In Sept., 1765, Mayhew sent Hollis a number of public prints about the Stamp Act and in May, 1766, several copies of his sermon on repeal.

29. Tudor, *Life of James Otis*, pp. 44, 145.

30. Adams (*Life and Works*, IV. 29; X. 193, also p. 288), believed that Harrison Grey, to whom Mayhew bad been an oracle, would never have been a refugee, had Mayhew lived. Cf. Sprague, VIII. 26; Backus, *A Fish caught in his own Net*, p. 66, note; *Boston News Letter*, July 17, 1766, Aug. 20, 1767.

31. Adams, *Life and Works*, X. 271; P. Oliver, *Origins & Progress of American Rebellion*, p. 60.

32. C. Chauncey, Sermon, July 24, 1766, pp. 13–14, 19–21; J. Winsor, *Me-*

A Boston minister who was among the first to oppose the English acts, whose influence was unusually great, and who was particularly hated by the Tories and the British was the polished gentleman, Dr. Samuel Cooper of Brattle Street Church, the friend and correspondent not only of Franklin, Samuel Adams, and other American statesmen, but of Europeans as well. His counsel was constantly sought and earnestly weighed. In conversation and correspondence, in frequent articles to the *Boston Gazette* and *Independent Ledger*, in sermons from his pulpit, and even as an attendant and speaker at the secret meetings of the Sons of Liberty, Dr. Cooper exerted a powerful influence.[33] From the beginning of his ministry in Brattle Square in 1744 he had taken an active part in public affairs.[34] From the beginning he was utterly devoted to the American cause. One of the secrets of his influence

---

morial History of Boston, III. 123; N. Eng. Hist. and Geneal. *Register*, 1859, p. 131. Cf. the ballad on "The Boston Ministers" written in 1774:

> "That fine preacher, called a teacher,
>   Of Old Brick Church the first,
> Regards no grace, to men in place,
>   And is by tories curst,
> At young and old, he'll rave and scold,
>   And is, in things of state,
> A zealous Whig, than Wilkes more big
>   In Church a tyrant great."

33. Adams, *Life and Works*, X. 271, 274; Sprague, I. 443; Tudor, *Life of James Otis*, pp. 152–53. Cooper was chaplain to the General Court, 1758–70, 1777–83. See "Diary," *Amer. Hist. Rev.*, VI. 301–03, and "Letters to Pownall," *Amer. Hist. Rev.*, VIII. 301–30. Winsor, *Memorial History of Boston*, p. 123, quotes from Palfrey, *Sermon in Brattle Square*, 1824, pp. 16–17: "Of the writings which alternately stimulated and checked the public mind in that season of stormy excitement, there were perhaps none of greater efficiency than those of Dr. Cooper. If other hands launched the lightning, his guided the cloud." P. Oliver, *The Origin and Progress of the American Rebellion* (F. L. Gay Transcripts, M. H. S.), pp. 61–62, 103, tells of one of "those Night Garret Meetings," at which "the serpentine Dr. Cooper" presided. The weight was so great that the floor sank, but Cooper survived "to commit such atrocious Acts as will perpetuate his Name with indelible Infamy."

34. For the public activity of Cooper, see Winsor, III. 123; Tudor, pp. 152–53.

was his discretion and the quickness with which he worked.[35] In the London Political Register of 1780 there is the following opinion of Dr. Cooper and his brother.

> William Cooper . . . is one of the greatest knaves and most inveterate rebels in New England. He is a very hot-headed man, and constantly urged the most violent measures. He was prompted secretly by his brother, the Reverend Samuel Cooper, who, though a minister of peace and to all outward appearances a meek and heavenly man, yet was one of the chief instruments in stirring up the people to take arms. Hancock, and many leaders of the rebellion, were his parishioners . . . . This pastor . . . was of such remarkable popularity, that the aisles of the church would be thronged with eager listeners, and he was a favorite of royalists and rebels.[36]

A ballad of the day describes his skill in politics.

> There's Cooper too, a doctor true,
>   Is sterling in his way; . .
> In politics, he all the tricks,
>   Doth wonderously ken,
> In's country's cause and for her laws,
>   Above most mortal men."[37]

---

35. Tudor, pp. 152–53.

36. Loring, *Hundred Boston Orations*, p. 9. In Draper's *Boston News Letter* of Sept. 17, 1775, is the following: "Last week the Reverend Doctor Morrison received a call to the elegant new church in Brattle Street in Boston, vacated by the flight of Dr. Cooper; and to-day he delivered an excellent discourse to a genteel audience. His discourse tended to show the fatal consequences of sowing sedition and conspiracy among parishioners, which this pulpit has been most wickedly practicing ever since the corner stone was laid." Cf. Moore, *Diary of the Revolution*, I. 136. Cooper was often "lampooned and personally insulted" (Tudor, p. 153). For further activities, see succeeding chapters.

37. *N. Eng. Hist. and Geneal. Register*, 1859, p. 131, ballad on *The Boston Minister*. His "Diary," 1775–76, gives some idea of his large acquaintance.

These ministers may have been the most noted of the Massachusetts clergy who opposed the Stamp Act, but they were by no means all. It was more essential for the success of the American cause that the people in the country be aroused. Those in Boston and the larger towns were more immediately under the influence of the lay leaders and had greater access to the press. But in the villages the minister was of greater relative importance.

Of the country ministers in Massachusttes none is more interesting than the Rev. Jonas Clark, of Lexington, the friend of John Hancock and Samuel Adams and of other patriots who gathered often at his home to discuss politics.[38] Living simply among his people, their familiar friend and constant guide, he was yet a statesman, thoroughly familiar with constitutional arguments and theories. For years before the Stamp Act, he is said to have preached Sunday after Sunday and explained in many a town meeting the doctrines of natural and constitutional rights and the right of resistance. He is said to have written practically every public paper of the town from 1762 to the end of the Revolutionary war, and every instruction to the Lexington delegates to the General Court, some of which in his handwriting still remain. Instructions to the town's representative in 1765 gave reasons for resistance.

> We have looked upon men as beings naturally free," he wrote. "What of all most alarms us, is an Act commonly called the Stamp Act, the full execution of which we apprehend would divert us of our most inestimable charter rights and privileges, rob us of our character as free and natural subjects and of almost everything we ought, as a people, to hold dear . . . this Act . . . is imposed in direct opposition to an essential right or privilege of free and natural subjects of Great Britain, who look upon

---

38. Hudson, *History of Lexington*, pp. 161–63, 336, 338. Clark is said to have had at times a controlling influence on Hancock, whose cousin was Clark's wife. The night before Lexington, Samuel Cooper, as well as Adams and Hancock, was at his bouse. See Cooper, "Diary," *Amer. Hist. Rev.* VI. 303, note.

it as their darling and constitutional right never to be taxed but by their own consent, in person or by their Representatives.[39]

In these rights Clark included also that of trial by jury.

Another country minister was the Rev. Ebenezer Parkman, of Westboro, whose diary gives a vivid picture of his mental agitation during these early days. Late in August he speaks of himself as being greatly agitated over the situation, especially that of Boston, and as pitying the Governor and hoping that he was innocent. During July he had bought Montesquieu's *Spirit of Laws* and by September 6 had read Bishop Hoadly's *Measures of Submiss." to ye civil Magistrate* and felt prepared to preach the following Sunday a sermon which was double the ordinary length. When the town committee in October drew up their instruction to their representative they met in his home.[40]

Probably many of the other ministers in Massachusetts were reading eagerly during these months. Many of them are said by town historians to have taken an early and active part in town activities and in forming their people's minds.[41] When the Stamp Act was repealed, sermons of rejoicing were preached and eight

39. Hudson, pp. 88–89; See also pp. 342 ff.; *Proceedings and Addresses Commemorative of the Two Hundredth Anniversary of Lexington*, pp. 18–20. Quotations from many of his papers and sermons are given by Hudson.

40. Diary, ed by Harriette M. Forbes, 1899; C. H. Bell, *History of the Town of Exeter*, p. 79. Daniel Rogers of the Separate Church wrote in his diary, Nov. 1, 1765: "The infamous Stamp Act abhorred by all the British Colonies took place."

41. One of them was Samuel West, of Dartmouth, a classmate and friend of Hancock, with whom he had great influence, and a friend of Otis, Robert Treat Paine, and other leaders. He was poor and served a parish of plain, uneducated people. See Sprague, VIII. pp. 38–41. Another was David Sanford, of Medway; cf. Jameson, History of Medway, pp. 426–27. Jeremy Belknap, of Dover, N. H., wrote pamphlets and articles in New Hampshire Gazette and in Boston papers; cf. Moore and Farmer, *Coll. Topog., Hist. and Biog.*, p. 39. Henry Cummings, of Billerica, Mass., was "a man of the people" and leader in town councils; cf. Hazen, History of Billerica, pp. 227–28, 262 ff. Samuel Cooke, of Arlington, a friend of Hancock, Adams, etc.; cf. Parker, *Town of Arlington*, pp. 51, 190–91.

were published in Massachusetts alone, some of which went into several editions.[42] Two of the most fiery were those of William Patten, of Halifax, and Joseph Emerson, of Pepperell.

Patten defined in much detail natural liberty and equality and declared that as members of civil society men had a right to every branch of liberty, which they had not surrendered. That the British subject in America had equal rights with those in Britain and possessed them "as inherent and indefeasible" he thought beyond question. He described the perils through which their ancestors had fulfilled their side of the compact made with the king and the rights which were, in return, promised them; those of freeborn Englishmen, including a right to their own estates, taxation by their own representatives, trial by their peers, and the special privileges of freedom of conscience, and the freedom from all taxation from abroad in return for the fifth part of their gold and silver ore. He quoted Sydney in talking of government based on compact and consent, and Locke on the right of the people to judge as to whether wrong had been done them. He spoke of the luckless

---

42. See Love, *Fast and Thanksgiving Days of New England*, pp. 541–42 (8 in Mass., 1 in Conn., 1 in R. I., 1 in Ga.). A sermon by Nathaniel Appleton, of Cambridge, was printed at expense of Gen. Brattle and sent to de Berdt in London (*Mass. Col. Soc. Pub.*, XIII. 319). Others were by Samuel Stillman of the First Baptist Church in Boston, who Winsor says was "one of the powerful preachers of the Revolution. The unattached crowd thronged to his obscure little church at the North End" (Winsor, *Memorial History of Boston*, III. 125). A ballad of the day, printed in N. Eng. Hist. and Geneal. Register, p. 132, sings of him:

> "Last in my list is a Baptist,
>   A real saint, I wot,
> Though nam'd Stillman, much noise he can
>   Make when in pulpit got.
> The multitude, both grave and rude,
>   As drove by wind and tide
> After him hie when he doth try
>   To gain them to his side."

Others were published by Joseph Emerson, of Pepperell, Elisha Fish, of Upton, Wm. Patten, of Halifax.

Charles, of James "with his Andros, and Randolph and the rest of his crew in this government," and exhorted his people to stand fast in the liberty which had been given them by the God of nature and the British constitution.[43]

Even more vigorous and ardent was the sermon of Joseph Emerson. Its glowing words must have deeply stirred its hearers. Emerson painted the dangers of the Stamp Act in blackest dye and its repeal as a marvelous deliverance from slavery.[44] He emphasized the injustice of trial by courts of admiralty without a jury, which he believed directly contrary to Magna Charta.[45] He connected civil and religious freedom. He described the suspension of trade and other miseries and imagined the evils they would have suffered had not the repeal occurred, among others the possibility of having to support diocesan bishops and even of becoming tributary to Rome, and finally the horrors of civil war. "In the supposed case, we should have fought . . . . for our children, our wives, our liberty, our religion, for everything near and dear to us; and the issue might have been the destruction of the British empire."[46] At first indeed few saw the danger, he said, but "upon the spreading of

43. Patten, Thanksgiving Sermon, 1766, pp. 6–18: "Whoever in his senses, (unless he had the temper of a slave) ever submitted his liberty; to the absolute disposal of others, under the notion of their being the sole judges of right and wrong?" He deprecates recent violence but thinks some have cause to be thankful that only their effigies have been hung. pp. 18–20 ff.

44. Emerson, Thanksgiving Sermon, 1766, p. 9. "And what is the great, the mighty deliverance we have experienced? Does it deserve a commemoration? Yes, if anything great and good ever did. Is it worthy to be handed down to posterity? Yes, to be printed in a book and preserved with sacred care as long as time shall last. Is it of such value as to demand a whole day to be spent in praising God for it? Yes, our lives,—yea, eternity,—as it is what our Savior purchased for us, and as there are such glorious things, of a spiritual nature, connected with it. And what is it? A deliverance from slavery;—nothing less than from vile ignominious slavery."

45. *Ibid.*, pp. 10–11. Pepperell was on the borders of N. H., and Emerson may have been interested in the controversy between Conn. and N. H. over an admiralty judge. See J. T. Adams, Revolutionary New England, pp. 258–59.

46. *Ibid.*, pp. 11–14.

some nervous pieces," which made the matter clear, all were roused and a noble ardor ran from breast to breast. Believing that many, if not most of his hearers were ignorant of the history of the trouble with Andros, Patten described it at length, quoting Cotton and Increase Mather, and urged his people to teach their children the wonderful history of their ancestors, to train them in the principles of liberty, to tell them that they were of the same blood as those who stood so nobly against King Charles, "frighted his Son from the throne, and then declared it vacant," to tell them of the resolute stand in the year 1765 and charge them never to yield their privileges, even at the hazard of their lives.[47]

It is sometimes through the eyes of an enemy that a man's or a group's power can best be seen. Peter Oliver, the last Chief Justice under the colonial regime in Massachusetts, held the dissenting ministers in detestation as the henchmen of James Otis. Otis, says Oliver, saw from the beginning the necessity of securing "the black Regiment," if he were to rouse the people. He therefore made sure of the support of the leading Boston clergy who "had imbibed the principles of the people" and whose influence over the lesser ministers was extraordinary. Thus Otis had gained the support of the black coated order who, says Oliver, "like their Predecessors of 1641 . . . have been unceasingly sounding the Yell of Rebellion in the Ears of an ignorant & deluded People."[48]

Influential as were the ministers of Massachusetts in rousing and keeping alive opposition to the Stamp Act, those of Connecticut played even a more important part in these early days. In 1764

---

47. *Ibid.*, pp. 22–30. He also urged them to have a reverence for lawful authority and cultivate an affection for the mother-country (pp. 31–32).

48. P. Oliver, *Origin and Progress of the American Rebellion,* pp. 39, 58–60. "Mr. Otis and his Myrmidons the Smugglers & the black Regiment bad instilled into the Canaille, that Mr. Hutchinson bad promoted the Stamp Act . . . it was in vain to struggle against the Law of Otis, & the Gospel of his black Regiment" (p. 73). Oliver speaks of the great influence of the election and convention sermons and the annual meetings of the clergy at Boston. Not all dissenting ministers opposed the English government, nor, of course, did the Anglican clergy. See later chapters.

the Connecticut Assembly had decided to make the best defence possible to the proposed tax. It decided to collect arguments which were to be printed, sent to London, and dispersed throughout the colony.[49] By the summer of 1765, however, the educated classes in general had become somewhat lukewarm and inclined to submit to the inevitable. Certain of the ministers were alarmed at the lack of interest and resolved to awaken people to a realization of their situation, as the ministers saw it.[50]

Early in August the Rev. Naphtali Daggett, then professor of Divinity at Yale, wrote under the name of "Cato" an article to the Connecticut Gazette against those "vile miscreants," the American collectors of the stamp tax, who had "no slightest spark of love for their country."[51] He censured bitterly those who were complaining with the tongue and pen only. This article is said to have been

49. Stiles, *Itineraries*, p. 509. On the committee which had this in charge was John Hubbard, the father of Rev. Ezra Stiles, then pastor in Newport, R. I. Hubbard, considering himself unfit, turned to Stiles for help, and begged him to send whatever he could collect and suggest, saying that it would be well, provided R. I. were to engage in a similar scheme, to have the same arguments used by all the governments concerned. Noah Welles, in his Election Sermon, May 10, 1764, spoke of the blessings of liberty, and the necessity of cultivating a love for it if life, liberty, and property were to be secured (pp. 16–17). He spoke at length of the blessings oi the English Constitution.

50. Hollister, *History of Connecticut*, II. 130–31. Of the cultivated classes, the clergy "were for awhile almost alone in their opposition to the measure." Gordon (*History of . . . Independence of . . . America*, I. 117) says that tht. inhabitants were inattentive and the judges, perfectly secure, were unalarmed. Cf. Martha Lamb, "Lyme," *Harper's Magazine*, Feb. 1876, p. 19. *Massachusetts Gazette and Boston News Letter*, Aug. 29, 1765: "No domestic News in the New York and Connecticut Papers. We can't learn they have carried their Resentment in the Neighboring Government to any great Length against those who were appointed Stamp Officers." Cf. *Centennial Papers of General Conference of Connecticut*. p. 17. Fowler says that governor, legislature, and judges were indifferent, but that the people were opposed. The Election Sermon, 1765, by Ed. Dorr, of Hartford, is very different in tone from that of Andrew Eliot, of Boston.

51. E. Atwater , ed .. History of the City of New Haven, pp. 39, 49, 216–17. J. T. Adams (Revolutionary N ew England, p. 334) says Daggett had held for ten years a grudge against Ingersoll.

reprinted widely from New Hampshire to Pennsylvania and to have met with general approval. It was but the first of a series of articles by Daggett. He was soon joined by the Rev. Stephen Johnson, the "forgotten patriot" of Lyme.

Johnson had graduated from Yale in 1743 in the midst of the "New Light" trouble and was in 1765 pastor of the largest church in Lyme, a little village but one of some importance. In September, 1765, after having seen some papers, perhaps the Virginia Resolves, brought secretly from New York by his friend and neighbor, John McCurdy, he began a prolonged and successful attempt to arouse greater resistance to the Stamp Act.[52] He published under a pseudonym in the New London Gazette six carefully reasoned articles which, like Daggett's, were copied widely in other papers. [53] He is said to have written anonymous

52. Gordon, *History of . . . Independence . . . of America*, I. 117; Hollister, *History of Connecticut*, II. 130–31; F. Morgan, ed., *Connecticut as a Colony and as a State*, II. 43; Martha Lamb, "Judge Charles Johnson McCurdy," in *Mag. of Amer. Hist.*, XXVI. 331. John McCurdy was an Irishman of Antrim. He and Johnson lived on the post road, entertained many guests, discussed the independence of America, etc. Lyme had wide business interests, its store was the only one between New London and Guilford. It sent vessels to the West Indies, Holland, and Ireland. McCurdy, in 1765, had seen copies of the Virginia Resolves in N. Y., and is said to have brought one home. Articles by Johnson, which were published secretly, are said to have inspired the organization of Sons of Liberty. Cf. Lamb, in *Harper's*, Feb. 1876, pp. 19–20; Palfrey, *History of New England*, V. 516; E. E. Sill, *A Forgotten Connecticut Patriot*, pp. 8–9, 37–44. Johnson inherited the library of his father-in-law, Wm. Diodate, of New Haven, nearly 100 volumes. E. Stiles, *Itineraries*, pp. 265–67; Dexter, *Yale Biographical Sketches*, 1701–45. p. 739.

53. See note 52. Also Stiles's Papers, I, III, IV: six articles in New London Gazette, the first signed "Addison," others "A Freeman of the Colony of Connecticut," Sept. 6, Sept. 20, Sept. 27, Oct. 4, Oct. 11, Nov. 1; the first addressed to the Freeman of the Colony of Connecticut, the last five to the Printers. Sept. 20th is missing in Stiles's Papers, but was found copied in the *Boston Evening Post*, Oct. 14, 1765 and later numbers. The article of Sept. 6 was copied Sept. 23 and praised in the *Boston Gazette & Country Journal*. The *New London Gazette* for Sept. 20th is missing in the Yale Coll. On Nov. 1st, Stiles Papers IV, Stiles notes, "This is part of a publication in five New London papers by the Reverend Stephen Johnson." In these Johnson quotes Sydney, Selden, and others. Sill, p.

pamphlets and to have traveled through Connecticut and parts of Massachusetts arousing the people against the measure. In December he preached a most vigorous sermon to his own people and published it anonymously as a pamphlet.[54] In all the newspaper and pamphlet literature of the time none give more clearly the arguments' against Great Britain, none advocate more forcibly unqualified rebellion, and none speak more plainly of the threatened independence of the colonies.

In his first articles Johnson wrote warmly of the crisis as the greatest America had ever seen. He called the colonial charters compacts of such a nature that, if broken on the one side, no obligation lay upon the other. He spoke of the essential, fundamental constitution of England and the privileges guaranteed by it, of the rights which were antecedent to all earthly government, derived from the "great Legislator of the Universe," the loss of which would entail slavery upon their posterity. He urged the people not to be lulled into security, to choose representatives who would not be bought or cowed into submission, and to give these representatives their definite instructions. He urged a union of all the colonies. The other five articles were detailed arguments, setting forth the natural rights of man and the rights of Englishmen and their history. He suggested the scattering of pamphlets by the thousands in America, in England, Ireland, and France, urged that foreign manufactures be used as little as possible, and advocated free trade with England only on condition that the Stamp Act be repealed. He pleaded for spirited resistance, even to the sacrifice of lives and fortune, and foresaw danger of war.[55]

38, says the excitement caused by these papers was great, that fleet riders carried them to all the colonies and there they were reprinted.

54. *Some Important Observations, Occasioned by, and adapted to, The Publick Fast, Ordered by Authority, December 18th, A. D. 1765.* This was published in Newport, Dec. 1765 and was, according to Love, the only Fast Sermon published that year. Cf. Love, *Fast and Thanksgiving Days of New England,* p. 541.

55. *New London Gazette,* Sept. 6, 1765; also Stiles Papers. "O my Country! for you I have wrote; for you I daily pray and mourn, and to save your invaluable Rights and Freedom, I would willingly die" (Nov. 1st).

Johnson's Fast Day Sermon is one of the most interesting and most vigorous of all the Revolutionary pamphlets. He called the Stamp Act "high and aggravated injustice," the "enslaving of a free people." The abolition of their charters and privileges, he said, the annulling of their governments and legal securities, dissolved the connection of the colonists with Great Britain and left them "absolutely in a state of nature and independency."[56] Should such a thing happen, he saw no reason why they should not choose what government they wished, or connect themselves anew with Great Britain or any other power, although they would no doubt be careful "to place no undue confidence where grants, charter, and legal securities, are deemed but as waste-paper."[57] Independence, though not desired, had often been forced upon the oppressed, he said. It had happened in Rehoboam's time, it had happened in Holland, and it was possible that it might happen also to the British colonies. Certainly, if it came to a choice of slavery or independence, they would not hesitate.[58] No obedience was due to any edicts which were unconstitutional.

> It is a flagrant absurdity to suppose a free constitution empowers any to decree or execute its own destruction: For such a militating self-repugnancy in a constitution, necessarily carries its own destruction in it. No obedience is due to them by the law of God.[59]

Where executive and legislative authority exceed the bounds of the law of God and the constitution, then their acts are *ipso facto*

---

56. Johnson, Fast Day Sermon, Dec. 1765, p. 18, note. He could not, he said, understand English politics which tended to "alienate, impoverish, and ruin the colonies; and stab to the heart, the trade and manufactures of Great Britain . . . which must render the settled colonies unserviceable to Great Britain, in peace and war; and render, in a measure, useless those immense tracts of uninhabited crown lands in America" (pp. 16–17, note). This is the first mention of a possible return "to a state of nature."

57. *Ibid.*, p. 18, note.

58. *Ibid.*, pp. 19–20.

59. *Ibid.*, p. 21.

void. Men have not only no right to give up liberty, they cannot do it without betraying the invaluable rights of posterity. Referring to Locke, Johnson said any attempts to take away their natural rights constituted a state of war in which the people might reassume and defend these rights. He extolled the British constitution in which each part was bound absolutely by law and declared that Britain had been the first to break it, whereas the colonists were only supporting it. "May we not ask," he said, "who is the aggressor, he that invades the right of a free people, or they who defend only what is their own ?"[60] Events big with fate urged them to the strongest possible resistance,

> for who knows the fatal consequences (if relief fails) whether the British empire may not be shattered into parties, torn into pieces, and, in the end, broken up and ruined. "A kingdom divided against itself, cannot stand."[61]

Other clergymen soon took up the work—in eastern Connecticut Ebenezer Devotion, of Windham, who in 1765 was elected to the Assembly, Elizur Goodrich, of Durham, Philemon Robbins, of Branford, and many others; and in the west, Noah Welles, of Stamford, Cotton Mather Smith, of Sharon, Judah Champion, of Litchfield, as well as a few other "New Lights."[62] The movement

---

60. *Ibid.*, p. 26. See also pp. 5, 22, 31–32. The doctrine of subjection "is of dreadful consequences. . . . In the British empire, 'tis a doctrine of rebellion, it breaks up our allegiance, which we owe and have sworn to King George II" (p. 26).

61. *Ibid.*, pp. 38, 40, 56. etc.

62. Hollister, *History of Connecticut*, II. 130–31. "They impugned the Stamp Act in their sermons, they classed its loathed name in their prayers with those of sin, satan, and the mammon of unrighteousness." See Gordon, I. 117; Atwater, *History of City of New Haven*, p. 34; Larned, *Windham County*, II. 54. Devotion was noted for his political ability; Stiles thought his election "a very singular instance" (Sprague, I. 508–10); Goodrich was repeatedly delegate to Convention of Synod of Philadelphia and New York, had prepared many boys for college, had early studied arguments for right to resistance, preached them in the pulpit, was known for his zeal in American cause. Cf. *Love, Fast and Thanksgiving Days of New England*, p. 331; Huntingdon, *History of Stamford*,

seems to have been strongest at first in the eastern counties. Windham had been settled largely by people from Massachusetts, friendly therefore to Boston and trading with her. The East was the home of more industries and greater commerce. Morever, it was in these eastern counties that the "New Light" and "Separate" movement had been strongest and the people were more "uneasy" than in the west.[63] Local politics also entered to some extent into the movement. The "New Light" faction, strongest in the East and with a few adherents in Fairfield County, wanted to control the government and to oust Governor Fitch.[64] Undoubtedly the return in 1765 of the popular Colonel Putnam to Pomfret and his uncompromising hostility to the Stamp Act was one of the reasons for the prominence of Windham County in these early proceedings.[65] But whatever other causes may have been contributory, certainly the activity of Johnson and other ministers should not be overlooked or their influence underestimated.[66]

In these eastern counties, the Sons of Liberty grew rapidly in numbers and in power. From Windham and New London counties almost entirely came the band of five hundred excited patriots who met Ingersoll, the stamp agent, on his way to Hartford, forced him to shout "Liberty and Property" and resign his office.[67] From

Connecticut, p. 202; Headley, pp. 308–09.

63. Stiles, *Itineraries*, pp. 265–67; 283, 296–97, 299, 588; Tracy, Great Awakening, p. 315.

64. Stiles, *Itineraries*, pp. 509–10, 588. John Hubbard wrote in 1766: "Among other fine Devices to set people by the Ears a Man's religious Principles are made the Test or shall I say the badge of his political Creed. An Arminian, and a Favourer of the Stamp Act signify the same Man." The "New Lights" defeated Fitch and elected Pitkin. See Stiles, pp. 63, 492; *Centennial Papers General Conference of Connecticut*, p. 61. J. T. Adams, *Revolutionary New England*, pp. 260–62, speaks of another question which divided the people of Connecticut, that of land speculation and the Susquehannah Co. Fitch opposed the scheme, as did the English government. See also pp. 324–28.

65. Larned, *History of Windham County*, II. 4–5.

66. For full account of Stamp Act troubles see Gipson, *Jared Ingersoll*; J. T. Adams, *Revolutionary New England*. Neither lays any weight upon the influence of the clergy.

67. Stiles, p. 63: "The Western part were less vigorous and were awed by the

these towns came early and concerted action in common meetings. Their resolutions show clearly the effect of the teachings of the clergy.[68] Those of Lyme early in January reflect very evidently the influence of Johnson's sermon in December.[69]

If the published sermons, articles, and pamphlets of the New England ministers are a good sample of those which were heard from very many of the pulpits during 1765 and 1766, and there is no reason to suppose they are not, then they served to spread and to intensify a spirit of resistance among the people and to convince them that such resistance was but a carrying out of the ideals and practices of their ancestors. Every villager who attended church on the Sabbath day could talk learnedly of the reasons for refusing to pay the tax. Usually taxation at any time would have been displeasing to the colonists and above all just after the French and Indian war, but to have their displeasure at the tax and their resentment at other restrictions of their freedom approved by their ministers and based on constitutional and religious grounds must have given added force and determination to their mood. There was nothing new in these sermons. There was a greater emphasis on the contractual character of the charters and on trial by jury as a natural right, but they were the age-old arguments presented with greater particularity and vividness.[70]

Anti-American Measures." Also pp. 492, 509–10, letters from Rev. Chauncey Whittlesey, Benj. Gale, and John Hubbard; E. S. Lines, "Jared Ingersoll," *New Haven Colony Hist. Soc.*, IX. 192. For full account, see Gipson. By March of 1776, parts at least of the western counties had caught the fever. See *Massachusetts Gazette* and *Boston News Letter*, Mar. 13, 1766, *Connecticut Courant*, Feb. 3, 1766. The action of Wallingford was perhaps due in part to the Rev. James Dana. See Davis , *History of Wallingford*, p. 366.

68. *Massachusetts Gazette* and *Boston News Letter*, Nov. 28, 1765, gives an account of the meeting of delegates from the towns at Windham, Nov. 11. Among the delegates was the Rev. Ebenezer Devotion. For New London Resolves, see issue of Dec. 19, 1765. They repeat the constitutional arguments of Johnson and others, declaring that, when the lawful bounds of authority are exceeded, the people have the right to reassume their natural authority.

69. For Lyme resolves see Appendix A.

70. J. T. Adams in *Revolutionary New England*, pp. 312, 332, 440–43, says that the general use of the "natural rights" argument was not common during

the early years of the Revolution, but that the colonists were forced back to it as other arguments failed; that Samuel Adams was somewhat ahead of colonial thought in general in asserting "that the essential rights of the British constitution are founded in the law of God and nature, and are the common rights of mankind," and that the colonists therefore were also inalienably entitled to the same rights, etc. These were precisely the arguments advanced by many of the clergy not only long before 1765 but during that and all the following years. It seems to have been a fairly general argument at this time, in New England at least, although not so frequently used by the lay pamphleteers. For further illustrations, see Appendix A.

Eight

Keeping the Flame
Alive: 1766–1774

*I*n attempting to determine the influence of the clergy in the
years preceding the outbreak of war, it is difficult to decide
how far they were actually leaders, making and controlling
public opinion and action, and how far they were merely borne on
the tide of public excitement or even forced to play a part against
their open or secret inclination. This is especially difficult to determine for the majority of the dissenting clergy in the years between
1770 and 1774, although there are some, at least, about whom
there is no uncertainty. It would seem natural that many should
have joined with the conservatives who began to fear the increasing power of the populace, because the ministry is usually considered a conservative profession. But the truth seems to be that,
whether because of a dependence upon the majority in a town for
their salary, or because of a fear that English success might en-
danger their power and position, or because of a conviction of the
justice of the cause and an active sympathy for the people, the great
majority joined the popular side, and some were among its leaders.
They believed indeed that they were but supporting the traditions
of the past, that they were, in fact, the true conservatives. At the
same time there were signs of a growing impatience with too great
wealth and a growing faith in real democracy and freedom of action and spirit.

The repeal of the Stamp Act seemed, for a time at least, to quiet the fears of most of the clergy, as well as of the people.[1] The ministers did not, however, cease to preach the familiar political doctrines, although there was less excitement in their sermons. The Massachusetts and Connecticut election sermons of 1767, 1768, and 1769, as was usual, dealt with principles of government. They emphasized again the original equality and freedom of men in the state of nature, the inalienable rights which were superior to all authority, the formation of society and government by compact, and the good of society as the end of all government. The discussions of a constitution by Bridges and Shute were especially definite and interesting.[2] All of these men praised the British constitution which protected their rights, but Haven and, somewhat more forcibly, Salter and Williams considered the late acts of Parliament dangerous and threatening. Haven said that the colonists were loyal to the King and ready to obey Parliament in the exercise of due authority, but that certain acts of Parliament made it impossible for the

1. T. Adams, *Revolutionary New England*, pp. 342–43. It was, however, in 1766 that the consociated churches of Connecticut united with the Synod of Philadelphia and New York and discussed the threat of Episcopacy. Bridges, in his Massachusetts Election Sermon of 1767, says, "Such convulsions there have been, as have shaken the very foundations of government, but . . . things have been in a good measure appeased" (p. 46).

2. Sermon of 1767 by Ebenezer Bridges, of Chelmsford; of 1768 by Daniel Shute, of Hingham; of 1769 by Jason Haven, of Dedham. In Connecticut, the sermon of 1767 was by Ed. Eells, of Middleton; 1768, Richard Salter, of Mansfield; 1769, Eliphalet Williams, of Hartford. Shute, pp. 22–24, says that the right to govern is a right delegated by the whole. The right to choose rulers is inalienable. "A compact for civil government in any community implies the stipulation of certain rules of government. These rules or laws more properly make the civil constitution." The laws prescribing rights of prerogative and of people should be founded on principles promoting the good of society and be held sacred by both. They ought, therefore, to be as plain as possible. "Mysteries in civil government relative to the rights of the people, like mysteries in the laws of religion, may be pretended, and to the like purposes of slavery, this of the souls, and that of the bodies of men." People are bound to support those having delegated authority so long as the laws made answer the end for which officials were chosen, otherwise they are morally bound to resist.

people to enjoy their important rights and privileges. In this sermon, which was widely read and which met with special notice in England, Haven spoke of the fall of Charles I and of Andros, of the right of Massachusetts to elect its council—a right which he hoped might continue to the end of time—quoted Locke on the right of resistance to every encroachment upon natural and constitutional rights, and asserted the right of the people to call those in authority to account and take away their power when abused.[3]

Richard Salter, of Connecticut, who praised the "ingenious, generous, sensible, spirited, and loyal Farmer,"[4] spoke in 1768 with picturesque directness of the danger from rulers who were "weak headed, short sighted, muddy brained men," of the people's concern over the Declaratory Act, and of the Townshend Acts which threatened calamity "which can scarce be painted in too horrible and gloomy colors."[5] Both he and Williams in 1769 urged the Assembly to exert itself in defense of the constitutional rights of the people against the least encroachment upon the "rights founded in the law of nature, which is the law of God, eternal and immutable."[6]

It was not only in election sermons that the ministers between 1766 and 1770 encouraged resistance to unconstitutional power. The annual artillery sermons and those preached at the musters were another means of reaching the people which seems to have been used to the full, both then and later. They gave occasion to laud the early colonists and especially to justify war in defense of natural and constitutional rights, even to declaring it, as the clergy have done since time immemorial, in harmony with the divine law.[7]

---

3. Haven, pp. 6, 7, 9–11, 17, 26, 34, 37–43, 46–48. *Boston News Letter*, Nov. 23, 1769, quotes London comment and speaks of the sermon as being in the hands of many people in Mass. Cf. Hollis Papers, no. 161.

4. Salter, p. 39.

5. *Ibid.*, p. 32. See also Judah Champion, Two Fast Day Sermons, 1770, p. 29, who says that the acts are unconstitutional and have caused general uneasiness, and that he hopes for their total repeal.

6. Williams, p. 42. See also pp. 11, 34–35, and Salter, pp. 30–34.

7. Shute, Artillery Sermon, 1767, p. 27: "this kind of war is supported by the written revelation which God has been pleased to give mankind. . . . De-

Sermons were also preached and printed for the especial purpose of familiarizing men with the heroic deeds of their ancestors and of inspiring a love for the rights and liberties for which their ancestors fought. Some of the ministers felt this their peculiar duty since they believed the people knew little of the past. Judah Champion, of Litchfield, for instance, published two discourses in 1770 for this purpose. He said,

> The few histories of the settling of New England now extant, are very scarce among the people in general, and the rising generation in particular, are very much unacquainted with the distresses their ancestors encounter'd, whose zeal and virtue should not be forgotten.[8]

Among such sermons were two which attracted much attention. They were discourses on religious liberty by Amos Adams, of Roxbury, who was the son-in-law of Charles Chauncey and therefore doubtless especially interested in the supposed danger of an American Episcopate which so agitated Chauncey and was at its height about 1768. Adams' sermons were read by many in America and were published in London in 1770. They were sent by Eliot to Thomas Hollis, and Hollis considered then "among the best publications produced by North America."[9]

fensive war is then right, according to the constitution of God." See pp. 11, 19, 25. Also Jonas Clarke, Artillery Sermon, June 6, 1768. That the sermons of the day met with notice in America and abroad is proved by the newspapers and correspondence. For example, *Boston Chronicle*, Dec. 5, 1768, quotes note from London that a sermon, "rather too warm on the side of liberty," had lately been burned at order of ne of the governors in America. For mention of other patriotic sermons during 1767–1769, see *Boston Chronicle*, Oct. 24, 1768, July 6, 1769; *Boston News Letter*, Mar. 17, 1768, Dec. 7, 1769. See Headley, p. 59, on sermons at musters.

8. Champion, Two Fast Day Sermons, Preface.

9. "He and such like Men cannot be too much encouraged," (Hollis Papers, Nos. 140, 154). Cf. also Amos Adams, Religious & colonial Liberty, Two Discourses, Dec. 1767, p. 50. These give a full account of English and colonial struggle for liberty. There were many such sermons, and for this definite purpose, later. See Boston News Letter, Dec. 2, 1768, Feb. 15, 1770.

Adams most certainly believed that real religious freedom, the natural and inalienable freedom of conscience, was the precious possession of New England and especially of Massachusetts, and that it was lacking in England. Again and again he gloried in American liberty.

> Here we dwell in a land of light, a region of liberty . . . religious liberty is one of the most precious jewels on earth . . . a darling privilege which we cannot be too willing to give up. . . . Our liberties, both civil and sacred, are truly our own;—they are what our fathers dearly bought; they descend to us as a patrimony purchased at their expense.[10]

It is hard to reconcile such enthusiasm with the conception we hold today of the intolerance of Revolutionary New England. But Adams and many of his contemporaries believed that religious liberty could go hand in hand with taxation for the minister's support and with various other restrictive laws. There were also radical ministers in Massachusetts who preached a freedom far wider than the general practice of the day. There was an increasing interest in the subject, both among Baptists and Congregationalists. It is probable,

---

10. Adams, pp. 32, 39, 53. The discourses are full of such phrases. Illustrations could be multiplied. John Tucker in his Convention Sermon of 1768 discussed at length the "divine constitution" and Christian liberty. "Every subject of this kingdom, i. e., every Christian, has and must have a right to judge for himself of the true sense and meaning of all gospel truths, and that no doctrine therefore;—no laws;—no religious rites; no terms of acceptance with God, or of admission to Christian privileges, not found in the gospel, are to be looked upon by him, as any part of this divine system." Ministers are to explain truths to people, but leave them free to make their own deductions and to receive as truth only what they see to be founded in God's word (pp. 15–18). Tucker discouraged politics in the pulpit. In 1769 Rev. John Lathrop of Boston wrote to Rev. Ebenezer Baldwin of Connecticut that he had heard that Massachusetts ministers had decided to do a way with all creeds and confessions. Lathrop answered that they had been pretty generally laid aside, that a movement by Sewall and Pemberton to examine candidates as in Connecticut was voted down by a large majority. Cf. Sprague, VIII. 71.

however, that a fair number of such sermons and pamphlets were intended as propaganda to quiet the critics at home and abroad and to strengthen the position of the government. There is hardly a Massachusetts sermon of these days which does not mention liberty, yet there were clergymen in Massachusetts who had, as it seemed to them, personal experience of its absence and who therefore preached it with special earnestness. Beginning about 1764, there was a large increase in the numbers of Baptists and a great improvement in the intelligence and education of the Baptist ministry. They soon came into conflict with the laws requiring payment of rates to the Congregational minister of the town unless they had the witness of a certain number of Baptist ministers that they were bona fide Baptists.[11] The significant features of their articles, pamphlets, and petitions against this law are the arguments used and the growing belief in entire separation of church and state.

The leaders of the movement were Isaac Backus, of Middletown, Massachusetts, Hezekiah Smith, of Haverhill, Massachusetts, Samuel Stillman, of Boston, "the little man eloquent," and James Manning, of Providence. In their writings they quoted Locke and applied to their own situation the very same arguments used against the unpopular acts of Parliament. Very clearly they drew the parallel between their own relation to the colonial government and that of the colonies as a whole to England.[12] In 1773 they refused to meet any longer the requirements of the provincial

---

11. Guild, *Chaplain Smith*, pp. 79, 84, 88.

12. See *Minutes of the Warren Association*, 1769–1862; Backus, *Works*, I. II. 1754–1787. Backus in *An appeal to the Public for Religious Liberty*, written in 1773, pp. 3–11, seems not to accept the common idea that certain rights were given up when government was established. He says that the Bible clearly shows that man first lost his liberty by breaking the rules of government and that only by government can man secure any liberty at all. He is referring apparently to those who praise liberty and despise government, thinking liberty means that each shall act as he pleases. He says that certain of their opponents were trying to make it seem that Baptists were claiming to be in a state of nature. This he denies and says they base their claims on their rights as men, as Christians, as subjects of a free government, and on their charters (p. 36, note).

law and became, as time went on, increasingly and embarrassingly vocal in their protests.

In 1770 a committee of grievances had been formed by the Warren Association of Baptists, and Smith was appointed as agent to London. This was the cause of much discussion in newspapers and letters, the Congregationalists asserting vigorously that full legal protection was given to religious liberty and the Baptists giving instances of oppression.[13] By some the trouble was attributed to the Episcopalians. Because the Baptists would not join with Presbyterians and Congregationalists in opposing an Episcopate, they were accused of being unwilling to aid in upholding American liberty.[14] They were also accused by some of the Massachusetts ministers of exaggerated and inaccurate statements and of using the situation unfairly to gain their ends. Religious toleration did not seem to many Congregationalists and Presbyterians to demand that subscription to a minister's salary should be voluntary, and many of the petitions seemed to them and to the General Court to be only an attempt to break a sacred covenant and escape the payment of any kind of ministerial tax.[15]

13. *Boston News Letter*, Sept. 20, 1770; also Aug. 2, 1770 ff. This controversy ran through several years.

14. See Eliot, Letters, nos. 101, 104 (M.H.S.). In 1770 Ezra Stiles wrote that north of Maryland only the Presbyterians and Congregationalists were left to defend civil and religious liberty, that if the other sects took any part in the struggle it would be on the other side. Cf. Hollis Papers, nos. 173, 178 (M.H.S.). The Rev. Andrew Eliot wrote to Hollis that the sudden attack of the Baptists was a surprise, that he had not heard that the laws of Massachusetts were not satisfactory, and that the oppression must have been local and accidental. Evidently he did not wish Hollis to think New England intolerant. He said that he and other ministers had spoken to Cushing, Adams, and other members of the Assembly who had promised to alter the laws so as to give all reasonable satisfaction, but that even then the Baptists had chosen an agent to the King. In consequence the Sons of Liberty in Boston were roused against the Baptists and even many of the Baptists themselves in Boston were displeased. J. T. Adams, *Revolutionary New England*, pp. 359 ff., suggests that Samuel Adams may have fostered the scheme of appealing to the King in order to rouse the clergy. For the Baptist position, see Hovey's *Life of Backus*.

15. Bradford, *History of Massaclusetts*, I, 411. See Eccles. Papers; Letters

Whatever the truth may have been, this difficulty focused attention on the whole question of religious liberty and gave one more occasion to apply the old arguments. It may well have been one cause of the increasing emphasis upon the subject of religious liberty in the New England sermons. However lacking this freedom may have been in New England, even the Baptists agreed that there was more of it there than in the mother country, and were ready to support the colonies in their contest with England.

Yet another method by which the ministers promoted opposition to England in these years, as well as later, was through their association with the young men in the colleges. As teachers they inculcated the principles of government and permitted debates on questions which must have caused disturbance in Loyalist hearts. For example, in the new Brown University, the students debated in 1769 whether it were good policy for the Americans under present conditions to establish an independent state.[16] Andrew Eliot, a somewhat conservative man though constantly friendly to the American cause, said in 1769 that the Harvard students had imbibed the spirit of the times and that their declamations and debates were full of the spirit of liberty. This, he said, had been encouraged, even if some times it got out of bounds, because their tutors were afraid to check too decidedly a spirit which might thereafter fill the country with patriots.[17]

and Papers, 1761–76, no. 101 (M. H. S.); and Hovey's *Life of Backus*. In another interesting controversy over church government which brought out analogies between ecclesiastical and political thinking, Wise's two pamphlets of 1713 and 1717 were republished and 1000 copies of the 2nd edition were sold before publication. See Dexter, *Congregationalism as Seen in its Literature*, pp. 501–02; Chaplin, *A Treatise on Church Government*; *A Second Treatise on Church Government*, 1773; Whitaker, *A Confutation of Two Tracts*, 1773; a pamphlet called *Observations upon the Congregational Plan of Church Government*; Israel Holly, Sermon, at Suffield, 1773; and the *Boston News Letter*, 1773–74; *Essex Gazette*, Jan. 29, 1771; Ms. Letters nos. 773129.1, 773660, 774468.1, 774618.1 in Dartmouth College.

16. Guild, *Manning and Brown University*, pp. 77, 90.

17. Hollis Papers, no. 166. See *Boston News Letter*, July 25, 1766, Jan. 7, 1768, Jan. 14, 1768, July 21, 1768, Oct. 27, 1768, July 20, 1769, Sept. 7, 1769,

Individual clergymen, during these years, were often of great service to the American cause through their English correspondence. Such a one was Andrew Eliot, of Boston, who had become the successor of Mayhew in the confidence and affection of Thomas Hollis, of London. By constant interchange of books and pamphlets which were given by them to others, the Americans learned of English sentiment and sympathizers in England were kept in touch with America. From letters between them it appears that Hollis was vehement and persistent in advising first Mayhew and then Eliot to get control of the press as far as possible and that it was through his advice that Eliot and others made arrangements for the regular receipt in London of American news and articles.[18]

July 19, 1770, Sept. 13, 1770, *Boston Chronicle*, Nov. 14, 1768. Daggett and Stiles and others made Yale "a seminary of sedition, faction and republicanism." Cf. Dexter, "Notes on Some of the New Haven Loyalists," in *New Haven Colony Hist. Soc. Papers*, IX. 44.

18. Hollis Papers, nos. 158, 163, 165–73. There are many letters to this effect; see also Chap. I. On Nov. 14, 1766, Eliot wrote: "I entirely agree with you, that an interest in the public prints is of great importance. The Spirit of Liberty would soon be lost & the people would grow quite lethargic, if there were not some on the watch, to awaken and rouse them." In 1767 Hollis suggested, through Eliot, to all patriots, holding up to public shame in the press "all such Scrubs, civil or religious, as shall flagrantly offend against Truth & Liberty of any Kind, on either side of the Water." In 1767 Eliot wrote that the "G—nv—ll—n pamphlet" sent by Hollis was the only one sent from London; was in such great demand that after certain friends had seen it, it seemed best to have it printed; it was sure to occasion much political altercation. In 1769 he wrote that without matter sent by Hollis they would be quite ignorant of what was said against them in England. Eliot distributed this material among those who could make best use of it and inserted in papers extracts from English papers sent him by Hollis. But Hollis advised, rather, having Almon and Kearsley send them all the political publications as they appeared. Eliot had an arrangement made with Kearsley to do so and also to have the best American publications printed in London. In 1770 Eliot wrote that he had often been surprised that no care had been taken to know what was said for and against them in Great Britain. "Few of our Merchants are Readers and others are out of the way of procuring. Our accounts of things are chiefly by private correspondences. . . . The popular Side have depended chiefly on Governor Pownal, Mr. Eolian and Mr. de Berdt." He regarded the first as a thorough politician, the second as a man of learning

In March 1770 occurred the Boston Massacre, which greatly excited the populace. It roused certain of the clergy, also, notably the young Rev. John Lathrop of the Old North Church. He had studied at Princeton under the presidency of that great lover of human liberty, Samuel Davies, and was an ardent patriot, sharing from his installation in 1768 in all the Revolutionary activities. He preached the Sunday after the massacre a sermon on the text, "The voice of thy brother's blood cryeth unto me from the ground."[19] This was shortly published in Boston and London and was reprinted in 1771. London papers quoted from its preface Lathrop's conception of the purpose of government as the general good and his belief that a government which failed of its purpose should be abolished and a better one established, whatever the fate of the wicked men who were attempting to subvert the rights of the people. They noted especially that he thought his sentiments were entertained by all who upheld the "glorious Revolution" and the Hanoverian succession. Lathrop, so said the London notice, urged the American clergy to assert their sentiments on all proper occasions. Some few Bostonians, he admitted, had been displeased by the notice taken by the ministers of the recent disturbances in the town, but who could expect "the heralds of the Almighty whose

and integrity, the third as one who did what he could but likely to be deceived. But he had passed on Hollis' hint and several had made arrangements to have London prints sent to them.

Eliot was a friend and correspondent of many clergymen and laymen. At first he thought some of the American measures too rash, but by 1769 he had become convinced that vigorous opposition had been necessary. He began, then to talk of independence. "The treatment of the Colonies ... tends greatly ... to hasten that independency which at present the warmest among us deprecate— things will not be settled until we have an American Bill of Rights."

Samuel Cooper also was in constant correspondence with ex-Gov'r. Pownall and others. In 1769, he used the term, "the great American cause," a phrase which he used later also. "Letters to Pownall," *Amer. Hist. Rev.*, VIII, pp. 309, 313. Cooper said he was ashamed of the neglect of the Selectmen in not writing, but that writing was not their talent.

19. *Innocent Blood Crying to God From the Streets of Boston*. Boston, 1770. Account given to Pownall by Samuel Cooper, Letters, *A. H. R.*, VIII. 316–18.

Commission obliges them to cry aloud, and not to spare," to be silent "when the blood of the people of their charge is spilled as water, and their carcases strowed in the streets"[20]—an exaggeration well calculated to inflame his hearers.

Chief Justice Oliver was especially bitter against the clergy during these days. Before the trials of the man concerned in the Boston Massacre, he said: the "Pulpits rang their Chimes upon blood Guiltiness, in Order to incite the People"; and after the trials were over again the pulpits "rang their Peals of Malice against the Courts of Justice."[21] The cooler Hutchinson believed that the people were led by such sermons to feel that they might as lawfully resist the King's troops as those of a foreign enemy.[22]

---

20. *Boston News Letter*, June 21, Aug. 16, Aug. 30, 1770; Sermon Introduction, iii–iv. Lathrop preached an anniversary sermon in 1771 "to a large Auditory," *News-Letter*. Mar. 21, 1771; and several of his later sermons were famous. The paper notes also Anniversary Sermon by Whitaker of Salem to very numerous audiences. A Ballad quoted in *N. Eng. Hist. and Geneal. Register*, 1859, p. 131, says:

> "Lathrop so clever, Old North forever. . . .
> But when he treats of bloody streets
> And massacres so dire
> When chous'd of rights by sinful wights
> How dreadful is his ire."

21. Oliver, Origin & Progress of the American Rebellion, pp. 128–30. He says they "blew-up the Coals of Sedition." "Prayers & Sermons were interlaced with Scandal against the Laws & the Government; ye Clergy had forgot the Errand their divine Master had sent them upon, & had listed into the Service of the new Masters; & to them, were most faithfull servants:—in this Service they have continued to this Day, with Fidelity irreproachable."

22. In June, 1770, Hutchinson wrote to John Pownall: "It is certain that the present leaders of the people of Boston wish for a general convulsion, not only by harangues, but by the prayers and preaching of many of the clergy under their influence, inflame the minds of the people, and instil principles repugnant to the fundamental principles of government. At the Artillery Election Sermon, one minister in his prayers deplored the tragedy, etc., then prayed 'that the people might have a martial spirit, that they might be instructed and expert in military discipline, and able to defend themselves against their proud oppressors, and the men whose feet are swift to shed innocent blood.' Our pulpits are filled with such dark covered expressions and the people are led to think they

In May 1770, two well-known patriots preached the election sermons in Connecticut and Massachusetts, Stephen Johnson, of Lyme, and Samuel Cooke, of Arlington, and each presented in detail the old theories, applying them to the immediate situation. Cooke in Massachusetts rehearsed the well-worn story of Charles II, James II, and Andros. He declared troops in time of peace a most "improper safeguard, to a constitution, which has liberty— British Liberty, for its basis."[23] He stressed also the danger of making the Council dependent on the Governor.[24]

Cooke's sermon is especially interesting to one who is following the development of the American written constitution. At great length he discussed the origin of government, the natural equality of men, and the power of the people as a collective body. Their safety, he said, depended upon the establishment of definite rules or laws to which individuals and each part of the government were to be subject.[25] Since the whole community controlled their execution, the community therefore determined its own rights. Only the people as a collective body had a right under God to choose and to limit those in authority who were therefore strictly responsible. A balanced government, carefully confined and watched, was, he believed, the best type. Unless the constitution were maintained in its entirety a free state at once ceased to be free. Its benefits must extend to every branch and to every individual of whatever degree-thus every man might enjoy his property in quiet security.[26]

---

may as lawfully resist the King's troops as any foreign enemy. . . ." *Massachusetts Spy*, Aug. 9, 1775, quotes letter of June 8, 1770.

23. Cooke, p. 18.

24. Ibid., p. 37: "If this were done, Liberty here will cease. This day of the gladness of our hearts, will be turned into the deepest sorrow."

25. *Ibid.*, pp. 6–7, 13–14.

26. *Ibid.*, pp. 9–10, 13–15, 17, 18–19, 30. Cooke was intimately associated with that great theorist on government, Jonas Clark, of Lexington, and was the friend of many Revolutionary leaders. Sermons of the time glow with the spirit of resistance. Cf. Loring, *Hundred Boston Orators*, p. 125; C. S. Parker, *Town of Arlington*, pp. 51, 107, 190–91.

About this time the papers began to be filled with discussions concerning the activity of the ministers in politics, especially their attitude toward the new governor, Thomas Hutchinson. As early as January 1771 there appeared in the Essex Gazette the first of many articles signed "Johannis in Eremo." This thin mask hid the Reverend John Cleaveland, of Ipswich, who in his youthful days had been denied a Yale degree because of his interest in the radical "New Lights," and in later years had attacked the theology of Mayhew and now unsheathed his sword against Hutchinson and England. A "meer tool," he called Hutchinson, and characterized his administration as tending to deprive the colonists of all their most important rights.[27]

He inveighed against the removal of the General Court to Cambridge and in his second article exclaimed: "Could a Hillsborough himself desire, or even expect to find a more obsequious tool among all the tribe of Pensioners !"[28]

Such an attack brought forth a defense, and the battle was on. Cleaveland asked the reprinting of a series of questions propounded by "Clericus Americanus" more than two years before and proceeded to answer his opponents in two long articles.[29] He

27. *Essex Gazette,* Jan. 8, 1771
28. *Ibid.,* Jan. 15.
29. Queries in *Essex Gazette,* Feb. 26; Articles, Mar. 26, Apr. 9, 1771:
"1. Whether the Liberty of a Freeman or an Englishman, which distinguishes him from a slave, does not necessarily imply some sort of right and property of his own, which no man has or can have a right to without his consent or actual alienation of the same? . . .
5. Whether the political union . . . to the British empire . . . are not entirely founded in the covenants and compacts between Great Britain and these Colonies, which are contained in their Charters?
6. If such measures are taken on the part of Great Britain . . . which . . . tend . . . to reduce the Colonists into a state of Slavery; whether the political union . . . are not hereby entirely dissolved, and the Colonists reduced to a state of nature?
8. . . . Whether all these together don't necessarily imply an open infraction and vacating our charters, or at least, a leaping over all these covenants and compacts contained in them, which are the basis of our political union to Great Britain?" Reply to first two articles in *Massachusetts Gazette,* also in *News Letter*

talked of the state of nature and natural rights, of the formation of civil states by voluntary compact, and of the purpose of government. If, he said, men were deprived of their natural rights, the compact was violated and the injured might seek protection where they chose. Applying the argument to Massachusetts, he said that their subjection was founded on voluntary compact contained in the charter, that both parties were bound by it, and that a breach of it by either side inevitably meant its entire destruction. If the charters were then seriously violated, the political connections with Britain were entirely dissolved and the colonists were back in a state of nature. If this were true the American governor had no more authority over America than over Holland. Would it not therefore be wise, he asked, to apply to the King for a renewal of the compact that they might not be forced against their will to apply to some other state for protection?

Much the same idea was expressed in an article in the Boston Gazette of November 9, 1772 by a "Mr. Humanity," who was assumed by those who answered him to be a minister. He addressed those who were contending for God-given liberty. It is "my firm opinion," he said,

> that the Americans would be justified in the sight of Heaven and before all nations of mankind, in forming an independent government of their own, and cutting off every son of Adam that dared to oppose them by force—Great Britain has robbed them, sent her armies to enslave them, and totally cancelled all obligations to continue their connection with her another day—I am however for making the King of Great Britain the offer once more, and but one, to renew the compact.

If this was not written by a clergyman, it is at least significant that men should at once conclude that it must have been.[30]

of Feb. 7 and 21. Such language was called "highly unbecoming to the Cloth." Cf. *News-Letter*, May 16.

30. *News-Letter*, Nov. 12, 19, 1772. The author did not live in Massachusetts.

Chauncey, Cooper, and other clergymen were also accused of attacking the Governor through the press and aroused the hostility of the Tories by so doing.[31] But by no means all the Massachusetts clergy took this attitude toward Hutchinson. Many had read and frequently quoted his History and some at any rate were glad to have one born in the colony chosen as governor. Congratulations on his coming into office were addressed to him by the Episcopal and Baptist ministers of Boston, by the "Reverend Associated Ministers" including eight members,[32] by the Presbyterian church of which John Morehead was pastor, by the corporation of Harvard College,[33] by the "pastors of the northern part of the county of Hampshire" and by the "ministers of the Congregational Churches in Massachusetts in Convention," May 30, 1771.[34] This last address was the occasion of much bitterness. Many, including Samuel Adams, claimed that it was by no means representative, that only a few were present at the convention, and of those few not all voted, and that it was an outrageous attempt to make it seem that the clergy as a body supported Hutchinson. Others said that a larger number were present than was at first supposed

31. *Boston News-Letter*, Aug. 8, 1771. The copy in M. H. S. has names of those referred to given in handwriting in margin—Otis, Joseph Greenleaf, Dr. Young, and Dr. Chauncey. The writer says she is horrified to see some of the sacred Order "pouring out their low dirty Ribaldry, disgraceful even from the Mouth of a Porter." Oliver, "Origin & Progress of the American Rebellion," p. 136, speaks of press "too often hovered around by that worthy Divine, Dr. Cooper & others of the same Cloth—from the Labors of their Brains would often issue a Bonfire, a Mob, & a tarring & feathering." *Essex Gazette*, Dec. 15, 1772, in an article signed "A Bostonian" (said by Cushing to be a frequent pseudonym of Chauncey) reprinted from the *Boston Evening Post*, Dec. 14, urges to union against paid judges, etc. *Boston News-Letter*, Dec. 5, 1771, contained an article wishing the clergy would be more concerned with morals and religion and engage less zealously in political matters. Tyler, *Literary History of American Revolution*, II. 304: "Many of the most trenchant articles" in *Boston Gazette* were written by Cooper.

32. *Boston News-Letter*, Mar. 21, 1771.

33. *Ibid.*, Mar. 28.

34. *Ibid.*, June 6.

and that it was as representative as the conventions usually were.[35] Certainly the desire of Adams and others for the support of the ministers and the frequently expressed disgust of the Loyalists at pulpits filled with sedition attest the influence of the clergy. Had they not been really influential, there would have been greater indifference to their attitude.[36] The years before the Boston Port Bill saw the publication of a number of radical sermons and pamphlets by the ministers in which principles of government and resistance were again thoroughly discussed. One of the most rebellious was preached at the Second Baptist Church of Boston, after the Gaspee affair, by the Rev. Isaac Skillman, who the next year became the pastor of the church. This pamphlet, called An Oration Upon the Beauties of Liberty, Or the Essential Rights of the Americans, was dedicated to the Earl of Dartmouth and went through five editions within two years, being published in Boston, New London, and Hartford.[37]

---

35. *Ibid.*, June 23, July 11, July 18; *Boston Gazette*, July 1; Samuel Adams, *Writings*, II. 174 ff.; also many articles signed "Candidus," written for the *Boston Gazette*. Adams was angered at what he thought the indifference and caution of too many of the clergy. See J. Adams, *Works*, p. 374, also *A Ministerial Catechise*, 1771, p. 6.

36. Samuel Adams' articles in the summer of 1771 may have stiffened the weaker brethren among the Congregational ministers. Certainly they would be likely to stiffen the determination of the more radical parishioners to see to it that their own ministers played the patriot. Perhaps this may have been one reason why so many refused to read Hutchinson's thanksgiving proclamation in November. Of the Boston clergy only the elderly Dr. Pemberton and one young newcomer read it. There seem to have been more outside of Boston who yielded, but the word went out that a great number refused. See *Boston Gazette*, Jan. 13, 1772, quoting from *Connecticut Courant*, Dec. 24; *News-Letter*, Nov. 14, 22; *Essex Gazette*, Nov. 12; S. Adams, *Writings*, II. 275; Cooper's "Letters," *A. H. R.*, VIII. 325–26. Cooper says that had the ministers been inclined to read it, it would not have been in their power, "a circumstance w'ch never [took] Place among us"; also that through want of attention and consultation, it was read in a majority of country parishes. For articles in newspapers and references in sermons, etc., to the influence of the clergy, see *Boston Gazette*, May 18, 25; Sept. 28, 1772; *Boston News-Letter*, May 21, June 4, 1772.

37. Isaac Skillman, *An Oration*. . . . The pamphlet was signed "A British

To a Loyalist, this must have seemed rank treason. Like Cleaveland, the author insisted that the King was the rebel, not the colonists. King, Commons, nor Lords could lawfully violate the rights of the people, he said. "For violating the people's rights, Charles Stewart, King of England, lost his Head, and if another King, who is more solemnly bound than ever Charles Stewart was, should tread in the same steps, what can he expect?"[38] If the King should become a tyrant, then the people must resume their delegated authority and call him to account. Such was the constitution of England. It was surely the King's ministry and Parliament, said the author, who were rebels to God and to mankind in attempting to overthrow the laws of Rhode Island. He argued at some length that the colonies could not break the laws of England, but their own laws only.

Therefore they must be tried under their own laws and in their own land. He exclaimed,

> I would be glad to know, my Lord, what right the King of England has to America? it cannot be an hereditary right, that lies in Hanover, it cannot be a parliamentary right, that lies in Britain, not a victorious right. . . . Then he can have no more right to America, than what the people have by compact, invested him with, which is only a power to protect them, and defend their rights civil and religious; and to sign, seal, and confirm, as their steward, such laws as the people of America shall consent to.[39]

Bostonian" but copies in J. C. B. L. give the author as Skillman. Evans, IV. 394, says this may possibly be ascribed also to John Allen; Sabin, vol. XX, Parts CXV–CXVI, pp. 54–56 attributes it to Skillman. The later edition had corrections and additions. In 1773 Skillman published *The American Alarm, or the Bostonian plea, for the rights, and liberties of the people.* This Evans and Sabin ascribe first to Skillman, but say it was also ascribed to Allen. M. H. S. catalogues *An Oration. . . .* under Allen. A sermon by Allen is noted in *New London Gazette,* Dec. 18, 1772, but the text is not that of *An Oration.*

38. Skillman, p. 5. See also pp. 6, 14–22. Like other reverend authors, he uses the illustration of Rehoboam.

39. *Ibid.,* p. 8. "Does the King ask for tall masts? Let him have them, but as a

He asserted the right of the Americans, if they united as he thought there was good prospect of their doing, to resist any military or marine force, a right which they had "by the law of God, of nature and of nations."[40]

> Where his Majesty has one soldier, who art in general the refuse of the earth, America can produce fifty, free men, and all volunteers, and raise a more potent army of men in three weeks, than England can in three years.[41]

This is a striking example of the belief in American power and youthful force as contrasted with the decadence of England and Europe; a belief which was often expressed at the time and has been so lasting and powerful a tradition. Very skilfully the reverend author suggested that not only tea, imports, etc., might be taxed, did they not resist, but lands, cider, soap, everything, even the light of the morning. "Stand up as one man for your liberty," he cried, "Stand alarm'd, O ye Americans."[42]

gift; that British streets be paved with American gold? let him have it but by way of trade, not taxation; for courts of Admiralty, that women spare their husbands to be sent confined in horrid men of war and sent back to tyranny? that judges be appointed by King? Never!" (pp. 15–18).

40. *Ibid.*, p. 10. This author carries the law of nature to extremes. Cf. Dedication, p. 3: "As a fly, or a worm, by the law of nature, has as great a right to Liberty and Freedom, (according to their little sphere in life,) as the most potent monarch upon earth."

41. *Ibid.*

42. *Ibid.*, p. 23. In 4th ed. he adds, "on Rum." This edition also has appendix on immediate abolition of slavery, pp. 21–22. "That it is not rebellion, I declare it before God, the congregation, and all the world, and I would be glad if it reached the ears of every Briton, and every American. . . . Shall a man be deem'd a rebel that supports his own rights? it is the first law of nature, and he must be a rebel to God, to the laws of nature, and his own conscience, who will not do it." See S. Howard, Artillery Sermon, 1773. Men have retained all rights not expressly given up; they can never give up certain ones; regard to religion makes war in defense of liberty obligatory. See N. *Eng. Hist. & Geneal. Register*, XXXI. 249. Howard often set forth, 1772–74, "the true grounds of dispute." Cf. J. Scales, *History of Strafford County*, N. H., pp. 182–83. A sermon of Rev. Jeremy Belknap of Dover at a military review speaks of "hostile invaders" and says, "Must we tamely

Other addresses, not so violent but equally insistent on natural and charter rights and the legality of resistance, were given on
various occasions. The Rev. Charles Turner's Election Sermon in
Massachusetts, 1773, dwelt long on the importance of a constitution which should determine just what powers were given to the
rulers by the people and what retained, a constitution which must
then be sacredly observed but which the people had an inalienable
right to alter when and how they would. Protestant ministers of
the gospel, he said, were forced to be friends to liberty. They could
not properly expound the Scriptures without supporting liberty as
well as proper loyalty.[43]

An illustration of the less public influence of certain ministers of the time is found in the friendship of Franklin for the Rev.
Samuel Cooper. Their correspondence continued throughout the
war and shows that Franklin considered Cooper's knowledge and
wisdom of very real value. They sent pamphlets, articles, sermons,
etc. to each other and gave them to others to read. From London
Franklin wrote confidentially to Cooper and asked his advice on
various matters.[44] In 1770 Franklin wrote,

> You have given, in a little Compass, so full and compre-
> hensive a View of the Circumstances on which is found-
> ed the Security Britain has for all reasonable Advantages

yield to every lawless usurper and suffer tyrants to sport with the lives and estates
of mankind?" The Second Regiment asked to have it printed.

43. Turner, pp. 6–7, 13–14, 16–18, 37–40. He discusses the first charter
which had been "murdered," the God-given right of the people to choose their
own officials and to hold them to account, the right of the people to judge when
resistance is necessary, the iniquity of profound secrets in government, the long
training of the people in devotion to the House of Hanover and a constitutional government, the close connection between civil and religious freedom.
This sermon was widely read. Cushing sent a copy to Franklin. S. Adams sent
a copy to Arthur Lee. Cf. S. Adams, *Writings*, III. 44–45. Turner also preached
at Plymouth Anniversary, 1773, and a "glorious spirit of liberty . . . breath'd thro'
every sentence" (*Essex Gazette*, Feb. 8, 1774).

44. Franklin, *Writings*, ed. Smyth, vols. V and VI (many letters between
1769 and 1776).

from us, tho' things were put into the same State in which they were before the Stamp Act, that I cannot refrain communicating an extract of your Letter, where I think it may be of Use; and I think I shall publish it.[45]

Again in 1771 he begged for further letters, saying; "Your candid, clear, and well written Letters, be assured, are of great use. . . ."[46] In 1772, Franklin wrote that Cooper had furnished him with a new and very good argument against the dependence of governors upon the Crown. "Your Reasonings," said Franklin, "against the Instruction are unanswerable, and shall appear here just before the meeting of Parliament."[47] During 1773, Franklin again begged a continuance of Cooper's letters and news, saying that they were "highly useful" to him and pleasing everywhere. At that time and later Cooper was Franklin's confidential correspondent in Boston.[48] Others whose correspondence was of special value were Ezra Stiles, of Newport, Chauncey and Eliot, of Boston, Jeremy Belknap, of Dover, N. H., and Benjamin Trumbull, of Connecticut.

The preceding illustrations and others of like sort prove the influence of many of the New England clergy, especially the Congregationalists, in stirring and keeping alive a spirit of active resistance to the acts of Great Britain between 1765 and 1774 and in developing and spreading abroad the arguments on which it was

45. *Ibid.*, V. 286.

46. *Ibid.*, V. 299.

47. *Ibid.*, V. 357–58. His argument was "that this propos'd Independence is impolitic on the part of the Crown, and tends to prejudice its Interest, even considered separately from that of the People, as it will prove a strong temptation to Governors to hold a Conduct that will justly lessen their Esteem and Influence in the Province, and consequently their power to promote the service of the King." For Cooper's influence see Tyler, *Literary History of American Revolution*, II. 302–06; Winsor, *Memorial History of Boston*, III. 123–24; Sprague, I. 442–44 See also Cooper's letters to Pownall, *Amer. Hist. Rev.*, VIII. 301–30.

48. Franklin, Writings, ed. Smyth, VI. 107–09; X. 248. See N. C. Bruce, *Benjamin Franklin*, I. 21, 353. Cooper was one of three to whom Franklin sent Hutchinson's letter. He wrote to Franklin that he had kept the trust inviolable (*Writings*, VI. 57–59; *Bowdoin and Temple Papers*, I. 434).

based. They also were already developing and teaching, on the basis of the traditional theories, the conceptions of a fixed constitution and of the organization of a free government which were later to lead to the demand for a constitutional convention and a written constitution.

Nine

Resistance at All Costs: 1774–1776

I n May of 1774, a gentleman of New York wrote to his friend in London excoriating the clergy of New England[1] for their

most wicked, malicious and inflamatory harangues . . . .
spiriting their godly hearers to the most violent opposition to Government; persuading them that the intention
of the Government was to rule them with a rod of iron,[2]
and to make them all slaves; and assuring them that if

---

1. Force, *American Archives*, 4th Ser. I. 301–02. The writer inveighs against the Presbyterian pulpits, "especially to the eastward." The term Presbyterian was very commonly used to describe both Congregationalists and Presbyterians. Hutchinson believed that the Congregationalists had been most extreme, generally wishing independence, while Baptists, Quakers, Presbyterians, and Methodists, be thought were neutral. See J. H. Allen, "Remarks on the Religious Situation in the American Colonies before the Revolution," (*Mass. Col. Soc. Pub.*, III. 42). At a later date than the letter referred to, the Synod of New York and Philadelphia declared that its members had not used their pulpits for political discussions. It is probable, I think unquestionable, that the writer referred chiefly to the Congregational clergy of New England. Oliver, *The Origin and Progress of the American Rebellion*, p. 148, says of the years 1774–76: "As to their Pulpits, many of them were converted into Gutters of Sedition, the Torrents bore down all before them. The Clergy had quite unlearned the Gospel, & had substituted Politicks in its Stead."

2. This was a phrase used during this year by Rev. Thos. Allen of Pittsfield.

they would rise as one man to oppose these arbitrary schemes, God would assist them to sweep away every ministerial tool, . . . from the face of the earth; that now was the time to strike, whilst Government at home was afraid of them; together with a long string of such seditious stuff, well calculated to impose on the poor devils their hearers, and make them run into every degree of extravagance and folly, which, if I foresee aright, they will have leisure enough to be sorry for.[3]

If there was some measure of truth in this complaint early in 1774, it was assuredly increasingly true as the American drama quickened. In passing the Boston Port Bill and succeeding acts, Parliament exercised its right to control the colonies in all ways whatsoever, a right which, though asserted in 1766, the colonists had hoped would be forever dormant. In the crisis the leaders on both sides recognized the power of the clergy. And well they might!

Led by the old, fiery Dr. Chauncey, the Boston ministers refused to read any proclamations of the governor and council[4] and, when General Gage refused to appoint a day of fasting and prayer because "the request was only to give an opportunity for sedition

---

3. The author says that in general, the Church of England people had been truly loyal, without any public oratory to spur them on. By writing and argument they had done all they could to stop sedition. The Episcopalians of Boston, and other Massachusetts towns, congratulated Gage on his appointment, declaring it their duty to cultivate "a Spirit of Loyalty to the King," and of "Obedience to the Rulers" that were over them. Cf. *Boston News-Letter*, May 26, 1774. The Baptists, as a whole, seem to have been suspected, in New England at least, of lukewarm attachment to the American cause and of trying to embarrass the New Englander. Rev. Hezekiah Smith, for example, heard the Election Sermon of Gad Hitchcock which so angered Gage by its seditious spirit, and then dined with Gage in an effort to procure his assistance in getting complete liberty for the Baptists. See *Minutes of the Warren Association*, 1774–76; Backus, *History of New England; Truth will Prevail*; Guild, *Chaplain Smith*, pp. 160–61. Backus and the other leaders declared their adherence to America, and when the break came in 1775 all the Baptists apparently gave active support.

4. Love, *Fast and Thanksgiving Days*, p. 334.

to flow from the pulpit,"[5] these associated ministers proposed that July 14th be observed.[6] Quick was the response. Political sermons, some of them violent in tone, were preached from Boston to the frontier.[7] The Provincial Congress of Massachusetts requested the clergy to advise strict obedience to the Continental Congress and to "make the question of the rights of the colonies and the oppressive conduct of the mother country a topic of the pulpit on week days."[8] The Continental Congress, recognizing the value of these politico-religious sermons, advised the setting aside of special days of fasting and of thanksgiving. These were observed in all the New England colonies and on each day the ministers set forth in greater detail the old theories, established from Holy Writ the legal right of resistance to unconstitutional action and, often in burning phrase, urged their people to resist even to bloodshed. Many of these sermons were published as patriotic pamphlets.[9]

---

5. Headley, p. 58. Gage, who had been unexpectedly present at the Election Sermon of 1774, had been infuriated by Hitchcock's bold plea for resistance.

6. *Ibid.*; Love, p. 335; *Boston News-Letter*, June 23, 1774.

7. *Boston News-Letter*, Aug. 11, 1774; Love, p. 335. See, for example, Timothy Hilliard, *The Duty of a People, The Substance of Two Sermons, Delivered at Barnstable, July 14th, 1774*; Peter Whitney, *The Transgression of a Land Punished by a Multitude of Rulers . . . two Discourses, Delivered July 14, 1774*, at Northborough (remarkably direct and powerful,—his father, the Rev. Aaron Whitney, of Petersham, was a Tory). Peter Whitney, from 1774–76, preached many patriotic sermons, (the texts of which are given on p. 70 of C. Kent, Northborough History) which were of great influence in the town; S. Webster, *The Misery and Duty of an oppress'd and enslav'd People . . . . at Salisbury*; J. Belknap, Dover, N. H. See J. Scales, *History of Strafford County*, N. H., pp. 182–84.

8. Thornton, xxxvii–xxxviii; Headley, p. 23; Griffith, *Historical Notes of the American Colonies & Revolution*, Appendix, p. 293; Love, pp. 336–38. For Address to Clergy, Dec. 6, 1774, see Force, 4th Ser., I. 1000.

9. Ebenezer Baldwin, Thanksgiving Sermon, Nov., 1775 (Love, p. 336, says Thanksgiving Sermons of Dec., 1775, preached in Bradford, Eastham, Hatfield, Marblehead, Roxbury, and Boston, were all published); J. Lyman, Thanksgiving Sermon, Dec. 15, 1774 (the town thanked him and ordered it printed. See Wells, History of Hatfield, p. 186); P. Whitney, Fast-Day Sermons, 1775 (not published; see C. Kent, *Northborough History*, p. 70); J. Lathrop, *Discourse*, Dec. 15, 1774 at Boston; William Gordon, *Discourse*, Dec. 15, 1774 at Bos-

There were many other occasions also to call forth such sermons, not only artillery and general election days, but the Plymouth
anniversary, the anniversary of the Boston Massacre and after 1775,
that of the battle of Lexington, etc.[10] But political sermons were not
confined to special occasions. One can well imagine that many a
minister was glad to discuss week by week subjects which he knew
would fill his church. In country districts sermons were preached
on English and colonial history and on the difficulties with England, as well as on theories of government. Two such which were
most interesting were delivered by Samuel Sherwood of Fairfield,
Connecticut, in August, 1774 and published with an appendix by

ton (preached again the same day,—very political and extreme, and called forth
pamphlets in opposition. See Love, p. 337); R. Ross, *A Sermon in which the
Union of the Colonies is considered and recommended*, Nov. 16, 1775; Eleazar
Wheelock, Liberty of Conscience, Nov. 30, 1775 (also preached Nov. 16); Henry Cummings, Sermon, 1775 (Sprague, VIII. 157); S. Williams, *Love of Our
Country*, Dec. 1774 (that we should resist the English Acts but preserve peace
and loyalty. See Kingsbury, *Memorial History of Bradford*, p. 101).

10. Election Sermons, Connecticut, 1774, by Samuel Lockwood, of Andover; 1775, by Joseph Perry, of East Windsor; 1776, by Judah Champion, of
Litchfield. Massachusetts: 1774, by Gad Hitchcock, of Pembroke; 1775, by
Samuel Langdon, of Portsmouth; 1776, by Samuel West, of Dartmouth. Gordon, *History of . . . Independence . . . of America*, I. 273, says passages in election
sermons most adapted to promote and spread the love of freedom had been
sent far and wide through the newspapers and "read with avidity and a degree
of veneration, on account of the preacher and his election to the service of the
day"; and that thus they had helped not a little in forwarding and strengthen-
ing opposition to the parliamentary claim. The sermon of Champion in 1776
was printed by the Assembly within three weeks of its delivery, in an edition of
500 copies. Cf. Bates, "Fighting the Revolution with Printer's Ink," *New Haven
Colony Hist. Soc. Papers*, pp. 149–50.

Anniversary Sermons: of Plymouth, by Gad Hitchcock in 1774, by Samuel
Baldwin in 1775; of Lexington, by Jonas Clark in 1776 (this sermon attracted
a great crowd including militia and strangers; among others the Rev. J. Marrett,
of Woburn, rode over to hear it), and another by Peter Whitney, of Northborough; of the Boston Massacre, by Peter Thacher in 1776 (preached in Boston
and greatly applauded; see *Boston Town Records*, 1770–1777, pp. 225–26); of
the evacuation of Boston, by Ebenezer Bridge in 1776 (see Moore, *Diary of the
Revolution*, I. 225).

Ebenezer Baldwin, of Danbury. They were preached and published to arouse the people of western Connecticut who seemed to these clergymen too ready to listen to specious arguments and "to lose their liberty and sink into slavery." Of the same sort were the six sermons of the radical Dan Foster, of Poquonnock, preached in October, 1744 in a country church near Winsor, Connecticut, not to those who had read widely but to the common people.[11]

Sometimes a minister was called upon to preach at town meetings, at county conventions, and provincial conferences.[12] The Rev.

11. Sherwood, *A Sermon, Containing Scriptural Instructions to Civil Rulers, and all Freeborn Subjects. In which the Principles of sound Policy and good Government are established and vindicated* . . . An appendix states grievances and pictures consequences. See Foster, *A Short Essay on Civil Government*, and R. Ross, *A Sermon on the Union of the Colonie*, preached to a country audience, Nov. 16, 1775. G. W. Balch, in an article on Rev. Benj. Balch, in *Danvers Hist. Coll.*, VI. 88, says: "During the entire Revolutionary period the latter were leaders and the most potent factors in resistance to British oppression. . . . In the absence of a numerous newspaper press, the political education of the people then as now in sparsely settled regions was conducted largely from the pulpit—or the stump." Sherwood, Baldwin. and Foster all speak of the lack of knowledge among their people concerning the cause of trouble. Baldwin in his Appendix, p. 47, says western Connecticut is "remote from public intelligence," few have opportunity to read papers and other writings, are therefore little acquainted with their danger, do not yet feel "the weight of oppression," etc. He proceeds to recount British Acts and give suggestions as to what to do in the "alarming crisis." Other men whose work was especially notable in this respect were Thos. Allen, of Pittsfield, Joseph Lyman, of Hatfield, Cotton Mather Smith, of Sharon, Conn., Moses Hemmenway, of Wells, Me., Peter Powers, of N. H., Moses Morrill, of Biddeford, friend of James Sullivan, Elizur Goodrich of Durham, Conn.

12. Town Meetings. *To Corporation of Freemen in Farmington*, Connecticut, Sermon on "Liberty described and recommended . . . ," Sept. 20, 1774, by Levi Hart of Preston. There are many others in town histories, etc., for example, James Dana, at Wallingford, Conn., Nov. 29, 1774 (*Wallingford Revohttionary Records*, p. 2); Joseph Lyman in Hatfield (Wells, *History of Hatfield*, p. 182); Samuel Eaton, in Brunswick, Me., Apr. 1775 (Wheeler, *History of Brunswick*, pp. 673–80; Sprague, I. 615); Rev. Dr. Williams, at the request of the selectmen, opened the town meeting of Lebanon, Conn., on July 18, 1774, called to discuss the alarming situation and to help Boston; about 300 freeholders were present (R. R. Hinman, *Historical Collections from official records, files, etc. of the part sustained by Connecticut. . . .* p. 69). Peter Thacher, of Malden, preached similarly at

Ebenezer Chaplin, who had defended the works of Wise and had upheld democracy in church and state, was especially asked to attend the meetings of the Worcester Convention,[13] and the addresses of Reverend Elisha Fish of Upton before this Convention were printed and distributed at the expense of the Convention.[14] Such addresses were not perfunctory, conventional affairs, but breathed conviction and enthusiasm and, occasionally, a passionate devotion to cause and country.

There was one kind of occasion during these years, as well as later, in which the clergy were of special service. When the militia mustered or recruiting was to be done, it was the custom to have an address by the pastor. In the months before the battle of Lexington, minister after minister, as if in preparation for the coming struggle, called upon the men to be of stout heart and good courage, ready to wield the sword of the Lord. On numerous occasions a fiery minister of the Gospel won more recruits and filled more empty regiments than could the men of war.[15] For

---

Watertown, Mar. 5, 1776. See Niles, *Principles and Acts of the Revolution.*

13. At least three clergymen attended the Worcester Co. Convention in 1774. Two others were probably there and perhaps more. Ebenezer Chaplin, of Sutton, Benj. Conklin, of Leicester, Joseph Wheeler, of Harvard, went as delegates. Elisha Fish, or "Mr. Paine," was asked to preach; the pulpit was that of Thaddeus Maccarty. Cf. *Journals of Each Provincial Congress of Mass.,* pp. 628, 631, 635–36, 649, 651.

14. *Journals of Each Provincial Congress,* p. 651. Elisha Fish, *A Discourse delivered at Worcester,* March 28th, 1775, at the desire of the Convention of Committees for the County of Worcester.

15. Examples of such sermons: Levi Hart, Apr. 19, 1775, at Preston, Conn.; Z. Adams, Jan. 2, 1775, at Lunenburg (preached to the militia after a large dinner; there were many spectators; the next day the town voted 100 L. M. for arms, etc. See *Essex Gazette,* Jan. 24, 1775); Ebenezer Baldwin, to a company of 100 men, Mar., 1775, at Danbury; William Emerson, Jan. and Mar. 1775, to the militia at Concord (Shattuck, *History of Concord,* p. 93); John Urquhart, after Lexington, to the men of Rockland and South Thomaston, Me. (Eaton, *History of Rockland,* I. 114); J. Belknap to the men at Dover, June 14, 1775 (Scales, *History of Strafford County,* p. 184); David Avery, after Lexington, at Gageboro, Vt. and again on his way to Boston with recruits (Headley, pp. 287, 291 and Chase, *History of Dartmouth College,* I. 308 note).

example, soon after Falmouth was burned in August, 1775, a re-cruiting officer who was vainly trying to raise men in Harpswell, Maine, asked Samuel Eaton, the patriotic minister of the town, to speak on Sunday morning to his people. Unwilling to do this at the communion service, he promised to address them in the evening. So after sundown, out of doors before the meeting-house steps, he preached on the text, "Cursed be he that keepeth back his sword from blood," and before the night was over forty men had volunteered.[16] Again, the recruiting officers had worked four days in vain to raise a company in Boothbay, Maine, when Pastor John Murray was asked to try his hand. He spoke in the Presby-terian Church and kindled such enthusiasm that in two hours the entire company was filled.[17]

In all these and like sermons and addresses the chief aim seems to have been to state clearly and repeatedly the arguments by which men could be certain that they had inalienable rights and to define these rights; to set forth in detail the requirements of a legally constituted government and to show that the English and colonial governments, if unabused, were such; to enumerate and enlarge upon the acts by which King and Parliament had abused their power, and to establish beyond a doubt the legal right and moral necessity of resistance.

As in earlier sermons, both before and after 1763, the inti-mate connection between theology and political theory is appar-ent. Like their predecessors these men also preached of the fixed constitution of God, of the Bible as establishing and illustrating great principles of civil government, of the natural and Christian rights of men which were given by God, certain of which could not be given up and in violation of which laws were null and void. These rights were discussed in more detail, for the most part, than before 1763, but with few additions.[18] One of the most significant

16. Sprague, I. 615; Wheeler, *History of Brunswick*, p. 736.

17. Greene, Boothbay, Southport and Boothbay Harbor, p. 233; Sprague, I. p. 615.

18. Sherwood, 1774, p. 11; Foster, 1774, pp. 18, 25, 35; Champion, 1776, p. 12; West, 1776, pp. 11–12; Hitchcock, Sermon at Plymouth, Dec., 1774, pp.

features is the interest shown in the mechanism of setting up governments and making constitutions, in the relation of the executive to the legislative power, and in the power of the people. Very shortly the states of New Hampshire and Massachusetts were to establish new governments and the clergy to exercise an influence in determining their character. By their careful and frequent discussions of principles the ministers were gaining the reputation which gave them their later influence. Thus in speaking of reserved rights, the Rev. Dan Foster included

> a voice in all public discussions concerning peace and war with other states; making alliances with other powers; sending and receiving embassies; entering into natural leagues and compacts; settling and regulating trade and commerce, &c. &c.[19]

In these the people must share either in person or by representatives. The assertion of religious liberty was increasingly frequent and comprehensive. West in 1776 said;

> No principles ought ever to be discountenanced by civil authority, except such as tend to the subversion of the state. So long as a man is a good member of society, he is accountable to God alone for his religious sentiments.[20]

A clear and succinct definition of the right of property was given by Elisha Fish. It meant, he said, the right of each individual to enjoy his own earnings, a right with that of life and liberty given him by God and stampt upon the human soul. He prayed that God would grant the "enslaved nations of the world a more clear and full sight of this human birth right, that is unalienable by man."[21]

For the most part, when natural equality was discussed, the reverend authors meant the equality and freedom of action which

18, 33–34.
19. Foster, pp. 48–50.
20. West, p. 45.
21. Fish, p. 8: see also p. 21.

they imagined men to have possessed before the foundation of society and government, when no one had any authority over another,—a freedom which could be limited only by consent and always for the common good. Now and then, however, the more practical though revolutionary suggestion was made of the desirability of greater economic equality. Stephen Johnson and others had spoken against supporting "idle drones,"[22] and against concentrating the wealth of the world in the hands of ruler and minister.[23] Benjamin Trumbull favored dividing property as equally as possible, not allowing a few persons to hold all the wealth of a country. He warned against adopting any law or precedent with such a tendency because of the danger that such persons would purchase or by undue influence obtain all important positions in the government and so oppress their fellowmen, who would thus become servile and little by little lose their true liberty.[24]

An increasing number of ministers seem also to have realized the inconsistency of claiming freedom as a natural right and of the clamor against a slavery threatened by England when there existed in the colonies a slavery which seemed to give the lie to their sincerity.[25] Only a few were radical in this sense; by far the larger

22. Johnson, Connecticut Election Sermon, 1770, p. 20.

23. C. Turner, Massachusetts Election Sermon, 1773, p. 8: such pride and luxury "on spoils violently extorted or slily drained from the people, is altogether foreign to the design of God, in setting them up." Peter Whitney, in two discourses in July, 1774, says civil rulers and ministers "should not ingross the wealth of the world to themselves as they have done in many ages and countries," and that pensions and too many officials weigh too heavily on the poor (pp. 14, 25–26). Parts of Whitney's sermons sound as if quoted almost word for word from Turner.

24. Trumbull, Sermon, 1773, pp. 30–31. Rev. Ebenezer Baldwin thought that the greater equality of fortune in America at the founding of the nation might make for greater liberty than the world had ever known. See also Webster's Election Sermon, 1777, p. 30, against monopolies; Phillip's Election Sermon, 1778, which favored a "great distribution of property and the landed interest not engrossed by a few"; Dana's Connecticut Election Sermon, 1779, and Ezra Stiles' of 1783 which urged free tenure of land, equable distribution of property and no large landed estates.

25. See *Boston News Letter*, March 25, 1773. Samuel Cooke's Election Ser-

number confined themselves to the issue with England. There was, however, sufficient radical democracy in a number of sermons to prove that the "levelling" spirit of New England which aroused fear in men of other colonies was not to be found alone among the poorer classes.[26]

There was prolonged explanation of government by consent. Certain of the sermons applied this doctrine to the right of the majority and to the making and changing of constitutions. Compacts and their sacredness were a constant theme, especially emphasized because of the argument that the King in permitting the charters to be broken had been guilty of breaking of compact and had therefore released the colonies from allegiance. By this break, so said some, the colonists were necessarily thrown back into a state of nature and resumed all rights which they had originally possessed.[27] Broken covenants and unconstitutional invasion of the rights upon which the English throne itself was founded could be and must be met by steady resistance. The legal right of resistance was discussed in great detail, perhaps the more warmly because Anglican clergy were preaching of loyalty and the unquestioning obedience to authority demanded by the Scriptures.[28] Old

mon of 1770 was one of the earliest to oppose slavery. Among those noted for opposition to slavery was Rev. David Osgood, of Medfield. The town in December, 1772, and January, 1773, instructed its representative to do his utmost to have the slave trade abolished. Others of note were Rev. Samuel Hopkins, of Newport, Rhode Island, Ebenezer Baldwin, Levi Hart, young Jonathan Edwards, Jeremy Belknap, David Avery, Elam Potter, Nathaniel Emmons, Andrew Eliot, Isaac Lewis, Ezra Stiles. Belknap and others wrote articles for the press opposing it.

26. John Adams, *Life and Works*, II. 330; I. 151.

27. See *Essex Gazette*, July 13, 1775, articles by Rev. John Cleaveland under name of "Johannis in Eremo." Sherwood, Foster, Cleaveland, Whitney, Webster, Thacher, and others speak of the charters as compacts and the breaking of them as a specially heinous violation of their rights. Hitchcock, Whitney, Lathrop, Sherwood, Hart, Foster, Backus, Fish, West, and others discuss all government as compact which all parties are bound to observe. For quotation, see Appendix A.

28. This study does not deal with the activities of the Anglican clergy in New England. Much can be found in Cross's Anglican Episcopate and Sabine's *Loyalists in the American Revolution*. Practically all of the Episcopal clergy of New England were loyal to England and some, at least, wrote and preached

and New Testaments, classic writers, modern and ancient philosophers and divines and often "the great Mr. Lock" were cited
in proof of the duty as well as the right to resist tyranny and any
attack upon the rights of men.[29]

It must be clearly understood that to these reverend authors
resistance to unconstitutional acts did not mean refusal to obey
constitutional authority. Far from it. Though recognizing the prov-
ocation to violence and though sometimes encouraging abuse of
the Tories, there was many a minister who drew careful distinction
between liberty and license. It was the liberty which was to their
minds inextricably associated with constitutional, ordered government for which they were fighting.[30]

It is evident that some of the New England ministers, especially of the Congregationalists, were preaching independence and

vigorously against rebellion. There was much answering of arguments. In Sept.
1774, directly after the meeting of the Continental Congress, Dr. Seabury and
Dr. Wilkins published *Free Thoughts on the Proceedings of the Continental Congress*, setting forth its errors, etc. Sherwood and Baldwin published their pamphlets in 1774, partly to counteract such teachings. See Pascoe, *Two Hundred
Years of the S. P. G.*, pp. 71–77; Dexter, "Notes on some of the New Haven
Loyalists," in *New Haven Colony Hist. Soc. Papers*, IX. 33; W. H. Munro, *History of Bristol, R. I.*, pp. 212, 222. At the outbreak of the Revolution there were
nineteen Episcopal clergymen in Conn., fifteen being Yale graduates.

29. Hitchcock, pp. 19, 22–25, 46–47; Foster, pp. 70–71; Gordon, 1774, pp.
26–27; Baldwin, 1775, p. 29; Wheelock, Wheelock Papers, no. 775305. There
are too many references to give. Many assert the right of the people to judge,
etc. I have references to thirteen sermons which discuss it more or less in detail
between 1774 and July, 1776.

30. For examples of the vigorous language of the clergy, see letters by "Johannis in Eremo" [Cleaveland] to General Gage, Essex Gazette, July 1775, and
a sermon by the Rev. William Gordon, December 1774, part of which was
repeated at a Boston lecture and which called forth pamphlets in opposition.
One such, Remarks upon a Disconrse Preached December 15th, 1774, asked,
"Where could this reverend politician—Christian sower of Sedition—war far-
ing priest—have learnt to preach up doctrines of sedition, rebellion, carnage
and blood? . . . I most heartily wish, for the peace of America, that he and many
others of his profession would confine themselves to gospel truth." The author
believes this address tends directly to bring on civil war (pp. 6–8). See also
Thornton, p. 196.

preparing for it long before 1776. As early as 1765 Stephen John-son had suggested that England might act so as to force the colo-nies into independence. From that time it had been mentioned as possible by an increasing number and in the later years as probable and even desirable.[31] The Rev. Cotton Mather Smith, of Sharon, Connecticut, is said to have prepared his parishioners for indepen-dence long before Lexington.[32] The Rev. Timothy Dwight advo-cated separation in 1775, using the same arguments as were later approved, but found that most of those with whom he talked were either too hostile or too timorous, even after Lexington.[33] The Rev. Ezra Stiles long expected and wished it.[34] The Rev. John Cleave-land in the Essex Gazette of June 7, 1774, said of Great Britain, "she is become cruel as the Ostrich, more cruel than Sea-Monsters towards their young ones! her Measures tend not only to dissolve our political Union to her as a Branch of the British Empire, but to destroy our Affection to her as the Mother State."; and on April 20th, and July 13th, 1775 he declared all connections were broken and allegiance totally dissolved.[35] On July 14, 1774, the Rev. Peter Whitney, of Northboro, asserted that the colonies were the pillars of England, that Ireland was calling for help, and that the attempt to enslave America might be the end of England.[36] By the spring

31. Sherwood, 1774, p. 13; Thacher in his Watertown Address, Mar. 5, 1776, welcomed it eagerly. He is also said to have written the instructions of the town to its representative, on May 27, 1776, saying, "it is now the Ardent wish of our Soles that America may become free & Independent States . . . we . . . Renounce with Disdain our Connection with a Kingdom of Slaves, we bid a final adue to Britain, Could an Accomadation be now affected we have Reason to think that it would be fatal to the Libertyes of America . . . we are Confirmed in ye oppinion that the Present age will be Deficient in their Duty to God their Posterity & themselves if they do not Establish an american Republick. . . ." (Corey, *History of Malden*, pp. 762–65).

32. Headley, pp. 308–09.

33. *Ibid.*, pp. 177–78.

34. *Ibid.*, pp. 205–06; Sprague, I. 475–77.

35. See also Force, *American Archives*, 4th Ser., II. 369.

36. Kent, *History of Northboro*, pp. 67–68. See also Sermon, p. 68. The resolution of Northboro in favor of independence, passed on June 3, 1776, is said to have been due to the influence of the Rev. Peter Whitney. Rev. Nathaniel

of 1776 other clergymen were advocating independence. On April 19th, 1776, the Rev. Jonas Clarke, of Lexington, preached in favor of it to a large audience,[37] and in his Election Sermon of May, 1776, Samuel West said that Providence was plainly pointing out to America the expediency and even the necessity of becoming an independent state.[38]

Yet there were numbers of New England clergy who did not approve of so radical a position. There were perhaps some who secretly desired independence but thought it unwise to make open avowals of any such intention or desire. Men of other colonies in 1774–1775 feared what they called the wish of Massachusetts for independence. In the cause of unity the Massachusetts delegates to the Continental Congresses urged great prudence. This may have accounted for the expressions of loyalty in the Massachusetts Election Sermon of 1775 and in certain other sermons during that year.[39] There were others who did not wish to break with England but who supported America loyally when the break did come.[40] A

Emerson, of Wrentham, alienated some of his parish by advocating it (Sprague, I. 695); the Rev. Peter Thacher of Attleborough was on a committee drawing up an unanimous recommendation in May, 1776 (Daggett, *History of Attleborough*, p. 122). The Rev. Thomas Allen of Pittsfield early advocated it. There were various others: Moses Morrill, of Biddeford, John Adams, of Durham, N. H., both friends of James Sullivan, Benj. Pomeroy of Hebron, etc. See also Moore, *Diary of the Revolution*, pp. 43–44.

37. Clarke, Sermon, Apr. 19, 1776, p. 22.

38. West, pp. 20–21. On Mar. 17, 1776, Samuel Cooper wrote to Franklin that Paine's *Common Sense* was read with eagerness (*Calendar of Franklin Papers*, I. 19). Thos. Allen also read Paine with avidity.

39. Adams and Perry in sermons of Jan. and May, 1775, asserted loyalty to King; Langdon in May, 1775 in Massachusetts Election Sermon prayed for reconciliation with all rights preserved. See J. Adams, *Life & Works*, I. 151.

40. Rev. Eleazar Wheelock was not one of early advocates of independence, though he believed in assertion of rights. By April, 1775 he saw little chance of reconciliation. See. *Memoirs*, pp. 330, 332, note; Chase, *History of Dartmouth*, pp. 317, 324–26; Wheelock Papers, no. 775279. Thos. Darling, Benj. Woodbridge, Nehemiah Strong of Conn. were never ardent. See Dexter, "Notes on some of the New Haven Loyalists," *New Haven Colony Hist. Soc. Papers*, IX. 40–41.

few succeeded in avoiding politics entirely and yet held the affection of their people.[41] But there were certain Congregationalists who, like the Anglicans, disapproved heartily of the very thought of independence and who resented its advocacy by their brethren.[42] As the struggle grew hotter it became increasingly difficult for a minister to run counter to the will of his people. In some cases those suspected of open or secret loyalty to England were called before committees to clear themselves.[43] Some lost their churches and a few suffered in various other ways.[44]

What proportion of the ministers preached independence before 1776, whether they were in advance of their parishioners, and to what extent they influenced public opinion are questions hard to determine. There seems no doubt that a few advocated independence openly before it seemed expedient or even desirable to many of the leading laymen. Their words must have steadied the wavering and have given courage to those who were less daring. At the least they gave the sanction of the church to the movement.[45]

41. One such was the venerable Ebenezer Gay, of Hingham, whose indifferent patriotism was attacked in the press. Others were Sam'l West, of Needham, Sam'l Williams, of Bradford, who believed in peaceful methods of resistance, and Daniel Collins of Lanesboro. See *Boston News-Letter*, Nov. 26, 1772, Jan. 13 and Mar. 4, 1773; *Biographical Memoirs of Rev. Thos. Thacher*, pp. 9–10; Sprague, VIII. 4, 52; Kingsbury, *Memorial Historical of Bradford*, p. 101; Palmer, *History of Lanesboro*, pp. 12–13. 82.

42. See Sabine, *Loyalists in the American Revolution.* He mentions twelve Congregational ministers who were either lukewarm or out and out Loyalists. There were others, as well. Rev. Mathew Byles, of Boston, was one of the best known.

43. Among these were Asa Dunbar, of Weston, Sam'l Dana, of Groton, who in Mar., 1775 preached non-resistance, Timothy Harrington, of Lancaster, and Ebenezer Morse, of Shrewsbury. See *Essex Gazette*, June 8, Sept. 21, 1775; *Massachusetts Spy*, Nov. 24 and Dec. 15, 1775; Butler, *History of Groton*, pp. 178–79; and Marvin, *History of Lancaster*, pp. 304–05.

44. Peter Whitney, of Petersham, Abraham Hill, of Shutesbury, David Parsons, of Amherst, Benj. Parker, of Haverhill. See Crane, *Peter Whitney and his History of Worcester Co.*, pp. 9–10; Judd, *History of Hadley*, pp. 410–11; Chase, *History of Haverhill*, p. 579.

45. For the people to throw away their liberties, wantonly, without a life

In some cases the ministers brought fire and ardor to the hope of independence. They had faith that the scattered and ill-prepared colonists could meet triumphantly the arms of Great Britain. A young Peter Thacher said in 1776,

> The British nation is now become a great tame beast . . . instead of ravaging the American continent in a single campaign, with a single regiment, they have proceeded one mile and a half in the conquest of it. . . . Formidable as was once the power of the British lion he hath now lost his teeth. . . .[46]

Union and strict adherence to the will of the Continental Congress were urged. There is scarcely a sermon of these and later years which does not emphasize the necessity of union, and many newspaper articles urging it were written by ministers. Ross of Stratford devoted a whole sermon in 1775 to its necessity and blessing.[47] Among these men were a few of prophetic vision who believed that America was to lead the world in an understanding and a realization of democracy. With eager eyes they saw the America of the future, a great free country, a refuge to the oppressed of all nations, a golden land of Liberty. It was to be America's task and joy to reinterpret Liberty and to embody it in her institutions.[48]

---

and death struggle, said Judah Champion in his great Connecticut Election Sermon of May, 1776, could not be done "without incurring Jehovah's most tremendous indignation and curse. God, angels and spirits in glory all look on" (pp. 30–31).

46. Niles, *Principles & Acts*, pp. 25–26. See also Cleaveland, *Essex Gazette*, Sept. 20, 1774 (under the name, "Johannis in Eremo").

47. Robert Ross, *A Sermon in which the Union of the Colonies is considered and Recommended.*

48. The ministers seemed to feel that liberty was dead in England and in Europe. They waxed eloquent over the opportunity in America. See Hilliard, 1774, p. 30; Lathrop, 1774, p. 28; Champion, 1776, p. 16; Thos. Barnard, of Salem (*Journal Letters of the late Samuel Curwen*, letter of June 26, 1776); Baldwin, both in 1774 and in 1775. Baldwin went into much detail in his prophecies of a great American Empire, estimating population, etc. This would be founded on as yet unknown principles of Liberty and Freedom. He believed that the struggle

would cause such principles to be more carefully examined than in the foundation of any other state. He thought possibly there might be established such great
liberty that Christ might set up His Empire here. Cf. Sermon, 1775, pp. 38–40
and notes. He said, in 1775, it was fortunate that trouble had started in New
England, which best understood and enjoyed liberty and was better trained to
militia service. Had it started in the South it could have been more easily put
down. See also Appendix to Sherwood's Address, 1774. Thacher was perhaps
most ecstatic. Cf. Niles, p. 26. Other like sermons were preached during the war.
"From this day will be dated the Liberty of the world," said Jonas Clark in commemorating the battle of Lexington (Sermon, Apr. 1776, p. 81).

Ten

The Making of Constitutions

When the war with Great Britain began, and especially when the colonies declared their independence and attempted to reorganize their governments, the ministers of New England had an unusual opportunity to clothe their theories in flesh and blood. The principles which had been theoretical became practical, and the ministers insisted that the new governments be founded on the pattern they had so long been laying down. The constitutional convention and the written constitution were the children of the pulpit.

To the men of New England who had been nourished from their youth on the election sermons and who had been thoroughly enlightened by their pastors in theoretical and practical politics, it was but natural to turn to the ministers when they needed some one to express their ideas of government. Moreover, in many of the smaller towns the farmers had had little experience in writing, and the ministers were almost invariably educated men. Thus the clergy had an immense opportunity to push home their cherished convictions and to help in forming the new political institutions.[1]

---

1. The material for a study of this phase of ministerial influence is scattered through all kinds of colonial records and historical collections, especially town and county histories and records. Sometimes in a list of members of committees and conventions there will occur the name of one or more ministers but without

In this respect there were peculiar differences among the New England colonies. New Hampshire and Massachusetts records show that many towns availed themselves of their pastor's help, even making him their sole representative in provincial congresses and conventions. In Connecticut and Rhode Island, on the other hand, it is the rare thing to find a minister elected to any committee or congress. This may have been due in part, in Connecticut at least, to the somewhat general criticism of many of the clergy in that colony. There had been for years, as has been shown, a conflict, partly ecclesiastical and partly political, in which laymen often disapproved the action of the clergy. Yet the Connecticut ministers were, for the most part, active and influential patriots. In Rhode Island there was none of the alliance between church and state which troubled Connecticut, yet there also ministers did not to any extent serve on committees or in congresses. These two colonies carried on the new state governments under their old charters and there was no need for any new application of the theories of government. The contrary was true in New Hampshire and Massachusetts. It seems possible that the people of New Hampshire and especially of Massachusetts, realizing that their government must be made anew, wished to utilize the peculiar knowledge and wisdom of the ministers who had so long discussed before them the principles of government.

In general, it may be said that the clergy served chiefly on committees of correspondence and safety, on committees to draw up instructions to representatives, on committees to report upon proposed constitutions and to draw up suggestions for amendment or reasons for disapproval, and as delegates to assemblies and constitutional conventions. Their election to such offices is of

the prefix Reverend, and in such cases it is possible that the pastor may have had a son of the same name who was serving. Usually the Reverend is prefixed, however, and in this study only those who are definitely stated to be ministers are considered. Appendix B gives a list of some of those who were members of committees, etc. and names also the committees, etc., upon which they served. A more complete search would doubtless greatly lengthen this list, especially in Massachusetts and New Hampshire.

peculiar significance in any attempt to estimate their influence. It seems hardly likely that they would have been elected had their parishioners not been willing to seek their guidance and trust their judgment. It is true, of course, that many leading townsmen were away, either in the army or in other service, and possibly the minister's influence was therefore the greater. But the surprisingly large number of pastors who were chosen to assist in committee work and in constitution making is a striking testimony to the faith of the people in their knowledge and sympathy.

Again and again in these state papers, as in their sermons, the ministers express their confidence in the Continental Congress and their desire to abide by its decisions. For example, the committee of Attleborough, Massachusetts, of which the Rev. Peter Thacher was a member, in May of 1776 instructed its delegate as follows: "If Continental Congress should think it best to declare for Independency of Great Britain, we unanimously desire you for us to engage to defend them therein with our lives and fortunes,"[2] and the committee of Malden in a paper drawn up by another Rev. Peter Thacher declared in May 1776: "we have unbounded confidence in the wisdom and uprightness of the Continentall Congress."[3] Undoubtedly the ministers saw that union was indispensable to the cause and were instrumental in furthering it and in keeping alive faith in the Congress.

In many of their resolutions and instructions the ministers stressed the doctrines of natural and constitutional rights and fundamental law. They voiced the unalterable determination of the people never to yield them and, though they wrote for the whole

---

2. Daggett, *Sketch of the History of Attleborough*, p. 122.

3. Corey, *History of Malden*, p. 764. There are many other such illustrations. As early as June, 1776, Rev. Zabdiel Adams urged upon his cousin, John Adams, the need of a national constitution. John Adams answered "I am fully with you in sentiment that although the authority of the Congress, founded as it has been in reason, honor, and the love of liberty, has been sufficient to govern the colonies in a tolerable manner, for their defense and protection, yet that it is not prudent to continue very long in the same way and that a permanent constitution should be formed, and foreign aid obtained" (John Adams, *Life and Works*, IX. 399).

town or county, it is easy to catch the enthusiasm and conviction of the writers themselves.

But it was when they dealt with the proposed state constitutions that certain of the ministers were most determined to see their theories put into effect. They would tolerate no makeshift government set up by legislatures. The people, by breaking away from Great Britain, had placed themselves in a state of nature and could only set up a new government by a compact made by themselves in a constitutional convention called for that sole purpose. And in this constitution there must be a clear-cut declaration of inalienable rights. Their representatives were instructed to insist upon this. The ministerial eye was fixed watchfully upon the legislature, and when a constitution was presented to them that had not been formed in this fashion they led their townspeople to reject it, proceeded to give their reasons, and continued their demands upon the Assembly. For example, when the town of Billerica began in 1775 to consider the form of government to be adopted, it chose as one of its committee its beloved and democratic minister Henry Cummings, who had directed its earlier action against Great Britain. He served on various such committees thereafter, influenced the town to reject the constitution of 1778, and was elected to the constitutional convention of 1779, where he served on at least seven committees.[4] Cummings was but one of many clergymen who were active in procuring the rejection of the constitution of 1778 by their towns. Their disapprobation was sometimes expressed through the newspapers, more often in town instructions.

The restless Rev. William Gordon, of Roxbury, who had preached so vehemently against England in 1774 and 1775, now wrote frequent articles to the Independent Chronicle and other papers on the subject of government in general and the proposed constitution in particular and was finally dismissed in 1778 from his position as chaplain because of his free criticism of the

---

4. Hazen, *History of Billerica*, pp. 238–39. The town is said to have acted as if semi-independent until after the acceptance of the constitution. Cf. *Journal of the Convention*, pp. 91, 135, 173.

Assembly.[5] Others who actively opposed the work of the Assembly were Samuel Cooper, of Boston, Peter Thacher and Habijah Weld, of Attleborough, Joseph Willard, of Beverly, Peter Thacher, of Malden, Jonas Clark, of Lexington, and Thomas Allen and Valentine Rathbun, of Pittsfield.[6]

The chief reasons for objections were that the Assembly had not been chosen for the express purpose of drawing up a constitution and that no bill of rights was included. The insistent demand of the towns for a constitutional convention seems to have been due in part at least to the ministers. They who had for years been preaching that government originated in compact now insisted that when the old compact with England was abrogated the people must in person or through their representatives make a new one and that no government was truly legal until that had been done. They who had taught so long the sacredness of natural rights demanded that these rights be clearly defined and stated. One of the ablest of the town papers drawn up by clergymen and expressing the views held by many of his fellow ministers was that of Jonas Clark, of Lexington, written in June, 1778, giving the reasons for the town's refusal to accept the constitution offered by the Assembly. Clark wrote,

> It may be observed that it appears to us that in emerging
> from a state of nature into a state of well regulated society,
> mankind gave up some of their natural rights in order that others of greater importance to their well-being,
> safety and happiness, both as societies and individuals,

5. *Massachusetts Spy* or *American Oracle of Liberty*, Apr. 23, 1778. One letter, out of several, speaks of the "late motley convention" and disapproves of the constitution; wants a convention called which will not be the General Court. See also *Journal for the Constitutional Convention of Massachusetts*, 1719, p. 16; Bradford, *History of Massachusetts*, II. 157, note. Gordon was dismissed in Apr., 1778. He was an ambitious man, a politician.

6. See Daggett, *Sketches of History of Attleborough*, p. 126; Stone, *History of Beverly*, p. 68; Corey, *History of Malden*, p. 774, note; Headley, p. 156; Hudson, *History of Lexington*, pp. 262–64.

might be the better enjoyed, secured and defended. That a civil Constitution or form of government is of the nature of a most sacred covenant or contract entered into by the individuals which form the society, for which such Constitution or form of government is intended, whereby they mutually and solemnly engage to support and defend each other in the enjoyment of those rights which they mean to retain. That the main and great end of establishing any Constitution or form of government among a people or in society, is to maintain, secure and defend those natural rights inviolate.

He spoke then of the necessity of having the fundamental rights which were retained explicitly stated in a Declaration of Rights, so that Government and persons in authority might know the Limits of their powers and that all members of society might know when their rights were violated or infringed. Clarke then mentioned other objections. He conceived that, next to a Declaration of Rights, equality of representation was of the greatest importance to the preservation of the liberties of the subject and the peace and safety of society. He considered the proposed distribution of representation inadequate and feared that the small towns might become an easy prey to the corrupt influence of designing men, as, he said, had been frequently and notoriously the fact in England and many other states. A rotation of office he also believed desirable, and therefore advocated a limitation on eligibility. The Legislative and Executive he thought should not be blended and better provisions for amendment by the people themselves should be provided.[7] This minister, who held his people in the hollow of his hand and who was the friend and counsellor of statesmen, had, through years of meditation and study, worked out in fine detail the theories of government, and he greatly desired to see his state put them into effect. That his people appreciated his

---

7. Hudson, *History of Lexington*, pp. 262–64. *Lexington Town Records*, 1778 to 1791, record of June 15, 1778; Headley, pp. 76–77.

peculiar ability is evidenced by their choosing him in 1779 to serve as their representative in the Constitutional Convention.[8]

In his belief in rotation of office and his fear for the small town, Clark showed his tendency to sympathize with the democratic theories of the day. During these years of the Revolution there was more liberal and even radical thought among the New England ministers than one would expect who is accustomed to thinking of the Puritan clergy as stiffly conservative and intolerant. For example, it was not only prominent Baptists like Isaac Backus and Hezekiah Smith who fought in every possible way to bring about complete religious toleration in Massachusetts.[9] Although many of the Congregational clergy, like Chauncey, were thoroughly in favor of the old ways, others, like Avery and Allen, were as eager for reform as any Baptists. There can be little doubt that the sermons and papers of such men, as well as the many newspaper articles and addresses to the Assembly by Backus and other Baptists, did much to cause the fairly wide opposition to taxation for ministers' salaries and to obtain in the constitution of 1780 a greater tolerance than under the old provincial law. The arguments used were those of natural, constitutional, and Christian rights, and there was much quoting of Locke and comparison of the religious with the political situation.[10] Although taxation still continued Back-

---

8. *Lexington Town Records*, Meeting of Aug. 2, 1779. He was chosen unanimously.

9. See *Boston Gazette*, 1778 ff. Feb. 22, 1779, Backus wrote: "all our contests with the court of Britain have been to limit them to their constitution, so as not to tax us where we are not represented nor to impose judges upon us who are interested against us. And I challenge Dr. Chauncy, Mr. Payson and their whole party, to prove if they can, that I or my brethren have ever requested or tried for any other or greater liberty, than to have these rules of equity fully established here." In answer "Swift" said in *Gazette* of Mar. 8, 1779: "I love the Baptists, but I hate Backus and only for his unbounded thitst for slander. He has published the most palpable falsehoods against an innocent people." See also Backus, *Works*, 2 vols. One of his most interesting addresses is Government and Liberty Described and Ecclesiastical Tyranny Exposed, published in Boston in 1778. *The Life Of Backus* by Hovey gives a good account of his work.

10. Backus considered Chauncey the leader of the conservatives. *The Ga-*

us himself believed that the obnoxious third article of the Bill of Rights which permitted it was to a large extent nullified by its last clause, that no subordination of any one sect or denomination to another should ever be established by law.[11]

In the making of the new constitution the majority of the ministers seem to have been democratically inclined. They wished to weaken the powers of council and executive and to strengthen those of the lower house.[12] Some, both in Massachusetts and in New Hampshire, doubted the necessity of having any governor or council at all. Others did not believe in property qualifications either for voting or for office.[13] There seems to have been a fear that the populous and commercial towns would gain power at the expense of the more sparsely settled, agricultural communities.[14] This

---

zette and other papers, 1778–80, had many articles for and against complete religious liberty. The Baptists most influential were Backus, Smith, and Stillman, who preached the Election Sermon in 1779. Of the non-Baptists, Shute, Avery, and Allen are typical. In Dec. 1777, David Avery preached in favor of perfect liberty in all the states. For Shute, see sermons already quoted and Sprague, VIII. 19–21. In 1779 Rev. Isaac Foster, of West Stafford, published a *Defence of Religious Liberty* which was answered by Joseph Buckminister of Rutland; see *Massachusetts Spy* or *American Oracle of Liberty*, Oct. 28, Nov. 5, 1779; Apr. 13, May 18, 1780; *Boston Gazette*, May 22, 1780; also *Works of Backus*, etc.; and *Minutes of Warren Association*.

11. In 1783, in his Address to Friends and Countrymen, p. 6, Backus wrote: "The American revolution is wholly built upon this doctrine, that all men are born with an equal right to what Providence gives them, and that all righteous government is founded in compact or covenant, which is equally binding upon the officers and members of each community. And tho' many pleaded for this doctrine, who were averse to having the same reduced to practice among us, especially in religious affairs, yet God has taken the wise in their own craftiness, in such manner, as not only to disappoint their expectations, but also to exceed our hopes." He said that the last clause of the third article "overthrows the superstructure which was intended to have been built thereon."

12. J. Adams, *Life and Works*, IV. 273, note; *Mass. Hist. Soc. Coll.*, 1st Ser. VIII. 281.

13. See below.

14. See *Massachusetts Spy*, Nov. 13, Dec. 4, 1776; *Boston Gazette*, Sept. 6, 1779; letter from Samuel Cooper to Benjamin Franklin in *Franklin Papers*, Univ. of Pennsylvania Library; cf. J. T. Adams, *Revolutionary New England*, pp.

was especially true in the western sections of New Hampshire and Massachusetts. Certain abuses had grown up under the provincial government, and when they bade fair to continue under the new state control the discontented people of the back country defied the central government. As each movement was led by ministers and as each affected the making of the constitution, they are of special interest in any attempt to estimate the infhfence of the clergy.

In western Massachusetts the leading spirit, the man who put his whole heart and soul into the movement and aroused a people who were sometimes indifferent, was the Rev. Thomas Allen, of Pittsfield.[15] The people of Berkshire County had suffered because of the exactions of the lawyers and the courts. The judges had often been political appointees, and the people felt themselves obliged to pay unduly heavy fees and taxes to maintain them. Debtors also were harshly treated. Thomas Allen declared that "our fellow citizens in this county have been ruled with a rod of iron."[16] Men of this region preferred the old charter of 1629 to that of 1691 and when the war began looked for at least as free a government as that had been. When it seemed to them that the Assembly was setting up a form of government little better than the old they began to make a vigorous protest.

Thomas Allen was a man of great energy and of democratic spirit. He had studied Puritan principles of government as well as of religion and now he read many of the pamphlets and other writings of the day on government and politics and took up the task of arousing Berkshire against what he considered the dangerous tendencies that were showing themselves at Boston.[17] From 1775 until 1780 he never rested from his labors. Traveling through Berkshire he spoke in every town, preached sermons, wrote letters,

114–17, 123–25, 142–50, 200–209.

15. [Footnote missing in original.—JM]

16. *Ibid.*, p. 340. An excellent account of this system is given on pp. 338–40.

17. *Ibid.*, pp. 336–37. Morison says that Allen, "for his straight thinking on constitutional questions, and his great influence on the movement, . . deserves a high place in the history of Massachusetts" (*Manual for the Constitutional Convention*, 1719, p. 14). See also Headley, p. 156.

called conventions, and drew up resolutions. Smith, the historian of Pittsfield, says that "a single address by him was sometimes sufficient to revolutionize the entire sentiment of a town against the wishes of its own most prominent citizens," and that "his teachings impressed upon the people of Berkshire political characteristics which remain strongly marked to this day."[18] The petitions and memorials which he drew up to the Massachusetts Assembly state his convictions and prove his earnestness. On the twenty-fifth of December, 1775, the town adopted a petition to the General Assembly at Watertown, written by Allen, in which they declared their "abhorrence of that constitution now adopting in this Province." The old charter of King William had been "lame and essentially defective," especially in the appointment of the governor by the king, by which means all manner of disorders had been introduced into the constitution, one of the worst of which had been the want of the privilege of confessing judgment in case of debt. In the present crisis they had been led to hope for new privileges which they still hoped to obtain, or remain, so far as they had done for some time past, "in a state of nature," and they declared that they would be restless in their endeavor that they might obtain the privilege of electing their civil and military officers. "If the right of nominating to office is not vested in the people," they said, "we are indifferent who assumes it,—whether any particular persons on this or the other side of the water." They asked that a new constitution be formed and hoped "in the establishment of such new constitution, that regard will be had for such a broad basis of civil and religious liberty, as no length of time will corrupt as long as the sun and moon shall endure."[19]

To make their protest effective the court of Quarter Sessions was forbidden to hold any session. Not all the towns were agreed to this step, and Mr. Allen, who had been reading *Common Sense*, undertook to convince them. He spoke to the people of Richmond

18. Smith, p. 342.

19. The entire petition is given by Smith, pp. 343–45; the original, in Allen's handwriting, is in the State archives.

and to the convention delegates met in Pittsfield at his summons, to such good effect that "no court was suffered to sit, and all commissions of civil officers upon which hands could be laid were taken away."[20]

Thus the rebellion began. The trouble spread to Hampshire County and the authorities were in a quandary. They appointed a committee of investigation, but the town of Pittsfield sent on May 29, 1776, an explanation of their proceedings, drawn up by their pastor.[21] They had not until last fall, he said, expected much beyond the restoration of the charter, but now, believing that it was impossible ever again to be dependent upon England and realizing that this was the only time that they might ever expect to have for securing their liberties and the liberties of future posterity "upon a permanent foundation that no length of time can undermine," they had with great pain decided to suspend the courts again and wished to present to the legislature their principles in what they had done and the objects they had in view:

> We beg leave, therefore, to represent that we have always been persuaded that the people are the fountain of power; that, since the dissolution of this power of Great Britain over these Colonies, they have fallen into a state of nature.
>
> That the first step to be taken by a people in such a state for the enjoyment or restoration of civil government among them is the formation of a fundamental constitution as the basis and ground-work of legislation; that the approbation, by the majority of the people, of this fundamental constitution is absolutely necessary to give life and being to it; that then, and not till then, is the foundation laid for legislation. . . .
>
> What is the fundamental constitution of this Province?

---

20. Smith, p. 347.
21. The whole document is given by Smith, pp. 351–54.

What are the inalienable rights of the people? the power of the rulers? how often to be elected by the people, etc? Have any of these things been as yet ascertained? Let it not be said by future posterity, that, in this great, this noble, this glorious contest, we made no provisions against tyranny among ourselves.

We beg leave to assure your Honors, that the purest and most disinterested love of posterity, and the fervent desire of transmitting to them a fundamental constitution, securing to them social rights and immunities against all tyrants that may spring up after us, has moved us in what we have done. We have not been influenced by hope of gain, or expectation of preferment and honor; we are no discontented faction; we have no fellowship with Tories; we are the staunch friends of the union of these Colonies, and will support and maintain your Honors in opposing Great Britain with our lives and treasure. But even if commissions be recalled, and the king's name struck off them; if the fee-table be reduced never so low, and multitudes of other things be done to still the people,—all is to us nothing while the foundation is unfixed, the cornerstone of government unlaid. We have heard much of government being founded in compact: What compact has been formed as the foundation of government in this Province? . . .

We beg leave to represent these as the sentiments of by far the majority of the people of this county, as far as we can judge. . . . Without an alteration in our judgment, the terrors of this world will not daunt us. We are determined to resist Great Britain to the last extremity, and all others who may claim a similar power over us. Yet we hold not to an imperium imperio; we will be determined by the majority. . . .

In 1777 the Assembly ordered the courts to sit. Hampshire yielded but Berkshire refused to do so until a constitution was actually adopted. The towns voted by large majorities against it.[22] Early in 1779 the legislature passed a resolution of full pardon;[23] this was indignantly refused by Pittsfield, however, which instructed its representative to exert himself to the utmost for its repeal, and directed:

> [A]s you are chosen to represent the town of Pittsfield, we expect that you will represent it as a town of a county which has acted as firmly and consistently as any county in the State; and, as you know the sentiments of the county, that you act conformably thereunto; and, if you are not treated with the same respect with representatives of other counties, that you return home, and give us the pleasure of your company.[24]

The original draft of these blunt instructions is in the handwriting of the indignant Thomas Allen.

When the question of a constitutional convention arose in 1779 Pittsfield voted unanimously in its favor and elected as two of its committee of instruction Thomas Allen and the Baptist minister Valentine Rathbun, who had ably seconded Allen in his exertions.[25] In the instructions given, their delegate is required to demand a Bill of Rights which is extraordinarily comprehensive, including a statement that

> as all men by nature are free, and have no dominion one over another, and all power originates in the people, so, in a state of civil society, all power is founded in compact; that every man has an unalienable right to enjoy his own opinion in matters of religion, and to worship God . . .

22. Smith, p. 360.
23. *Ibid.*, pp. 362–63.
24. *Ibid.*, pp. 363–64.
25. *Ibid.*, pp. 178, 365.

without any control whatsoever, and that no particular mode or sect of religion ought to be established . . . that no man can be deprived of liberty, and subjected to perpetual bondage and servitude, unless he has forfeited his liberty as a malefactor . . . that, as all men are equal by nature, so, when they enter into a state of civil government, they are entitled to the same rights and privileges, or to an equal degree of political happiness. . . . These and all other liberties which you find essential to true liberty, you will claim, demand, and insist upon, as the birthrights of this people.[26]

He was to endeavor to obtain annual elections, constant attendance of representatives in the House, utmost equality in taxes, no negative upon the voice of the House of Representatives,— all disputed points to be settled by the majority of the whole legislature.

Although not all these demands and desires were met, the County of Berkshire accepted the new constitution of 1780.[27] For the time the struggle in western Massachusetts to work out their political theories into actual practice and to remedy their grievances was ended. In the conflict this radical Congregational minister of the back country and his Baptist colleague had carried their opposition to any government other than one founded on a true constitutional basis with the inalienable rights of the people guaranteed, to the extreme of aiding and abetting disobedience to the acts of a government which they believed had no legal existence. In

---

26. *Ibid.*, pp. 366–67. Instructions are given in full p. 368. Smith, says that in the original instructions, as drawn by the Committee, the delegate was to consent to the nomination and choice of Supreme Court Judges by the Governor, Council, and House of Representatives. In the copy attested by the moderator, this is changed to an election "by the suffrages of the people at large." Mr. Rathbun did not sign the report and Smith suggests that the change may have been suggested by him and that Mr. Allen was not so radical as the "dominant sentiment of the town."

27. *Ibid.*, p. 370.

leading the opposition and in presenting their arguments so ably and so steadfastly they played no small part in forcing the summoning of the constitutional convention and in determining the character of its work. There is no better illustration than this of the influence of the minister upon the Revolution.

To the Massachusetts constitutional convention of 1779–1780 at least thirteen clergymen were sent as representatives from their towns, among them the very radical Ebenezer Chaplin, of Sutton. Some of them served on numerous committees of importance. The Rev. Noah Alden, a Baptist of Bellingham, was made chairman of a committee to reconsider the third article of the Bill of Rights after he had moved to have that article recommitted.[28] The Rev. Gad Hitchcock, of Pembroke, the Rev. Peter Thacher, of Malden, the Rev. Jonas Clark, of Lexington, the Rev. Henry Cummings, of Billerica, and the Rev. Samuel West, of Dartmouth, were of special influence, if one may judge by the number and character of the committees upon which they served.[29] Hitchcock and West were members of the committee to draw up the constitution, and West of that to write the address to the people. Father West, as he was called, is said to have had great influence.[30] Some were radical and expressed themselves forcibly in the convention. The Rev. Peter Thacher pleaded eloquently that the office of governor should be done away with, and after that was decided against him that at least the executive should not be given the aristocratic title of Excellency.[31]

When the time came to vote on the constitution of 1780, again the ministers played their part. Many served on committees for

28. *Journal of Convention*, p. 40; Guild, *Chaplain Smith*, p. 120, note. This was the article dealing with the taxation of the people of a town for the support of church and pastor. Alden was chairman and Rev. David Sanford, of Medway, a member of this committee of seven. See Jameson, *History of Medway*, pp. 57–58, 124, 426, for account of Sanford.

29. *Journal of Convention*. For other clerical members, see pp. 8–19, 41, 171.

30. *Ibid.*, pp. 26–29, 130; Sprague, VIII. 38–41. Several of these, as well as other clergymen, were members of the convention to ratify the Federal constitution, and West is said to have had much influence then over Hancock.

31. Sprague, I. 720–21.

report and discussion.[32] A delightfully simple account is that of the Rev. Ebenezer Parkman, of Westborough. He was at that time seventy-seven years old and had not attended the town-meeting of May 22, 1780, which was to discuss the constitution. But three men from "ye Town Meeting" waited upon him to beg him to "pray with ym & give ym my Advice, they being assembled upon ye very important Affair of ye Plan of Government."[33] So the old man went with them, and joined them in discussing and voting upon each article of the constitution. He strenuously insisted that the governor should be not only a Christian but a Protestant and finally prevailed upon all but two of those present to vote the insertion of the word. For several days he assisted in drawing up the reply to the convention and later in September he was again asked by the town to meet with them to vote for the new governor. When the new government went into operation he wrote in his diary:

> We esteem this ye Day of ye Commencement of ye honorable Revolution, The New Constitution of Government now begins The Election of Governor &c. It is exceedingly to be desired and prayed for, yt ye minds of ye People were properly affected with ye great Importance of this so unexampled Time! direct ye weighty Affairs of it and grant an happy Issue to His Glory and ye Public Weal![34]

In May of that important year, the Rev. Samuel Cooper was chosen Election preacher and his sermon was considered so eloquent and of such importance that it was translated into foreign languages and printed in the same volume as the Massachusetts constitution.[35] When the first election sermon under the new

---

32. See Appendix B.

33. Parkman, Diary, pp. 236–37. In the meeting to elect the governor, his vote was the only one out of sixty-two to be cast for James Bowdoin.

34. *Ibid.*, pp. 239, 265, 280.

35. E. E. Hale, *The Centennial of the Constitution*, p. 3: "The discourse itself was received with enthusiasm. It was read in Europe with profound interest,

government was to be preached, the Rev. Jonas Clark was chosen. A wiser choice could not have been made. Once again this political philosopher stated the great principles of government in which he believed and for which he had worked. It is a noble .document, ringing with sincerity and profound conviction. Again the social compact was exalted as God's own way of establishing government. By common consent only, said Clark, could it be amended, but by common consent it could at any time be altered or dissolved. Equality and independence he declared the just claim, the indefeasible birthright of men. "Nothing short of them," he said, "ever had or ever would satisfy a man or a people truly free—truly brave." His closing words rang eloquent:

> these colonies hesitated not a moment, but . . . greatly
> dared to be free! . . . God . . . hath . . . given us a name
> among the nations of the earth . . . . All may yet be lost,
> if we rise not as. one man to the noble cause. . . . Forbid
> it, righteous Heaven! . . .[36]

The New Hampshire movement, similar to that of western Massachusetts, which had its part in the formation of the constitution of New Hampshire, centered in the so-called New Hampshire Grants on both sides of the Connecticut River and especially in Hanover and Dartmouth College. Grafton County had been recently settled and, to a large extent, by men of eastern, "New Light" Connecticut. The very names of Connecticut are repeated: Lyme, Plainfield, Lebanon, Windham, Hebron, Enfield, Canaan, etc.[37]

---

with such interest, I think, as awaited no other American document of that time, excepting the Declaration of Independence. It was translated into most of the important languages of Europe." Franklin, *Writings*, ed., Smyth, VIII. 256–57, says it was much admired in France. Franklin wished it printed at Geneva, with the Massachusetts constitution. Swift, "Massachusetts Election Sermons," *Mass. Col. Soc. Pub.*, I. 428, says it was translated into Dutch and put into a collection of documents from the thirteen United States of America.

36. Hudson, *History of Lexington*, pp. 339–41, gives much of this sermon. For extracts, see Appendix.

37. See Lawrence, *New Hampshire Churches*, pp. 432, 539, 549–50, 565;

These men had come from towns where "Separates" had been fighting for exemption from taxes to support pastors and churches not their own. Among them was Elisha Paine, of Plainfield, the son of the great "Separate" minister of Canterbury.[38] There were among them men of education and of means. All believed in the election of their own officials and in the town as the unit of government. Hanover, where the Rev. Eleazar Wheelock, of Lebanon, Connecticut, had recently established Dartmouth College, whose students and teachers were largely Connecticut men,[39] was the intellectual center of the country, and the young Dartmouth the only institution of higher learning in the state.

The towns on both sides of the Connecticut River had been incorporated under special grants given by Governor Wentworth and had never been represented in the Assembly, although they had asked for representation. In 1774, for example, the people of Hanover had petitioned, saying that they regarded representation as an inestimable privilege, inseparable from taxation and inherent in the British constitution.[40] The Assembly was unfriendly, however. The government was in the hands of the seaboard towns and the Assembly was afraid of extending representation to the back country. In 1775, forty-three towns were represented, while about one hundred were not.[41] To the college the legislature seemed especially unfriendly. It would not permit the institution to organize as a separate township, would not make roads in its neighborhood, never gave for its support more than five hundred pounds.[42]

When the Fourth Provincial Congress was called in May

Larned, *History of Windham County, Connecticut*, p. 77; Chase, *History of Dartmouth College*, I. 422; Stackpole, *History of New Hampshire*, II. 157–58, says they were radical, and believed in manhood suffrage.

38. Larned, pp. 71–72, 77.

39. Wheelock was himself a prominent "New Light," a friend of Elisha Williams, whose *Seasonable Plea* has been quoted, of Benjamin Pomeroy, etc. A number of the students and graduates of the college had been born in Windham County, Connecticut.

40. MS Letter, no. 774900.5 (D. C. L.).

41. Stackpole, *History of New Hampshire*, II. 157.

42. MS Letter, no. 775209 (D. C. L.); Chase, I. 271–77.

1775, the towns of Grafton and Cheshire county responded, each town which could afford it sending one delegate. It was to this congress that nine clergymen were sent by various towns.[43] The act of November 14th, arranging for election to the next congress, was very unfavorable to the Connecticut valley towns, many of the small towns being grouped together, the Hanover group being entirely unrepresented, and the control again in the hands of the east. On December 5th, Wheelock wrote: "We are in a State of Nature, the Constitution thrown out of Doors."[44]

In the next congress, whether because of discontent with the method of representation or because of poverty and the war, not so many towns were represented. It was this Assembly that on the fifth of January, 1776, "took up civil government" and adopted a temporary constitution, by which representatives were to be chosen, not one from each town but by a method of grouping which gave the eastern, longer settled, and more populous towns a large majority of delegates.[45] The Council was not to be elected at large; instead five were to be chosen in the county of Rockingham, two in Hillsborough, two in Strafford, two in Cheshire, and one in Grafton, again giving the majority to the east.[46] Moreover, the representatives and councillors were to be limited to men having real estate to the value of two hundred pounds.[47]

In July 1776, delegates from the dissatisfied towns involved met at College Hall, Hanover, and began an agitation against the government which lasted until 1784. Although of great interest, the details of the struggle, the refusal to pay taxes, the temporary union with Vermont, the attempt to establish a new state with its capital at Hanover, the ultimate reunion of the towns east of the Connecticut with New Hampshire, must be passed over.[48] The

43. *Provincial Papers, N. H.*, VII. 468–70, 668. See Appendix B.
44. MS Letter, no. 775651, (D. C. L.); Chase, I. 423–25.
45. Stackpole, p. 161.
46. *Provincial and State Papers, N. H.*, X. 232.
47. *Ibid.*, pp. 235–36.
48. For details, see J. L. Rice, "The New Hampshire Grants," in *Mag. Amer. Hist.*, VIII. Rice, p. 12, says the greatest influence of the college lay to the west of

significant facts for this study are rather the part played by the clergy, the arguments presented so forcefully and the influence of the movement upon the new constitution.

It is hard to tell how far the ministers were responsible for the agitation. Their enemies believed that the whole movement was due to the ambition of Wheelock and his friends for political power and their desire to have Hanover the capital either of New Hampshire or of a new state formed from the new towns on both sides of the Connecticut.[49] There was even a suggestion now and then that the British were behind the trouble.[50] Wheelock himself tried to seem neutral, but the term "College Party" was used continually and certainly Wheelock must have known and approved and to some extent have guided the movement.[51] The leaders were men closely associated with the college. The College Hall was frequently the meeting place of delegates from the towns of Grafton and Cheshire counties, and it was from College Hall that the memorial went which was accepted by the towns as best expressing their protest.[52] Meshech Weare, President of the Council, attributed the initiation of the movement to the College. In December, 1776, he wrote to the delegates at Exeter:

> I enclose you an Address of Several Towns in the County of Grafton to the people at large (fabricated I suppose at Dartmouth College) and calculated to stir up Contention & animosities among us at this difficult time; Especially as our Government is only temporary & the state of matters not allowing a Revisal. However

the river. He believes the college intended from the beginning to make Hanover the capital of a larger state. See also Chase, I.

49. State Papers Vermont Controversy, pp. 235–37, 241; Weare Papers, no. 105; Chase, I. 445–46.

50. State Papers Vermont Controversy, pp. 209, 237.

51. Chase, I. 445 ff. Wheelock had sided with settlers west of the river in the earlier controversy with New York and tried to have land "receded back to New Hampshire" (pp. 435 ff. and *New Hampshire State Papers*, VIII. 314).

52. That of July, 1776. See *Provincial and State Papers*, N. H., X. 229–35.

this Pamphlet with the assiduity of the College Gentlemen has had such an effect that almost the whole
County of Grafton if not the whole, have refused to
send members to the new Assembly, which is to meet
next Wednesday.[53]

Chase attributes the College Hall Address of July 1776, as well as
that of October 1776, to Bezaleel Woodward, professor in the college and son-in-law of Wheelock, and says that they were "widely
circulated and produced a profound impression."[54]

These addresses and the reasons given by the towns for their
refusal to send delegates are among the most interesting of Revolutionary documents. They bristle with the assertion of natural
rights; they declare the towns in a state of nature, demand a constitutional convention and a bill of rights, assert the right of each
town to its own representative, refuse to listen to such methods of
electing a council, question the wisdom of having any council at
all, and declare that any man, whether possessed of two hundred
pounds or not, should have the right to sit as representative. The
defiance of these little towns and their utter faith in the truth of
their theories is amazing. The memorial begins:

> The important Crisis is now commenced wherein the
> providence of God; the Grand Continental Congress;
> and our necessitous circumstances, call upon us to as-
> sume our natural right of laying a foundation of civil
> Government within and for this Colony. . . . We think
> it of the utmost importance, that every inhabited town
> have the liberty, if they please, of electing one member,
> at least, to make up the legislative body—As it may be
> much questioned, if any one distinct corporate body be
> neglected, or deprived of actual representation, whether,
> in that case, they are any ways bound, or included by
> what the others may do: Certainly, if they are considered

53. *Ibid.*, X. 228.
54. Chase, I. 426, note.

in a state of nature, they are not. No, not even an individual person. But suppose it should be thought prudent at any time, by the legislative body, to restrict, or lessen the number of representatives; it is absolutely necessary that the whole should be active in the matter, in order to surrender their privileges in this case, as they cannot be curtailed without . . . . We readily agree, that it is a thousand pities, that when we are engaged in a bloody contest, merely to oppose arbitrary power without us, we should have occasion to contend against the same within ourselves; especially by those who profess to be friends of liberty. . . . As for ourselves, we are determined not to spend our blood and treasure, in defending against the chains and fetters, that are forged and prepared for us abroad, in order to purchase some of the like kind of our own manufacturing.—But mean to hold them alike detestable. . . .[55]

Several meetings were held in Hanover at College Hall, and the towns sent resolves to the legislature stating that they accepted the above address and giving therein reasons for their refusal to send delegates. On November 27, 1776, the townmeeting at Hanover voted unanimously:

That we will not give in our Votes for a Counseller as directed. . . . Because we can see no important end proposed by their creation, unless to negative the proceedings of the House of Representatives, which we humbly conceive ought not to be done in a free state. . . .[56]

Acworth, December 9, 1776, voted: "we think every lawful elector is a subject to be elected . . . ."[57] Chesterfield, which had sent a representative, instructed him thus on December 12, 1776:

---

55. *Provincial and State Papers. N. H.*, X. 229–35.

56. *Ibid.*, X. 236–37.

57. *Ibid.*, X. 238.

We can by no means imagine ourselves so far lost to a sense of the natural rights and immunities of ourselves and our fellow-men, as to imagine that: the State can be either safe or happy under a Constitution formed without the knowledge or particular authority of a great part of its inhabitants ... you are ... to exert yourself to the utmost to procure a redress of the afore-mentioned grievances, and in case they will not comply, to return home for further instructions.[58]

At a meeting of Haverhill, Lyman, Bath, Gunthwait, Landaff and Morristown, December 13, 1776, they refused to elect a representative or to send in a vote for Councillor because "it is our humble opinion, that when the Declaration of Independency took place, the colonies were absolutely in a state of nature, and the powers of government reverted to the people at large. . . ."[59] And so it went, each town asserting the same rights in different phraseology.

The many documents repeated these arguments unceasingly, and the towns grew more defiant and more determined to have the principles of government in which they believed put into effect.[60] In 1777 an address of the United Committees signed by Woodward, as clerk, declared they were ready to resist Great Britain or any other who wanted to subject them to a state inconsistent with their natural and inherent rights, and shortly thereafter Hanover gave instructions to Woodward (which are in his handwriting) concurring in this address and approving the position taken in an anonymous democratic pamphlet of

---

58. *Provincial and State Papers. N. H.*, X. 240.

59. *Ibid.*; the paper is supposed to have been written by Woodward. Other memorials, petitions, and resolves of the towns are given in *Town Papers, N.H.*, XI. 23–24; XII. 57: "Ye Code of Laws made on that system are of ye same tenure of those we have Revolted from and for that reason we are Spilling our Blood and treasure for nothing" (New Grantham). See also XII. 573–74; XIII. 69, 282, 762–65.

60. Several of them refused to pay taxes and raised what money they needed for their own use. See Weare Papers, IV, no. 209; Chase, I. 459.

the time, *The People the best Governors,* which seems to have had much influence.[61]

Certain of the eastern towns, notably Portsmouth, realized that the western counties had real grievances and advised the legislature to redress them, but nothing was done for some time. At last, in 1778, a constitutional convention was called, but the old method of representation was retained and the constitution was rejected. In 1781, the Assembly decided on a new constitutional convention to be chosen more in accordance with the demands of the "college party."[62] The constitution drawn up was twice rejected, but after modifications was finally accepted and went into effect in 1784. Neither Hanover nor Dresden, as the college district was then called, had any part in making it, and many of the democratic ideas of the western towns did not carry. The union with Vermont and the later effort to found a separate state had lessened their influence.[63] The motives behind the revolt of the western towns are hard to determine and to estimate. It is possible that a desire to enhance the value of land along the river may have had something to do with it.[64] Certainly the ambition to increase the importance of the college played a large part. The natural independence of the frontier and its distrust of the older commercial towns must be taken into account. However complex the motives, there seems little reason to doubt the sincerity of the belief in the old theories of compact and natural rights and in the determination to carry them into effect, or to doubt that it was the ministers of the college district who

61. Weare Papers, IV, no. 35; Chase, I. 452; MS 777211 (D. C. L.). Cf. article by H. A. Cushing, *Amer. Hist. Rev.,* I. 284–87. See *Town Papers, N. H.,* XIII. 762–64, for meetings in June, 1777; Chase, I. 458 ff., for later circulars. A circular sent out by the College in Jan. 1777, the MS of which is in the handwriting of John Wheelock, is quoted in part in Appendix A.

62. Chase, I. 491.

63. *Town Papers, N. H.,* IX, Appendix, gives details about the Conventions. The town and the college separated in 1779; the college was more radical than the town. Of 5,760 acres, Wheelock, his family, and the college owned 4,000 (Chase. I. 459–63).

64. *Memoirs* of Wheelock, p. 303.

initiated and led the movement. The agitation at least hastened the calling of a constitutional convention and to some extent influenced the character of the constitution which was finally adopted.

Thus in both New Hampshire and Massachusetts, but especially the latter, the ministers played a larger and more direct part in determining the character of the new institutions than has been realized. This is especially significant in view of the long years through which they had been preaching the underlying philosophy.

Eleven

Varied Services During the War

*I*f any proof were needed of the sincerity of the support given the radicals by the evangelical clergy of New England, one would need only to study their deeds both before and during the war. Many of them served as chaplains, some for long periods, even when they had to pay more for their substitutes than they themselves received; some fought and fought well in single battles or campaigns; some did good service in recruiting men for the army or in keeping discouraged and weary soldiers from returning home; many gave freely of their scant substance and by their glowing sermons kept up the courage of those at home; some used their skill in describing battles and campaigns; others served in less usual ways.

Beginning with 1767 and continuing throughout the war the ministers did all in their power to encourage the non-importation agreements and home manufactures. There are many instances in each of the New England colonies of all-day spinning bees held in the rooms and on the lawns of the minister's home.[1] Frequently

---

1. Thos. Waters, *Ipswich in the Massachusetts Bay Colony*, II. 299; in 1769, 77 women spun all day in the home of Rev. John Cleaveland. Afterward he preached to them and told them how they "might recover to this Country the full and free Enjoyment of all our Rights, Properties and Privileges (which is more than the others have been able to do) and so have the Honor of building

before the end of the day the minister would address the women and girls on the issues of the time. From the pulpit also they urged careful observance of the non-importation agreements. One good clergyman during the war felt so keenly the need of clothes for the soldiers at Quebec that he excused the women of the town from afternoon service and set them all to spinning on the Sabbath day.[2] The power of their influence in this respect is attested by Englishman and Tory. Oliver wrote,

> Mr. Otis's black Regiment, the dissenting Clergy, were also set to Work, to preach up Manufactures instead of Gospel—they preached about it & about it, untill the Women & Children, both within Doors & without, set their Spinning Wheel a whirling in Defiance of Great Britain: the female Spinners kept on spinning for 6 Days of the Week; & on the seventh, the Parsons took their

not only their own but the houses of many Thousands and perhaps prevent the Ruin of the whole British empire." He urged living upon the produce of the country, not using any foreign teas, nor wearing clothes of foreign manufacture (*Essex Gazette*, June 27, 1769). In Newport in 1771 at the home of Rev. Mr. Hopkins, a "new and ingenious Construction," was used, "so calculated that near twice as much as on the common Wheel may be spun in the same space of Time" (*Boston News-Letter Supplement*, June 20, 1771). I have from *Boston Chronicle, News-Letter, Essex Gazette, Massachusetts Spy, N. Eng. Hist. & Geneal. Register*, and one or two town histories, alone, 32 examples either of such all day spinning parties or of large quanities of yarn or cloth presented to the minister; 20 of these are between 1767 and 1770. *Boston News-Letter*, June 15, 1769 speaks also of many others in various provinces; 6 in 1770–1774, 6 after 1774. See J. Lathrop, Artillery Sermon, 1774, p. 29, note, urging home manufacture of clothes. "The Lord of providence has put a price into our hands, and if we are not greatly wanting to ourselves, we may be free, we may be rich, we may be the most powerful people under the heavens. It is to be wished that societies were fanned in all the principal cities and towns on the continent for the encouragement of agriculture and manufactures."

2. Judah Champion, of Litchfield. He read from the pulpit of the taking of St. Johns and of the suffering of the Army in the cold northern winter; then afer service gave his permission for every woman and girl to go to her spinning; *Centennial Papers General Conference of Connecticut*, pp. 58–59.

Turns, & spun out their Prayers & Sermons to a long
Thread of Politicks, & to much better Profit than the
other Spinners; for they generally cloathed the Parson
and his Family with the Produce of their Labor—this
was a new Species of Enthusiasm, & might be justly
termed, the Enthusiasm of the Spinning Wheel.[3]

In this matter the ministers showed knowledge of human nature by arousing competition between town and town and between
churches in the same town, and even between married and unmar-
ried women, as well as by making the whole affair a great social occasion through having the men come to supper and join in an evening
of fun with music and singing of songs written by the Sons of Liberty.[4] Often many spectators came from town and country to view
the spinning and thus, as well as through sermons and newspaper
articles, the non-importation idea spread.[5] Even after the merchants
grew tired of their agreements and decided to resume trade, the "independent priests" were linked, by the hostile press, with the politicians and smugglers in keeping alive the movement.[6]

Many of the clergy supported vigorously the Solemn League
and Covenant of 1774.[7] On June 7, 1774, the Rev. John Cleaveland, of Ipswich, writing as usual under the pseudonym of "Johannis in Eremo," advised that the names of all merchants in the sea-
port towns who refused to enter the covenant be published so that
the country towns might have no dealings with them.[8] Oliver tells
of one country minister who attended the town meeting held in
the church, sat himself down at the communion table and roundly
declared that no one who failed to support the Covenant was fit

---

3. Oliver, *Origin and Progress of the American Rebellion*, p. 88.

4. *Boston News-Letter,* July 6, 1769.

5. *Ibid.,* Dec., 2, 1768, June 15, and July 6, 1769.

6. *Essex Gazette,* Mar. 19, 1771, quotes from an article in the *London Gazette* and *New Daily Advertiser,* Nov. 30, 1770.

7. *Massachusetts Gazette* and *Boston Post-Boy,* July 18, 1774; *Boston News-
Letter,* Oct. 13, 1774; *Essex Gazette,* June 7, 1774; and other papers of the day.

8. *Essex Gazette,* June 7, 1774.

to come to the sacred table. Certain of the Boston clergy, he says, traveled to the country towns, creeping into houses and leading captive silly men and women.[9] There were also a number of ministers who wrote frequently for the newspapers as well as some who worked quietly behind the mask of more popular names. Such were Dr. Samuel Cooper who is said to have written Hancock's fifth of March oration,[10] and the Rev. John Adams, of Durham, New Hampshire, who aided Sullivan, his intimate friend.[11] The statesman minister, Dr. Samuel Cooper, gave most distinguished service of an unusual kind all through the war. He who knew much of the heart of Samuel Adams,[12] and was the intimate friend

---

9. Oliver, *The Origin and Progress of the American Rebellion*, pp. 147–48, 151: "Neither their Cloaths, their Shoes, or their Throats are as yet worn out; the Faction deceived them; they have helped to deceive the People."

10. Wm. Bentley, *Diary*, I. 52; not only this but other papers of Hancock are commonly ascribed to him. In 1783 he was called by Samuel Dexter "The Prime Minister" (*Bowdoin and Temple Papers*, Pt. II, p. 29): he was hated by Loyalists. See Winsor, *Memorial History of Boston*, III. 123–24; Sprague, I. 442–43; Moore, *Diary of the Revolution*, I. 136; Tudor, *Life of James Otis*, pp. 152–53; Sabin, IV. 516. On Apr. 3, 1776, S. Adams wrote to Cooper: "I wish your Leisure would admit of your frequently favoring me with your Thoughts of our publick Affairs. I do assure you I shall make use of them, as far as my Ability shall extend, to the Advantage of our Country." Cf. S. Adams, *Writings*, III. 273, 303; IV. 106, 108, 123, 148, etc. Franklin, *Writings*, ed. Smyth, VII. 407; VIII. 183, 256, etc. Washington was told by the Mass. delegates in 1775 that among various others he could also rely on Drs. Cooper, Chauncey and Langdon. Cf. *Writings of Washington*, ed. Sparks, III. 20.

11. Stackpole, *History of New Hampshire*, II. 70–71. Among others were Rev. Wm. Gordon, of Roxbury (see J. Buckingham, *Specimens of Newspaper Literature*, I. 215; Tyler, *Literary History of the American Revolution*, II. 423–28); Rev. Joseph Lyman, of Hatfield (L. Coleman, *Genealogy of the Lyman family*, pp. 179–80); Rev. Thos. Allen, of Pittsfield, especially in *Connecticut Courant* (see Smith, *History of Pittsfield*, and later references); Rev. Jeremy Belknap, of Dover, N. H. (Sprague, VIII. 75; G. B. Spalding, *The Dover Pulpit during the Revolutionary War*; Farmer and Moore, *Coll. Topog., Hist. and Biog.*, I. 39); Rev. Samuel Cooper (Sprague, I. 442; Tyler, *Literary History of the American Revolution*, II. 302–06); Rev. John Cleaveland for many years in *Essex Gazette*; Rev. Zabdiel Adams, and others; some writing under pseudonyms hard to run down.

12. Adams, *Writings*, IV. 106. Many of their letters are in vols. III and IV.

of Benjamin Franklin realized, as perhaps few other clergymen, the vital importance of the French alliance. He received in his home and in many ways assisted the French generals and others who came to America during the war. There they met and talked with Americans and each learned to know the other better. That he might more successfully carry on this work, he was granted, says Faÿ, as was Thomas Paine, a thousand dollars a year by the King of France.[13] For three years he accepted this aid and succeeded so well in his design that after his death his work survived him as did the friendships he had created.[14] For many years this wise and cultured gentleman had been interested in politics and government and during the war he wrote freely concerning such subjects to Adams and Franklin. He kept Franklin while in France in touch with American sentiment, and his letters and pamphlets were quoted in France, where, according to Franklin, his name and character gave weight to his opinions.[15]

An illustration of the most violent articles written by the clergy is one against General Gage, by the fiery-tongued old preacher, John Cleaveland, of Ipswich. The virulence of his attack is almost incredible. On June 17, 1775, he wrote,

> Thou profane, wicked-monster of falsehood and perfidy . . . your late infamous proclamation is as full of notorious lies, as a toad or rattle-snake of deadly poison—you are an abandoned wretch. . . . Without speedy repentance, you will have an aggravated damnation in hell . . . you are not only a robber, a murderer, and usurper, but a wicked Rebel: A rebel against the authority of truth, law, equity, the English constitution of government, these colony states, and humanity itself.[16]

13. B. Faÿ, *L'Esprit révolutionnaire en France et aux Etats-Unis*, pp. 87–88.
14. *Ibid.*
15. Franklin, *Writings*, ed. Smyth, VIII. 256–58. Many letters in vols. VII, VIII, IX; also *Calendar of Franklin Papers*, I, II, III. See Bruce, *Benjamin Franklin*, I.21, 353.
16. *Essex Gazette*, July 13, 1775, but written June 17. An earlier "illiberal

This same John Cleaveland and many of his fellow ministers won the bitter enmity of the Loyalists and the English by their attacks upon the Tories, and seem to have been responsible for a part at least of the harsh treatment meted out to them by the patriots. Cleaveland published articles, evidently written at white-heat, on the 18th and 25th of April, 1775, in which he first suggested that it might be the "proper dictate of wisdom, as the way, and only way left us of our preservation and safety, as soon as we see the sword of Great Britain drawn against us to sacrifice every New England Tory among us";[17] and on the 25th he cried out,

> General Gage, pluck up stakes and begone; you have drawn the sword . . . the defensive sword of New England is now drawn; it now studies just revenge, and it will not be satisfied till your blood is shed, and the blood of every son of violence under your command, and the blood of every traitorous Tory under your protection.[18]

Admirably suited was this to stir up the hot passions of the crowd. Even in their prayers, the clergy consigned the Tories to strange penalties.[19]

---

letter" of June, 1774 had been noticed in the *Boston Post-Boy* of Aug. 8, 1774. Another letter of Sept. 20, 1774 says that it was unconstitutional to obey Gage or to hold office under him, etc. Other clergy had also written articles and preached sermons against Gage. See *Boston News-Letter*, Dec. 22, 1774.

17. *Essex Gazette*, April 18, 1775.

18. *Ibid.*, Apr. 25, 1775. Also Sherwood, Fast Day Sermon, 1774, p. ix. Rev. Nathaniel Whitaker of Salem was violent in attacking Tories, especially after 1776.

19. Oliver, *The Origin and Progress of the American Rebellion*, p. 147; A. K. Teele, ed., *History of Milton*, pp. 424–25; Force, *American Archives*, 4th Ser. II. p, 369; *Essex Gazette*, Apr. 18 and 25, 1775. Additional quotations in Appendix A. In the *Boston News-Letter*, Mar. 17, 1775, a clergyman laments that some of his brethren "strive to inflame the worst passion of the human mind" and asks, "Why do patriots continually wish and urge us to feed these unfriendly and malignant vices?" He would resign rather than adopt a course "so odious" in a clergyman. See also *Boston News-Letter*, Dec. 30, 1774.

Colonel John Peters, writing in 1778 to the Rev. Samuel Peters, the noted Tory, who was then in London, accused Dr. Wheelock, of Hanover, New Hampshire, with three laymen of having "put an end to the Church of England in the State, so early as 1775," of having seized "all the Church people for 200 miles up the river and confined us all in close gaols,[20] after beating us and drawing us through water and mud."[21] This account Stackpole considers somewhat exaggerated, but it shows that activity against the Tories was attributed to the Rev. Dr. Wheelock. The Rev. Samuel Eaton, of Harpswell, had an effect probably not intended, when he so excited the people of Harpswell and Brunswick during an address in the meeting house, April, 1775, that they seized one Vincent Woodside, a Tory holding a commission from the King, and proceeded to bury him alive, almost to his destruction; then spoiled the masts in the lumber yards, and finally went to Topsham and seized another suspected Tory, who also fortunately escaped their anger.[22]

It is impossible to determine what proportion of the New England clergy were radical revolutionists and what proportion were conservatives or Loyalists. It was difficult for the Loyalists among them to get a hearing. Certainly the press and publishing houses, run largely by radicals, would be slow to accept their articles and sermons. In some towns, ministers who were suspected of being Loyalists were called to account by local committees.[23] In some cases, as the strife continued, they lost their churches and suffered in other ways.[24] Among those refusing to bend to the

20. [An older form of the word "jails."—JM]

21. Stackpole, *History of New Hampshire*, II. 318.

22. Wheeler, *History of Brunswick, Topsham and Harpwell*, pp. 678–80; Sprague, I. 615.

23. Among these were Asa Dunbar, of Weston, Samuel Dana, of Groton, who in Mar., 1775, preached non-resistance, Timothy Harrington, of Lancaster, and Ebenezer Morse, of Shrewsbury. See *Essex Gazette*, June 8, Sept. 21, 1775; *Massachusetts Spy*, Nov. 24 and Dec. 15, 1775; Butler, *History of Groton*, pp. 178–79; Marvin, *History of Lancaster*, pp. 304–05.

24. Peter Whitney, of Petersham, Abraham Hill, of Shutesbury, David Parsons, of Amherst, Benj. Parker, of Haverhill. See Crane, Peter Whitney and his

storm were not only almost the entire body of Anglican clergy but certain Congregationalists as well. In western Massachusetts there was a little band of Tory clergymen who for a time had much influence. These were Daniel Collins, of Lanesboro, Abraham Hill, of Shutesbury, David Parsons, of Amherst, Roger Newton, of Greenfield, and Jonathan Ashley, of Deerfield. In this region there was a strong Tory element among the laymen, chiefly among the officers who had served in the French and Indian War and those who held commissions from the king. The Williams family was one of the most influential and had members in several towns.[25]

Into this frontier land came two young Congregational ministers, Joseph Lyman and Thomas Allen. Joseph Lyman was from Lebanon, Connecticut, and arrived in Hatfield in 1772. He found the Tory element in possession. In 1768, the town had unanimously voted to report to Boston that they did not approv, of her measures, but considered them "unconstitutional, illegal and wholly unjustifiable . . . subversive of government and destructive of the peace and good order which is the cement of society."[26] Wholeheartedly the young pastor threw himself into the work of changing their opinions. Sunday after Sunday, as well as in town meeting, he preached the doctrine of liberty and resistance. He was "of resolute will and indomitable courage" and he spoke "with burning words." In two years the Whigs won control of the town meeting and in December, 1774, they ordered his Thanksgiving sermon published and voted him the thanks of the town. Colonel Israel Williams, the

---

History of Worcester Co., pp. 9–10; Judd, *History of Hadley*, pp. 410–11; Chase, *History of Haverhill*, p. 579. This study does not consider the Anglicans except incidently. In the north and middle colonies they were almost to a man Loyalists, but in Virginia and the Carolinas and especially in Georgia, more of them were either neutral or adhered openly to the colonial cause.

25. C. J. Palmer, *History of Lanesboro*, pp. 12–13, 82; Wm. Bentley, *Diary*, I. 92–93; Judd, *History of Hadley*, pp. 410–11; Moore, *Diary of the Revolution*, II. 440; G. Sheldon, *History of Deerfield*, II. 677, 693–95, 710–11; F. M. Thompson, *History of Greenfield*, I. 255, II. 718.

26. D. W. & R. F. Wells, *History of Hatfield*, pp. 180–81; *Boston News-Letter*, Oct. 6, 1768.

head of the Tory party, was forced to sign the association test and later confined to his home lot. Thus the zeal and energy of this one minister won a whole town to the American side and doubtless his influence extended far beyond the town limits.[27]

Thomas Allen of Pittsfield was a man of remarkable power, dominating the whole region round about. A graduate of Harvard, in 1762, he went out in 1765 to be pastor of the small settlement on the Massachusetts frontier. Here too there was a strong Tory element, among its leaders Colonel William Williams and Israel Stoddard.[28] There must have been many bitter struggles between the Tory and Whig factions; and the part played by Mr. Allen can be judged from the accusations brought against him and the action of the town thereon. In 1774 the town "passed in full" the following resolutions:

> Whereas (the name of Colonel William Williams was here inserted but erased) Major Israel Stoddard and Woodbridge Little, Esquire, have exhibited several charges against the Reverend Thomas Allen, thereby endeavoring to injure his reputation, in respect to what he said and did in a late town-meeting, in defence of the rights and liberties of the people; wherein they charge the said Thomas with rebellion, treason, and sedition, and cast many other infamous aspersions, tending to endanger not only the reputation, but the life of the said Thomas.
>
> Voted, That all the foregoing charges are groundless, false, and scandalous; and that the said Thomas is justifiable in all things wherein he hath been charged with the crimes aforesaid; and that he hath merited the thanks of this town in everything wherein he hath undertaken to defend the rights and privileges of the people in this

27. Wells, pp. 182, 186–88. He is said to have declared to his mother who wanted him not to antagonize Col. Williams, "There is a man here now he cannot rule."

28. Smith, *History of Pittsfield*, pp. 174, 176–77.

Province, and particularly in his observations and animadversions on the Worcester Covenant.[29]

Somewhat later in 1774, the town requested the Tory minister of Lanesborough, Daniel Collins, to cease censuring and disapproving Allen "in regard to his conduct in some public affairs of late." Although Mr. Collins insisted that it would be well for "gospel ministers, in their public discourses, to avoid entering very far into a consideration of state policy,"[30] it is clear that the majority of the town was with their pastor. In 1774, Allen was made chairman of the correspondence committee and later was elected to other committees, drew up town resolves and instructions, ruined the plots of Loyalists, and harried the Tories into jail or with "hue and cry" drove them out of the country. He made journeys into New York, and wherever he went patriots sprang up. He said,

> I have exerted myself to disseminate the same spirit [of liberty] in King's district, which has of late taken surprising effect. The poor tories at Kinderhook are mortified and grieved, and are wheeling about, and begin to take the quick step. New York government begins to be alive in the glorious cause and to act with vigor.[31]

He was so successful that his name was sent to General Gage as that of "the most dangerous character to the King's cause in the western part of the colony."[32]

In the Revolution, as in all wars, the clergy served as chaplains in the army. Among so many who were enthusiastic in the cause, it is difficult to pick the most influential. David Avery, of

---

29. *Ibid.*, p. 198. The Worcester Covenant was an especially strict non-importation and consumption agreement, which seemed to some to include even buying from or selling greens and potatoes to country people. See S. Adams, *Writings*, III. pp. 131–32.

30. *Ibid.*

31. *Ibid.*, pp. 209–10; Headley, pp. 128–29, 132–34; *Essex Gazette*, May 18, 1775. Letters by Allen, May 1775, were published in various papers.

32. Headley, p. 132.

Gageborough, Massachusetts, was one who served long, encouraging the men with his clear, ringing voice through the weary winter at Valley Forge.[33] Abiel Leonard, of Woodstock, Connecticut, was one of the best loved and most influential. In March, 1776, Washington and Putnam wrote to his congregation at Woodstock asking them to give him up to the army, because his influence was so great and so valuable.[34] Among those who served for years was the great Baptist, Hezekiah Smith, of Haverhill, Massachusetts. Smith was the friend of Gates, Washington, and many of the New England officers, and occasionally served as aide-de-camp. It was he who enthusiastically called Saratoga "the grandest conquest ever gained since the creation of the world."[35] Many of the men already mentioned as radical preachers hastened to give their services in this way.[36] "Mr. Washington," says Oliver, speaking of the winter 1775–1776, "was provided with a Chaplain, who with a stentorian Voice & an Enthusiastick Mania, could incite his Army to greater Ardor than all the Drums of his Regiments."[37]

Before the actual hostilities began, these fighting parsons had their muskets ready. In September of 1774 an alarm spread through the country that a clash had come in Boston and handbills were read in the Connecticut churches on the Sabbath morning. At once the clergy responded. The Rev. Jonathan Todd, of East Guilford, marched with eighty-three of his parishioners, the Rev.

33. Chase, *History of Dartmouth College*, I. 308–09.

34. *Centennial Papers General Conferences of Connecticut*, p. 81; Larned, *History of Windham County*, II. 156–57, 161.

35. Guild, *Chaplain Smith*, p. 227; see also pp. 20, 51, 162, 165, 198; *Diary of Smith*, pp. 35 ff.

36. Stephen Johnson, of Lyme, present at Bunker Hill; Ebenezer Baldwin, of Danbury; Benjamin Trumbull, of North Haven; the aged Benjamin Pomeroy, of Hebron, some of whose people thought him altogether too deeply concerned with politics; Cotton Mather Smith, of Sharon, who is said to have written the patriotic hymns sung by his congregation; Judah Champion, of Litchfield; and others of Conn. Of Mass., John Cleaveland of Ipswich; Thomas Allen, of Pittsfield; also Peter Powers, of Haverhill, N. H.; and many others both better and less well-known.

37. Oliver, *The Origin and Progress of the American Rebellion*, p. 192.

Mr. May, of Haddam, and the Rev. Mr. Boardman, of Chatham, with one hundred each.[38] All that winter many were helping their people to be ready for any emergency. Some served as clerks or officers of military companies and alarm lists,[39] some took part in early expeditions to secure powder and arms. The Rev. John Adams, of Durham, New Hampshire, in December of 1774 went with others to take supplies from the fort at Newcastle and is said to have stored the powder under his pulpit.[40] The Rev. John Treadwell went into his pulpit with musket loaded, his sermon under one arm and his cartridge box under the other.[41]

When the news of Lexington and Bunker Hill arrived, parson after parson left his parish and marched hastily toward Boston. Before daylight on the morning of April 30, 1775, Stephen Farrar, of New Ipswich, New Hampshire, left with ninety-seven of his parishioners.[42] Joseph Willard, of Beverly, marched with two companies from his town, raised in no small part through his exertion.[43] David Avery, of Windsor, Vermont, after hearing the news of Lexington, preached a farewell sermon, then, outside the meeting-house door, called his people to arms and marched with twenty men. On the way he served as captain, preached, and collected more troops.[44] David Grosvenor, of Grafton, left his pulpit and, musket in hand, joined the minute men who marched to Cambridge.[45] Phillips Rayson, of Chelsea, is given credit for leading a group of his parishioners to attack a band of English soldiery that nineteenth day of April.[46] Benjamin Balch, of Danvers, Lieu-

38. Chase, *Beginnings of the American Revolution*, II. 38–39, quoted from Stiles, *Diary*, I. 484–85.

39. Crowell, *History of Town of Essex*, pp. 203–04; *Essex Gazette*, Mar. 14, 1775; *Provincial Papers, N. H.*, VII. 601; Tapley, *Chronicles of Danvers*, p. 69.

40. Stackpole, *History of New Hampshire*, II. 72.

41. Lewis and Newhall, *History of Lynn*, I. 340,346.

42. Chandler, *History of New Ipswich*, pp. 74–76.

43. Thayer, *Address delivered in First Parish*, Beverly, p. 54.

44. Headley, p. 291; Chase, *History of Dartmouth College*, I. 308 and note.

45. Pierce, *History of Grafton*, p. 188; Parkman, *Diary*, p. 93.

46. Chamberlain, *Documentary History of Chelsea*, II. 312, 425–27.

tenant of the third alarm-list in his town, was present at Lexington and later, as chaplain in army and navy, won the title of "the fighting parson."[47] Jonathan French, of Andover, Massachusetts, left his pulpit on the Sabbath morning, when the news of Bunker Hill arrived, and with surgical case in one hand and musket in the other started for Boston.[48]

A surprising number of preachers served as privates or as officers during the war.[49] Throughout the war, as earlier, they encouraged enlisting and often succeeded when the recruiting officers failed. The Provincial Congress of Massachusetts ordered that Phillips Payson, of Chelsea, and the eager young pastor of Malden, Peter Thacher, be furnished with "beating orders" for the purpose of raising two companies for defence of the sea-coast.[50] William Emerson, who had so aroused the men of Concord that many enlisted among the minute men in January, 1775, often used his power in like fashion in later years.[51] The story told of the Rev. Samuel Eells, of Bradford, Connecticut, is typical. When news

47. Balch, "Some Account of the Rev. Benjamin Balch," *Danvers Hist. Coll.*, VII. 86–93. They hastened to Boston, even from distant towns. Nathaniel Eells, of Stonington, Connecticut, for instance, and men from New Hampshire hurried to help. Cf. Wheeler, *History of Stonington*, p. 363. There seem to have been many neighboring ministers at Concord, some animating their men, some distributing ammunition, and some fighting. See Chase, *Beginnings of American Revolution*, III. 31, 61–62, 107.

48. Bailey, *Historical Sketches of Andover*, p. 454.

49. Details may be learned from Breed, Headley, *Centennial Papers, General Conferences of Connecticut*, etc. They served as privates, lieutenants, captains, and now and then as officers of higher rank. The Rev. John Martin fought at Bunker Hill, and Thos. Allen at Bennington. See Frothingham, *History of Charlestown*, p. 366; Sprague, I. 608–09. Quotations from Upcott, IV. 419 are to be found in Moore, *Diary of the Revolution*, I. 358: "So great is the rage of fighting among the Presbyterian preachers, that one of them has taken no less than seven different commissions, in order to excite the poor deluded men who have taken up arms, they know not why, to stand forth with an enthusiastic ardor, against their King and the constitution" (Dec. 1776). This refers to ministers of other colonies as well as to New England.

50. Chamberlain, *Documentary History of Chelsea*, II. 427.

51. Shattuck, *History of Concord*, p. 93.

arrived in 1777 that Washington needed help, he read the notice from the pulpit, stopped the service, adjourned to the green in front of the meeting-house, where a company was at once formed and the Rev. Mr. Eells made its captain.[52] The sharp-tongued John Cleaveland is said to have preached his whole parish into the army and then to have gone himself,[53] while the Rev. Thomas Allen, of Pittsfield, persuaded a whole discontented brigade in General Lincoln's army to remain in service.[54] There was many another pastor who encouraged recruiting and kept up the spirits of his people during days of suffering and discouragement. They pled for union and sacrifice and persistent effort until the war was won. "It is better to be free among the dead, than slaves among the living," said Zabdiel Adams in 1782.[55]

Besides serving as recruiting agents, chaplains, and fighters, the ministers helped in many other ways. John Murray, of Boothbay, Maine, who was peculiarly successful in preaching men into service, also carried messages for the armies while serving as chaplain, and a reward of five hundred pounds was offered by the British for his arrest.[56] Samuel Haven, of Portsmouth, the loved friend of the poor, on hearing of Lexington, sat up much of the night making bullets and soon started a manufactory of saltpeter so successful that it was noticed by "Junius" in the New Hampshire Gazette of January 9, 1776, who was opposing independence on the grounds that it could not be won and, if won, could not be maintained. In speaking of the lack of ammunition, he wrote,

I said without ammunition; but the making of Salt Petre

---

52. Baldwin, "Branford Annals," in *New Haven Colony Hist. Soc. Papers*, IV 328–29.

53. A. F. Stickney, *Mag. of Amer. Hist.*, XXVIII. 392.

54. Wm. Allen, *An Account of the Separation, . . .* , p. 68.

55. Swift, "Massachusetts Election Sermons," in *Mass. Col. Soc. Pub.*, I. 428. Among the most noted chaplains were Cotton Mather Smith, of Sharon, Conn., Nathaniel Robbins, of Milton, Mass., Peter Powers, of Haverhill, N. H., Moses Mather, of Stamford, and David Ely, of Huntingdon, Conn.

56. Greene, *Boothbay, Southport and Boothbay Harber*, p. 233.

has made such rapid progress, especially at Portsmouth, where both clergy and laity are employed six days in the week and the Seventh is seasoned with it, that I beg leave to subtract that.[57]

The learned Samuel West, of Dartmouth, raised the ire of the British by deciphering an important letter which had been written in a secret code.[58] In Connecticut, when the people, tired of Continental money, started a secret trade with the British on Long Island, the ministers determined to stop the trade and, in general, succeeded. One man is said to have been excommunicated from the church for thus selling oxen.[59]

These ministers also gave of their small salaries to help the cause of independence and union. Man after man sacrificed a part or, in some instances, all of his salary. It would perhaps have been difficult in some cases to collect the rates from a people heavily burdened, but ministers also felt the pinch of war and to remit a whole year's salary was genuine devotion. And in some cases they gave more than this. Such men were Nathaniel Taylor, of New Milford, Connecticut, Josiah Stearnes, of Epping, and James Pike, of Somersworth, New Hampshire, and the zealous David Sanford, of Medway, Massachusetts.[60] Another man of small means was the Rev. Thomas Allen, of the little frontier village of Pittsfield, yet he made large loans to the government, even selling his watch for the cause.[61]

Among those who wrote narratives of the war were David Avery, David Rowland, William Emerson, Peter Thacher, of Malden,

---

57. *State Papers, N. H.,* VIII. 26. See also Moore, *Collections, Topog. . . . , relating to N. H.,* II. 367–68.

58. *Old Dartmouth Historical Sketches,* 1903–1907, No. 7, Sept. 1904, p. 13.

59. *Centennial Papers General Conferences of Connecticut,* pp. 25–26. Authority for these statements is not given.

60. Sprague, I. 467–68; Farmer and Moore, *Hist. Coll.,* I. 259–60; Scales, *History of Strafford Co.,* p. 220; Jameson, *History of Medway,* pp. 426–27; Headley, p. 361. I have other like illustrations.

61. Wm. Allen, *An Account of the Separation, . . . ,* p. 68.

Ezra Stiles, and Thomas Allen.[62] One of Allen's letters to the Hartford Courant of September 1, 1777, described the Ticonderoga campaign, which he heartily condemned as reflecting "eternal shame and infamy upon the American Army."

An amusing bit of assistance to the patriot cause was given by the Rev. Wheeler Case, who described in rhyme Saint Clair's flight, Burgoyne's defeat, and other incidents of the war. His purpose in printing, so he said, was to help, if he might, "the glorious cause of Liberty." Like many another preacher he foresaw a great and teeming land.

> Our borders shall extend both far and wide,
> Our cords shall lengthen out on ev'ry side,
> State after State, the growing numbers rise,
> The greatest Empire this below the skies,
> In gloomy desert, e'en in distant land,
> Large cities shall be built, and churches stand.
>
> Where wolves now range and other beasts of prey,
> Where Indian tribe more savage far than they; ...
>
> Trade unconfin'd extensively shall grow
> And riches here from ev'ry nation flow.
> Our naval force, how great! our fleets abound,
> Our flocks and herds spread o'er the land around,
> Here ev'ry sort of fruit springs up and grows,
> And all the Land with milk and honey flows.[63]

---

62. Allen wrote an account of Bennington in *Connecticut Courant*, of Ticonderoga in *Hartford Courant*. Other letters of his were published and copied. See also Wm. Allen, An Account of the Separation, p. 68; Avery, *Thanksgiving Sermon*, Dec. 18, 1777, gives a glowing account of the war; Rowland, *Historical Remarks*, Providence, June 6, 1774; Swayne, *The Story of Concord*. Emerson wrote an account of the battle; Thacher wrote at request an account of Bunker Hill. Stiles helped to prepare an account of hostilities by ministry, army, navy, etc. See Letters and Papers, 1761–1776, no. 151 (M. H. S.).

63. Wheeler Case, *Poems, Occasioned By Several Circumstances and Occurrencies, In the Present grand Contest of America For Liberty* (C. H. S., no. 297).

Occasionally a minister was able to render an unusual service by giving important information to those in power. In his own estimation and in that of his biographer President Eleazar Wheelock of Dartmouth College was of signal service in sending frequent embassies to the Canadian Indians, in keeping up friendly relations with them, and in receiving and transmitting news from the northern frontier. He served as Justice of the Peace, organized the militia in Hanover, and kept in constant touch with influential friends, such as Governor Trumbull of Connecticut. His work was considered of such importance that he was given in 1776 a grant of five hundred dollars by the Continental Congress.[64]

These are but a few of the more striking instances of the activity of the New England ministers. There were many other men whose work was of equal importance, both those whose names are well-known and those of little fame. It is not possible to enumerate all their many services. Perhaps the most important from the point of view of a country at war was their unflagging interest, their support of the Union, and their confidence of success. Both in the army and in the home village they strengthened the hearts of their people and kept them often from yielding to the natural discouragement of a long war gladdened with few victories and darkened by military defeat and economic depression.

---

64. Chase, *History of Dartmouth College*, I. 87–88, 317 ff., 365; *Provincial Papers*, N. H., VII. 17, 547–48, 680; MS Letters, nos. 775378.1, 775378.3, 775478, 775408, 775578.1, 775216.2, 775217, 775220.1, 775222, 775306, 775352, 776116.1 (D. C. L.). Other clergymen gave information of importance. For examples of such service, see MS Letter of Rev. Richard Salter to William Williams (C. H. S.) and the Wheelock Papers.

Twelve

Conclusion

In the preceding chapters an attempt has been made to show one phase of the American Revolution about which little has been written. Such a study proves beyond question that the arguments used against England were not new ones; on the contrary they had a continuous history running far back into the past. They were the result of long discussions, of traditional belief, of continual reinterpretation of the Bible in the light of new philosophy; they grew out of theology and church polity, out of sharp ecclesiastical controversy as well as of more purely political theory.

For generations the ministers had kept alive the doctrines of the seventeenth century and had presented them to their people, now in one guise, now in another. Their devotion to the traditions of their ancestors, their need to defend the Hanoverian succession, their interest in keeping out the Anglican church, the custom of the election sermons, their interest in the political affairs of the colonies, all led them to study constitutional government and to relate it to the teachings of the Bible.

Out of reading and discussion, preaching and practice there had grown up a body of constitutional doctrine, very closely associated with theology and church polity, and commonly accepted by New Englanders. Most significant was the conviction that fundamental law was the basis of all rights. God ruled over men by a divine constitution. Natural and Christian rights were legal rights because a part of the law of God. The peculiar privileges of Englishmen were guaranteed by the constitution. Every part of the government was limited in power by the constitution. Any act contrary to the constitution was illegal and therefore null and void.

Probably the most fundamental principle of the American constitutional system is the principle that no one is bound to obey an unconstitutional act. The present study reveals that this doctrine was taught in fullness and taught repeatedly before 1763. The enquiry is sometimes made why the courts in America have the power of declaring laws void, why, in other words, the courts have accepted the principle that no one is bound by an unconstitutional act. No single idea was more fully stressed, no principle more often repeated, through the first sixty years of the eighteenth century, than that governments must obey law and that he who resisted one in authority who was violating that law was not himself a rebel but a protector of law.

The similarity between the political philosophy of the seventeenth century and that of the American Revolution has often been pointed out, but the lines of transmission have never been clearly traced. The teachings of the New England ministers provide one unbroken line of descent. For two generations and more New Englanders had heard their rights and the political philosophy underlying them carefully analyzed; they had been taught that these rights were sacred and came from God and that to preserve them they had a legal right of resistance and, if necessary, a right to resume the powers they had delegated and alter and abolish governments and by common consent establish new ones. Such principles had been used to define the relative power of rulers and people. They had been called upon to strengthen the hands of the colonists against over-bearing governors and councils, of church members against the tyranny of pastors, and of governing bodies, both civil and religious, against an unruly people. In such struggles, in defense of Hanoverian against Stuart, in the French and Indian war, these theories had been taken out of the field of abstraction and had become associated with cherished personal liberties and with the protection of home, church, and country. Thus they had been woven into the warp and woof of New England thought.

Perhaps the class most concerned with these theories before 1763 was the clergy. But the clergy were not a class apart. They were the fellow-students, the teachers and friends of professional and business men and the pastors and guides of less learned farmers. If Mayhew and Eliot read Locke and Sydney and found their teachings deepened and strengthened by the Bible, it is probable that they talked over their convictions with Otis and Thacher and other friends. If Jonas Clarke preached frequently on government he surely discussed it with Hancock and Adams and others who met in his hospitable home. All through the New England colonies the ministers were helping to spread the theories of the philosophers and to give them religious sanction. Thus when the trouble with England came to a head, New Englanders were accustomed to thinking and to arguing for their rights in terms of natural law, the constitution, government by consent, and the right of resistance, and believed that by so doing they were following the injunctions of God.

The significance of this background of Revolutionary thought has never been adequately appreciated. Historians have sometimes believed that these theories were exotic and were foisted upon the people by a few book-learned political leaders when the Revolutionary ferment began. A study such as this of the teachings of the ministers proves rather that a New Englander could not have helped thinking in terms of natural and fundamental law and constitutional right. Government by consent and the illegality of an unconstitutional act were to him as unquestioned as the divine law which gave them sanction. There is not a right asserted in the Declaration of Independence which had not been discussed by the New England clergy before 1763.

The motives which led so many of the New England ministers to support the American cause when the break with England came would be impossible to determine. The younger ones, graduated from college after 1763, had been educated in an atmosphere of opposition to Great Britain. They were likely to sympathize with movements of revolt and to fall in with popular tendencies. Most of the non-conformist clergymen who were Tories were old men, and yet there were young college graduates among the revolutionists. The country clergy were likely, then as now, to follow the example of the leading city ministers, to accept their decisions and to echo their words, and the Boston clergy of greatest influence were friends of the "Faction." The ministers were, as they themselves said, men and citizens, and felt the common impulses. The hard times and scarce money affected them as it did their parishioners. One very strong motive was the fear, acute after the Quebec Act of 1774, of an Episcopate and the possible loss of their own independence and prestige. They were firmly convinced that civil liberty and religious liberty were inextricably tied together. All their traditions were opposed to appointed clergy, clerical courts, etc. All their history taught them resistance to the domination of government over church. Doubtless also there were ministers whose chief desire was not to alienate their people and lose their church and income. Such waited to see which way the tide was running and were mere reflections of the word and will of their people.

Yet with all that can be said of this or that motive, there seems no doubt that one at least, and a very strong one—indeed the controlling one in many cases—was a sincere conviction of the validity of the old theories of government in which they had been brought up and in their special duty, as ministers of God, to support them against all unconstitutional attack.[1]

1. Samuel West's request to the clergy in his Massachusetts Election Sermon, 1776, to study civil government and to teach its principles to the people is typical. The article by Chauncey A. Goodrich in 1856 (Sprague, I. 509–10) on Rev. Elizur Goodrich, of Durham, Connecticut, says that the zeal of the clergy was not merely a feeling caught from their people or received from politicians, but was the result of long discussions of some years by leading ministers in social and ecclesiastical meetings. Elizur Goodrich, for example, had studied the right of resistance with President Clap, had later studied Cumberland's *Law of Nature*, Grotius, Puffendorf, etc., and grew passionate, in the pulpit only, on

The alliance of the ministers with the leaders of the agitation against England was one reason for its success. They were organized and could easily communicate with each other. They were able and zealous propagandists with a remarkable opportunity for reaching the people. All through the struggle they used every means at their disposal to present the old arguments with new force. No clever lawyer, no radical mechanic gave more warmth and color to the cause than did some of these reverend divines. With a vocabulary enriched by the Bible they made resistance and at last independence and war a holy-cause. To have won their support was, so said their enemies, the "master-stroke" of the politicians.[2]

Resistance thus become a sacred duty to a people who still were, on the whole, a religious people. The urge of restless discontent with conditions, with high taxes and hard times, the impatience of control and the independent spirit of the frontier, the travail of a nation in birth, were given legal and religious sanction. Daniel Leonard exclaimed,

> What effect must it have had upon the audience to hear the same sentiments and principles, which they had before read in a newspaper, delivered on Sundays from the sacred desk, with a religious awe, and the most solemn appeals to heaven from lips, which they had been taught from their cradle to believe could utter nothing but eternal truths![3]

It would be hard to measure the value of their service in the war. But of equal value was their help in constitution making. These ministers believed in the theories they preached and intended to see that the unique opportunity before them was not lost. That the new governments should be formed according to

---

the religious duty of resistance to Great Britain. See also Barry, *History of Massachusetts*, II. 27 5; III. 12–13.

2. *Boston News-Letter*, December 22, 1774.

3. J. Adams, *Life and Works*, IV. 55, note. For comments by Adams, see pp. 55–56; for other comments, Boston News-Letter, March 17, 1775.

right principles they were determined. The only way in which they could conceive of government set up by compact was through the calling of the constitutional convention. To define the natural rights retained by the people meant a bill of rights. To separate and limit the powers of each part of the government so that the rights of each should be exactly determined and carefully preserved meant the drawing up of a written constitution which could be changed only by the people themselves. The insistence of the ministers on these and other points seems to have had a decided influence on the course of events. A few years later, when Massachusetts was in the throes of adopting the Federal Constitution, General Lincoln wrote to Washington, "It is very fortunate for us, that the clergy are pretty generally with us. They have in this State a very great influence over the people."[4] So might the leaders of the Revolution have said not only in Massachusetts but in all the New England Colonies.

The right to life, liberty, and property has been written into our constitutions. Their meaning has changed with the years and sometimes in ways far from the thought of the men of 1776, but we can think of no government without them. The right of religious freedom is another dearly cherished right, though at times endangered. Americans reverence the written constitution, drawn up in a convention called for this purpose only, and carefully separate the powers of government. As we search for the origin of these and other fundamental constitutional doctrines and the reasons for America's devotion to them, one line of search runs back to the New England ministers who for a hundred years and more accepted and taught them with unquestioning faith and, to a religious people, gave them the sanction of divine law.

4. *Writings of Washington*, ed. Sparks, IX. 330, note.

Appendix A

Supplemental Primary Source Material

Examples of Covenants

Church Covenant

Examples of the church covenant are given in many published church and town records. Walker, *Creeds and Platforms*, also gives examples of simple and more elaborate covenants.

The Charlestown-Boston Covenant (Walker, p. 131) is as follows:

> In the Name of our Lord Jesus Christ, & in Obedience to His holy will & Divine Ordinaunce.
>
> Wee whose names are herevnder written, being by His most wise, & good Providence brought together into this part of America in the Bay of Masachusetts, & desirous to vnite our selves into one Congregation, or Church, vnder the Lord Jesus Christ our Head, in such sort as becometh all those whom He hath Redeemed, & Sanctifyed to Himselfe, do hereby solemnly, and religiously (as in His most holy Proesence) Promisse, & bind orselves, to walke in all our wayes according to the Rule of the Gospell, & in all sincere Conformity to His holy Ordinaunces, & in mutuall love, & respect each to other, so neere as God shall give us grace.

Covenant with Minister

For discussion and examples of this type of covenant as a binding contract, see *Plymouth Church Records*, 2 vols., published by New England Society, N.Y., 1920–1923, especially vol. I, pp. xxvi–xxvii; also *Records of the Town of Plymouth*, vol. I, Plymouth, 1889; *Connecticut Historical Society Collections*, II, 51–125. An example of a binding letter of acceptance is that written by the Rev. Avery Hall to the church at Rochester, New Hampshire, after they had agreed to pay him a salary of £80 (Franklin McDuffee, *History of the Town of Rochester, New Hampshire*, 2 vols., ed. and revised by Silvanus Hayward, Manchester, 1892; I. 89–90).

> To the Church of Christ in Rochester & to the Congregation in s^d Town Avery Hall sendeth Greeting. Dearly beloved in our Lord Jesus Christ.
>
> Where as in your destitute State, being deprived of a settled Gospel Minister, God in his Providence hath pointed out me, to preach ye Gospel to you, & you have made choice of me (1. as ye least of all Saints) to be your gospel Minister; to take the charge of your Souls; Seeing your Unanimity, & having implored ye divine Guidance in this important affair & being moved as I humbly trust by the Spirit of God, I think it my Duty to accept the call; & I do freely accept ye Call to ye Work of the gospel ministry among you & stand ready to be introduced into ye Sacred Office according to gospel Order in a convenient time, confiding in your Goodness that you will be ready to afford me all needful helps & Assistances, f.or my comfortable Support among you; expecting also that you allow me a suitable time for Journeying once a year to visit my Friends abroad—& now I beseech ye God of all Grace to bless us with all spiritual Blessings in heavenly things in Christ Jesus; and that ye Word of the Lord may have free Course & be glorified among us.

Town Covenant of Exeter, N.H.

   (*New Hampshire Hist. Soc. Coll.* 1st. ser., I. p. 321.)

   Whereas it hath pleased the Lord to move the heart of our dread sovereign Charles, by the grace of God, king, &c. to grant license and libertye to sundry of his subjects to plant themselves in the western parts of America. We his loyal subjects brethren of the church in Exeter, situate and lying upon the River Pascataqua, with other inhabitants there, considering with ourselves the holy will of God and our own necessity that we should not live without wholsom lawes and civil government among us, of which we are altogether destitute; do in the name of Christ and in the sight of God, combine ourselves together to erect and set up among us such government as shall be to our best discerning agreeable to the will of God, professing ourselves subjects to our sovereign lord king Charles according to the libertys of our English colony of Massachusetts, and binding of ourselves solemnly by the grace and help of Christ, and in his name and fear to submit ourselves to such godly and christian lawes as are established in the realm of England to our best knowledge, and to all other such lawes which shall upon good grounds be made and enacted among us according to God, that we may live quietly and peaceably together in all godliness and honesty. Mo. 8. D. 4, 1639, as attests our hands." Thirty-five signers, John Wheelwright the first one.

Additional Quotations

   The following quotations are given here, because sources are so scattered and difficult, therefore, for the average historical student to use.

E. Pemberton, *On the Power and Limitations of Magistrates.*
Massachusetts Election Sermon, 1710:

> The Power of the greatest Potentate on Earth is not In-
> herent in him, but is a Derivative. . . . For God is the
> Source and Original of all Power; there is no Power but
> what is derived from him, depends on him, is limited
> by him, and is subordinate to him, and accountable. . . .
> Rulers are to be the Guardians of their Peoples' Religion
> and Property, their Liberties, Civil & Sacred. . . .

God, the Lord Paramount of Heaven and Earth, governs not
by unaccountable will but by stable measures

> Hence Rulers, of all Orders, ought to conform to and
> regulate themselves in all their Administrations, by this
> Divine Standard . . . They must govern themselves by
> unalterable principles, and fixed Rules, and not by unac-
> countable humours, or arbitrary will . . . It is a Statute of
> the Great Law-giver of the World, that they which Rule
> over Men be Just . . . Rulers have Power, but it is a limited
> Authority; limited by the Will of God, and Right Rea-
> son, by the General Rules of Government, and the par-
> ticular Lawes Stated in a Land . . . Hence, this Character
> of Rulers [Gods] requires . . . That they take care that
> Righteous Laws be Enacted, none but such, and all such,
> as are necessary for the Safety of the Religion & Liber-
> ties of a People . . . Rulers must be . . . Just to the Laws
> and the Established Constitution they are under: . . .
> God Himself has called you Gods; but those that are
> not skilful, thoughtful vigilant and active to promote the
> Publick Safety and Happiness, are not Gods but dead
> Idols. . . .

Honor and reverence are due to Rulers as God's delegates:

[I]t can never go well with a People, when Government is brought into Contempt. Government has something too Divine in it to be insulted, and rudely treated.

So the seeds of faction and sedition must be carefully suppressed:

> I am not Ignorant to what an extravagant height the Doctrine of Submission to Rulers has been carry'd by some, and I wish I could see no danger of the Contrary Extream of depressing it to a meer Nullity. Extreams on both hands are to be avoided; for both are dangerous to a State. The One may Expose a People to the Oppression of Sullen Tyranny; the Other to the Confusions of Lawless Anarchy: ... Doubtless God has not left a State without a Regular Remedy to Save itself, when the Fundamental Constitution of a People is overturned; their Laws and Liberties, Religion and Properties are openly Invaded, and ready to be made a Publick Sacrifice. But on the other side it is beyond me to imagine that the God of Order has ever invested any men of a Private Station, who can with a Nodd inflame and raise the Multitude with a Lawless Power, on pretence of Public Mismanagements, to Embroyl the State, Overturn the Foundations of Government.[1]

J. Barnard, *Massachusetts Election Sermon,* **1734, pp. 23–27:**

> For where, (as in mixed Government especially,) there are peculiar Rights and Powers belonging to the Throne, and some peculiar Rights and Priviledges belonging to the People; and where, again, the Rights and Powers of

---

1. Pemberton favored the establishment of a Synod. The Connecticut Election Sermon of 1712 by John Woodward is so much like this that it seems as if he must have read Pemberton. However, he lays less weight on the dignity of rulers and more upon the good of the people.

the Throne are branched out, and divided among the several Partners in Rule, to each their proper Portion; nothing is more plain than that, Righteousness requires, that no one invade the Right that peculiarly belongs to another. . . . So that it is the first Point of Righteousness in a State, to act upon the Constitution; because every Part of the Government, . . . have as full and just Right . . . in and to that Part of Power, or to those Priviledges, which are assigned and made over to them, in the very Foundation of the Government, as any Man has, or can have, to what he calls his own; . . . the Rulers are to govern according to Law.

When the Kingdom was founded in Israel, Samuel wrote the Manner of the Kingdom in a Book, and laid it up before the Lord, . . . that it might be their Magna Charta, the fudamental [*sic!*] Constitution of the Kingdom, and the standing Rule of their Government for the future. . . . Thus it will be found, . . . an equal departure from the Rule of Righteousness, to wrest the Sword out of the Hand of him to whom the Constitution has committed it, as to snatch the Purse from those that have the keeping of it. . . . Thus Righteousness in Rulers requires them to adjust all the Parts of their Administration to the true Rights, Liberties, and Priviledges of the Subject. These are various in their Kind, and more or less, in Number, and Degree, according to the Nature of the Constitution, and are in wrought into it; . . . There is nothing a people are more tender of than These . . . . will not be persuaded easily to part with them . . . . No Sum would be tho't too much to be given for the peculiar Priviledges of some People, nor can they be defended at too dear a Rate; and therefore These ought to be preserved inviolate, . . . Hence it is the highest Point of Righteousness, in the Rulers of a People, the primary

Design of whose Institution was to secure the Community in their Rights, to be very careful to maintain entire, and untouched, those natural and civil, Liberties, and Priviledges, which are the Property of every Member of the Society. . . .

J. Eliot, Connecticut Election Sermon, 1738, p. 36:

Eliot defines the difference between a legal and a despotic government. All such as have "true Sentiments of Liberty," he asserts, "must have terrible Ideas of Arbitrary & Despotick Government" but the difference between them is not thoroughly understood.

Arbitrary Despotick Government, is, When this Sovereign Power is directed by the Passions, Ignorance & Lust of them that Rule. And a Legal Government is, When this Arbitrary & Sovereign Power puts itself under Restraints, and lays itself under Limitations, in all Instances where they see it Either possible or probable, that the Exercise of this Sovereign Power may prove or have proved Prejudicial or Mischievous to the Subject: Even this is an Act of Sovereign Power. This is what we call a Legal Limited & well Constituted Government. Under such a Government only there is true Liberty.

C. Chauncey, *Massachusetts Election Sermon*, 1747, pp. 15–16:

In speaking of the British constitution Chauncey says, "If the prerogatives of the King are sacred, so also are the rights of Lords and Commons." If either oversteps its rights or invades those of another part,

the law of righteousness is violated: . . . if one part of the government is really kept from exerting itself, according to the true meaning of the constitution, . . . the designed ballance is no longer preserved; and which side soever the scale turns, whether on the side of sovereignty, or

popularity, 'tis forced down by a false weight, which by
degrees, will overturn the government, at least, according to this particular model.

And the case is the same in dependent governments, especially where the derived constitution is divided into several ruling
parts. Here also the constitution is evidently the "grand rule to all
cloathed with power, or claiming priviledge, in either branch of the
government."

E. Williams, *A seasonable Plea* . . . 1744, pp. 2–6:

Reason teaches us that all Men are naturally equal in
Respect of Jurisdiction or Dominion one over another.
Altho true it is that Children are not born in this full
State of Equality, yet they are born to it. . . . For God
having given Man an Understanding to direct his Actions, has given him therewith a Freedom of Will and
Liberty of Acting, as properly belonging thereto, within
the Bounds of that Law he is under: . . . So that we are
born Free as we are born Rational. . . . This natural Freedom is not a Liberty for everyone to do what be pleases
without any Regard to any Law; for a rational Creature
cannot but be made under a Law from its Maker: But
it consists in a Freedom from any superior Power on
Earth, and not being under the Will or legislative Authority of Man, and having only the law of Nature (or in
other Words, of its Maker) for his Rule. . . .[2]

But because in such a State of Nature, every Man must
be Judge of the Breach of the Law of Nature and Ex-
ecutioner too (even in his own Case) and the greater
Part being no strict Observers of Equity and Justice; the

---

2. "The Rights of Magna Charta depend not on the Will of the Prince, or
the Will of the Legislature, but they are the inherent natural Rights of Englishmen; secured and confirmed they may be by the Legislature, but not derived
from nor dependent on their Will" (p. 65).

Enjoyment of Property in this State is not very safe. Three Things are wanting in this State (as the celebrated Lock observes) to render them safe; viz. an established known Law received and allowed by Common Consent . . . a known and indifferent Judge . . . a Power to back and support the Sentence when right. . . . Now to remedy these Inconveniences, Reason teaches Men to join in Society, to unite together into a Commonwealth under some Form or other, to make a Body of Laws agreeable to the Law of Nature, and institute one common Power to see them observed. . . . It is they who thus unite together, viz. the People, who make and alone have Right to make the Laws that are to take Place among them; or which comes to the same Thing appoint these who shall make them, and who shall see them Executed. . . .

Hence then the Foundation and Original of all civil Power is from the People, and is certainly instituted for their Sakes; or in other words, . . . The great End of Civil Government, is the Preservation of their Persons, their Liberties and Estates, or their Property. . . . I mean not that all civil Governments (or so called) are thus constituted: (tho' the British and some few other Nations are through a merciful Providence so happy as to have such.) 1. There are too too many arbitrary Governments in the World. . . . These are not properly speaking Governments but Tyrannies; and are absolutely against the Law of God and Nature. But I am considering Things as they be in their own Nature, what Reason teaches concerning them.

Arguments Concerning the Stamp Act

The Rev. Ebenezer Devotion not only preached against the Stamp Act but also issued in 1766 a pamphlet in answer to one from London.[3] This was a terse, sharp reply, extreme in sentiment

---

3. E. Devotion, *The Examiner Examined*, 1766.

and hinting at disunion. Answering the claim that Parliament had jurisdiction over the colonies in all cases whatsoever, Devotion said that were it true it would involve the slavery of millions.[4] He argued that by their charters the colonial assemblies had the right of taxation and that ten thousand violations of it could not abridge the right.[5] In annulling these rights, Parliament had been guilty of a breach of faith. "What but compact," he said, "annexes the colonies to the british empire, rather than to the states of Holland?" He ridiculed the arguments of early discovery. If one part of these contracts is annulled, the whole is destroyed. Men who claim the contrary "cut the hand of union, and would maim the british empire."[6] If England must control the colonies for their protection, certainly she could well do so merely for the sake of the trade. France, Holland or Spain would surely be glad to offer protection for such trade. Such an argument must lead eventually to the loss of the colonies to the empire.[7]

A meeting was held in Lyme, Connecticut, on the second Tuesday of January, and its resolves were sent to the New London Gazette and published in other papers. This meeting followed the December sermon of Stephen Johnson and shows great similarity of argument.

> 1. That we have an inviolable Right by the God of Nature; as well as by the English Constitution, (and is unalienable even by ourselves) to those Privileges and Immunities which by the Execution of the Stamp Act we shall be forever stript and deprived.

> 2. That we are unalterably fixt to defend our aforesaid Rights and Immunities by every lawful Way and Means, against every unjust Attack.

---

4. *Ibid.*, pp. 3–7. "The subjects of the most absolute despotick prince upon the globe, are not more finish'd slaves."

5. *Ibid.*; also pp. 7–10, 15–17.

6. *Ibid.*, pp. 13–14.

7. *Ibid.*, pp. 23–24.

3. That our Aversion and Threats to any Person in public Character, or others in the Colony, is and shall be on Account and according as they are more or less engaged and active, directly, or indirectly, to carry into Execution the detestable and oppressive Stamp Act, which would be an indelible Stain to England's Glory, and perpetual Chains to American Liberty. . . .

7. That whereas we conceive the general Safety and Privileges of all the Colonies to depend on a firm Union in the support of the British Constitution, we therefore do Declare we will do our utmost to resist all such Enemies to His Majesty and the British Constitution as shall attempt to disposses the Colonies of their most sacred Rights, and will be ready on all Occasions to assist our Fellow Subjects in the neighboring Provinces to repel all violent Attempts which may be made to subvert their & our Liberties.[8]

D. S. Rowland, Thanksgiving Sermon, Providence, 1766:

Taxed at a time when they were fatigued and financially exhausted by a long war, they naturally wished to question its equity and when it appeared contrary to the principles of the English Constitution their zeal was aroused to prevent the blow.

It is certain we are free born, and that this our native freedom, cannot be alienated but by conquest, or voluntary consent. . . . As this is our native right, antecedent to any politic system, so it is the criterion and glory of every state, founded on just and reasonable principles. . . . It is our happiness under English government to enjoy whatever we have a natural right to. . . . (p. 27).

He urged loyalty to King and Parliament "wherever it doth

---

8. *Conn. Courant,* Jan. 27, 1766. *Letter* on Jan. 23, 1766 in the supplement.

not evidently infringe its fundamental principles," and declared one advantage of the trouble to be a better understanding of their essential connection and dependence and the nature of their rights and their ability to defend them. (pp. 25, 30).

Arguments, 1774–1781

Letters by Reverend John Cleaveland to *Essex Gazette*, April 18 and 25, 1775, showing his reaction to Lexington and Concord and his inflamatory attack on Tories:

> To the Inhabitants of New England, Greeting. Men, Brethren and Fathers:
>
> Is the time come, the fatal era commenced, for you to be deemed rebels, by the Parliament of Great Britain? Rebels! Wherein? Why, for asserting that the rights of men, the rights of Englishmen belong to us. . . . But subdue us to a subjection unto the supreme legislation and taxation authority of the British Parliament over the Colonies without their consent, they will not, they shall not! . . . Great Britain, adieu! No longer shall we honor you as our mother; you are become cruel; you have not so much bowels as the sea monsters towards their young ones . . . by this stroke you have broken us off from you, and effectually alienated us from you. . . . O Britain ! see you to your own house.
>
> King George the Third, adieu! No more shall we cry to you for protection. . . . Your breach of covenant; your violation of faith; . . . have dissolved our allegiance to your Crown and Government. . . . O George! see thou to thine own house. . . .
>
> O my dear New England, hear thou the alarm of war! The call of Heaven is to arms! to arms! . . . Behold what all New England must expect to feel, if we don't cut off and make a final end of those British sons of violence,

and of every base Tory among us, or confine the latter to Simsbury mines. . . .

We are, my brethren, in a good cause; and if God be for us, we need not fear what man can do. . . .

O thou righteous Judge of all the earth, awake for our help. Amen and Amen.

A circular letter issued by "College Party," Jan. 30, 1777, signed "Republican" (Chase, *History of Dartmouth College*, I. 431 ff.[9])

We have set out to defend the rights of human nature against invasions from abroad; but what is our condition in the mean time at home? A bare conquest over one enemy is not enough; and nothing short of a form of government fixed on genuine principles can preserve our liberties inviolate. . . . Believe me, my Countrymen, if we do not settle our affair at home as to the principles of free government while we are settling them abroad, it will finally be too late. . . . We have doubtless among us tyrants enough at heart, though not unalterable in power. And if we follow the advice of puny patriots, we shall exchange the gallows for fagots. . . . It is observed by Mr. Burgh, in his Disquisitions, that a time of danger is the most favorable to correct abuses in a civil state. Apply that thought to the present case. Examine every corruption, and especially of that fundamental principle, the mode of representation. lstly. Has each incorporated town any distinct powers? 2dly. Is each incorporated town vested with any legislative privileges? If so, then let it have an independent weight in the legislature of the State, as far as the said distinct privileges may intitle. 3rdly. Has one incorporated town as much power

9. Chase, I. 431, note, says that there is only one copy in existence; it is in the writing of John Wheelock, but the "style indicates a different author."

in itself as another? Then it may claim the same weight in government. 4thly. Does every State, small as well as large have equal weight in the American Congress? If so then every town incorporate has the same right in the assemblies of each State. In short, a political body that superintends a number of smaller political bodies ought necessarily to be composed by them, without any regard to individuals.

We proceed to observe that the declaration of independency made the antecedent form of government to be of necessity null and void; and by that act the people of the different colonies slid back into a state of nature, and in that condition they were to begin anew. But has it been so in the government of New Hampshire? I ask how shall we know that independency has been proclaimed, if we only consult the civil oeconomy of this state? ... I ask again, what advantage independency has been of to this government, since it had the same legislature before as after the declaration? Think on these matters: and though it is now late, yet that very consideration proves the necessity of dissolving soon the present unconstitutional legislature and planting the seed anew.

But if it be still asserted that the legislative constitution is founded on independency, it will prove, if anything, that this very constitution established independency itself, before it was proclaimed by the congress. All power originates from the people. A state of independency before a plan of government is formed, supposes the whole right to be vested in them who by a full representation are to rear a new fabric. But it has not been so in the present case; for this very assembly, which was in being before the declaration of independency, has dictated the regulations, that took place afterwards. The grossest absurdity, which will appear in one word [is], viz., the legislature over the people before independence was unconstitutional, and deprived them of their rights, yet this very unconstitutional legislature has marked out their liberties for them in the state of independency. As much as to say, an unconstitutional body have made a constitutional one. Wauld to God that you might carefully weigh these matters, and that every one would measure them by the feelings in his own mind.

The paper then discusses the question of expense to small towns if each has its representative and says such an argument is absurd. "It is no fantom, but on this very point the foundation of your liberties stand." It urges no yielding in right of each incorporated town to a representative and in demanding a convention called to "fix on a new plan of government, which can be the only proper seal of your concurrence in independency."

Jonas Clark, Massachusetts Election Sermon of 1781 (Hudson, *History of Lexington*, pp. 339–341):

'Tis not indeed pretended that any one man or number of men have any natural right or superiority, or inherent claim of dominion or governmental authority over any other man or body of men. All men are by nature free and equal and independent in this matter. It is in compact, and in compact alone, that all just government is founded. The first steps in entering into society, and towards the establishment of civil government among a people, is the forming, agreeing to, and ratifying an original compact for the regulation of the state-describing and determining the mode, departments, and powers of the government, and the rights, privileges and duties of the subjects.

This must be done by the whole body of the people, or by leaders or delegates of their choice. This right of the people, whether emerging from a state of nature, or the yoke of oppression, is an unalienable right. It cannot be disposed of or given up by a people, even though ever so much inclined to sell or sacrifice their birthright in this matter.

> While the social compact exists, the whole state and its members are bound by it; and a sacred regard ought to be paid to it. No man, party, order, or body of men in the state have any right, power, or authority to alter, change, or violate the social compact. Nor can any change, amendment, or alteration be introduced but by common consent. It remains, however, with the community, state or nation, as a public, political body, at any time, at pleasure, to change, alter, or totally dissolve the constitution, and return to a state of nature, or to form a new government as to them may seem meet. These principles being admitted, it is evident that no man or body of men, however great or good—no nation, kingdom or power on earth, hath any right to make or impose a constitution of government upon a free people.
>
> Equality and independence are the just claim—the indefeasible birthright of men. In a state of nature, as individuals, in society, as states or nations, nothing short of these ever did or ever will satisfy a man or a people truly free—truly brave. When opportunity offers, and power is given, it is beyond dispute the duty of the subjected nation to assert its liberty; to shake off the foreign yoke, and maintain its equality and independence among the nations.
>
> The principles of reason, the laws of nature, and the rules of justice and equity, give men a right to select their form of government. Even God himself, the supreme ruler of the world, whose government is absolute and uncontrollable, hath ever paid a sacred attention to this

important right—hath ever patronized this interesting claim in the sons of men. The only constitution of civil government that can plead its origin as direct from heaven, is the theocracy of the Hebrews; but even this form of government, though dictated by infinite wisdom, and written by the finger of God, was laid before the people for their consideration, and was ratified, introduced, and established by common consent.

Gad Hitchcock, *Massachusetts Election Sermon*, 1774, pp. 46–47:

> Our danger is not visionary, but real—Our contention is not about trifles, but about liberty and property; and not ours only, but those of posterity, to the latest generation. . . . For however some few . . . . even from among ourselves, appear sufficiently disposed to ridicule the rights of America, and the liberties of subjects, 'tis plain St. Paul, who was a good judge, had a very different sense of them—He was on all occasions for standing fast not only in the liberties with which Christ had made him free . . . but also in that liberty, with which the laws of nature, and the Roman state, had made him free from oppression and tyranny.

S. West, *Massachusetts Election Sermon*, 1776, p. 51:

> They are robbing us of the inalienable rights that the God of nature has given us . . . and has confirmed to us in his written words. . . ." (p. 12)

> [T]yranny and arbitrary power are utterly inconsistent with, and subversive of the very end and design of civil government, and directly contrary to natural law, which is the true foundation of civil government and all politick law; Consequently the authority of a tyrant is of itself null and void.

J. Lathrop, *Artillery Sermon*, 1774, p. 15:

> [The] original compacts . . . which lie in the founda-
> tion of all civil societies, may not be disturbed. A single
> article may not be altered but with the consent of the
> whole body. Whoever makes an alteration in the estab-
> lished constitution, whether he be a subject or a ruler,
> is guilty of treason. Treason of the worst kind: Treason
> against the state. . . . That we may and ought, to resist,
> and even make war against those rulers who leap the
> bounds prescribed them by the constitution, and at-
> tempt to oppress and enslave the subjects, is a principle
> on which alone the great revolutions which have taken
> place in our nation can be justified. A principle which
> has been supported by the most celebrated Divines as
> well as civilians.

Note. "Luther, Calvin, Melancthon, Zuinglius, . . . and the reformers in general" (pp. 23–24).

Elisha Fish, *A Discourse at Worcester*, 1775, pp. 13–14:

> The covenant between prince and people most naturally
> represents the covenant between God and his creatures.
> God creates his people, therefore they are bound to a
> sacred regard of the covenant of their creator: But the
> people in a political sense create the prince; therefore
> this covenant should be maintained with the greatest re-
> gard of any social covenant of a civil nature on earth, and
> the breach of this covenant is greater on the side of the
> Prince than the people, for it is against the whole body.
> . . . If the prince sin against the subjects, it is against his
> political creators, and in that view highly aggrivated.

Appendix B

Clergymen on Town Committees and in Provincial Congresses and Conventions[1]

New Hampshire

John Adams, Durham.

Committee to send help to Boston. Letter written by him, perhaps with assistance of Major John Sullivan, who was also on Committee. (Stackpole, *Hist. of N. H.,* II, pp. 70–71.)

Benj. Bridgham, Fitzwilliam.

Only delegate to Fourth Prov. Congress. (*Prov. Papers,* VII, p. 470.)

Jacob Emery, Pembroke.

Chosen Nov. 26, 1776 delegate to state convention at Exeter to consider state of country. Chairman of Com. to prepare proclamation for day of fasting and prayer (Carter & Fowler, *Hist. of Pembroke,* pp. 110, 111, 269).

Repres. in. Legis., Dec. 1776. (p. 269).

Stephen Farrar, New Ipswich.

Only delegate from town to Fourth Prov. Cong. (*Prov. Papers,*

---

1. The following lists are very incomplete. Those men concerned with constitutional questions are starred. Some of same may have been members of constitutional conventions, but the title Rev. is not given in partial lists preserved. Some of the names are the same. I have added some who were in the conventions to ratify the Federal Constitution merely to show that their interest and influence in constitutional questions continued. Abbreviations have been used where the meaning is clear.

VII. 470.) On com. to prepare plan for ways and means of furnishing troops. Three clergymen on this com. with several laymen (p. 474).

Com. to prepare letter to Continental Congress (p. 480).

Com. to make draft empowering Com. of Pub. Safety and Com. of Supplies to act in recess of Congress and to recommend Commissary (p. 484.)

"Chosen to meet with deputies from town to choose delegates to represent the province in a Continental Congress at Phila." (*N. H. Hist. Soc. Coll.,* V. 15.)

Elijah Fletcher, Hopkinston.

Only delegate to Fourth Prov. Cong. (*Prov. Papers,* VII, p. 470.)

Com. to prepare draft to be sent to towns concerning Tories (p. 474).

Com. to draw up recommendations to save rags for use of. army (p. 535).

Com. to consider sum of money to be issued and plans for its emission (pp. 638–639).

Abiel Foster, Canterbury.

One of two delegates to Fourth Prov. Cong. (*Prov. Papers,* VII. 470.).

*Edward Goddard, Swanzey.

Delegate to Canst. Conv. 1781 (Read, *Hist. of Swanzey,* p. 872).

*Aaron Hall, Keene.

Only delegate to Canst. Conv. 1788 (*ibid.*).

*Wm. Hooper, Madbury.

Only delegate to Canst. Conv. 1788 (*ibid.*).

*Samuel Langdon, Hampton Falls and Seabrook.

Only delegate to Canst. Conv. 1788 (*ibid.*).

*Amos Moody, Pelham.

Only delegate to Canst. Conv. 1788 (*ibid.*).

John Page, Hawke.

Only delegate to Fourth Prov. Cong. (*Prov. Papers,* VII. 668).

James Pike, Somersworth.

Said to be "common scrivener for the whole parish . . . . Hardly a legal document during that period was made out in any other handwriting than his own" (Scales, *Hist. of Strafford Co.*, p. 220).

Jonathan Searle, Mason.

Member and Clerk of Hillsborough County Congress, May, 1775, held at Amherst, N. H.

On Com. of this County Congress to "act on any affairs that may come before them or any score of them to be a Corram to act till further orders" (*Prov. Papers*, VII. 449–50).

Com. of Public Safety; its duty was to keep the county from "declining into a state of Nature"; it was for a time the only local government (Boylston, *Hist. Sketch of Hillsborough County Congress*, p. 19).

Josiah Stearnes, Epping.

Member First Prov. Cong. (Farmer and Moore, *Hist. Coll.*, One of two delegates sent by town to Fourth Prov. Cong., meeting May 17, 1775 (*Prov. Papers*, VII. 469).

Com. to draw up rules (p. 471).

Com. to plan for ways and means of furnishing troops (p. 474).

Com. to make a Draught of a letter in answer to one from Congress of Mass. Bay to one to Continental Cong. On this Committee two clergymen and one layman (p. 478).

Com. to make draft empowering Com. of Public Safety and Com. of Supplies to act in recess of Congress and to recommend Commissary (p. 484).

Com. to draw up resolves for taking up deserters (p. 535).

*Benj. Thurston, North Hampton.

Only delegate to Canst. Conv. 1788 (State Papers N. H., X, 2–7).

Timothy Upsham, Deerfield.

Only delegate from town to Fourth Prov. Cong. (*Prov. Papers*, VII. 470).

Timothy Walker, Concord.

Member of First Prov. Cong. (Moore, Collections, Topog . . . . of N.H., p. 238).

Member of Third Prov. Cong., meeting Exeter, Apr. 1775. (*Prov. Papers*, VII. 454).

*Timothy Walker, Jr., Concord.

Licensed to preach; preaching occasionally in various towns, but not settled. Was frequently town clerk, selectman. Delegate to Provincial Congresses.

On Com. June 11, 1776 to make draught of Declaration of Independence to be transmitted to Delegates in Congress.

Member of Com. of Safety (Bouton, *Hist. of Concord*, pp. 267, 269).

Member of Council, 1777–1780 (Lyford, *Hist. of Concord*, I, 256, II, 1360) .

Samuel Webster, Temple.

Only delegate to Fourth Prov. Cong. (*Prov. Papers* VII, 470).

Com. to draw up rules (p. 471).

Com. to prepare plans for wa.ys & means of furnishing troops (p. 474).

Com. to make draft of letters to Cong. of Mass. Bay and to Cont. Cong. (p. 478).

Com. of Public Safety (p. 543).

Com. to bring in plan to regulate militia of colony (p. 546).

Com. to make draft for establishing & encouraging manufac tures (p. 548).

Eleazar Wheelock, Pres. of Dartmouth.

Served as Justice of Peace, 1773 (*Prov. Papers*, VII. 17).

Report of Com. of Safety of Hanover and Lebanon, of Jan. 2, 1775 in his handwriting (MS. Papers, Dartmouth College, no. 776102).

Paine Wingate, Hampton Falls.

One of two delegates to Fourth Prov. Cong., May 17, 1775, (*Prov. Papers*, VII. 476).

On Com. to prepare draft to be sent to towns concerning Tories. Two ministers and one layman on Com. (p. 474).

*Joseph Woodman, Sanbornton.

Com. chosen by town to draw up suggested amendments to

Constitution, 1782 (Runnels, *Hist. of Sanbornton*, p. 133).

Massachusetts[2]

*Jedediah Adams, Stoughton.

Delegate to Const. Conv. 1779 (*Journal of Convention*).

*Noah Alden, Bellingham.

Delegate to Const. Conv. 1779 (*ibid.*).

*Thomas Allen, Pittsfield.

Chairman of Committee of Correspondence. (Smith, *Hist. of Pittsfield*, pp. 190, 199, 215 note).

Com. of Instructions to delegate to Const. Conv. 1779, very remarkable paper (*ibid.*, pp. 365–67).

Drafted county memorial 1774 (*ibid.*, p. 193 and note).

Wrote petition to Legislature concerning a constitution, 1775 (*ibid.*, p. 343).

Wrote petition to legislature concerning constitution and posi tion of Berkshire towns, 1776 (pp. 351–355).

Wrote original draft of instruction to representatives, 1777 (*ibid.*, pp. 363–4).

Wrote address to judges adopted by county convention (364– 365). Also on Com. 1768 "to examine the Boston letter to the selectmen" (*ibid.*, p. 183).

*Ebenezer Chaplin, Sutton.

Delegate to Canst. Conv. 1779 (*Journal of Convention*).

Chas. Chauncey, Boston.

Com. to consider and report declaration "to be made by this town to Gr. Britain & all the World," 1774 (*Boston Town Records*, 1770–1777, p. 183).

*Jonas Clark, Lexington.

Delegate to Mass. Const. Conv. 1779 (Hudson, p. 409, and *Journal of Convention*).

On town Committee to consider Const. 1779–1780 (Hudson,

---

2. Committees of the Constitutional Convention of 1779–80 on which clergy served are too numerous to give. See Journal of the Convention.

Hist. of Lexington, pp. 409, 262–64). Drew up reasons for opposition.

Probably helped many town committees because all instructions to Repres. 1762–1776 were drawn up by him; also many of later date (*Proceedings, Commemorative of Two Hundredth Anniversary,* pp. 18–20; Hudson, *Hist. of Lexington,* pp. 87– 88, 342; Sprague, I, 517–18).

(I do not find his name on other committees in town records).

Benj. Conklin, Leicester.

Com. of Correspondence (Washburn, *Hist. Sketches of Leicester,* p. 94).

Member of a "patriotic convention." Probably on other committees.

*Henry Cummings, Billerica.

Com. of town 1775, to "draw up proper vote to present to the town" concerning drawing up of form of Government (Hazen, *Hist. of Billerica,* pp. 238–239).

Delegate to Const. Conv. 1779 (*ibid.,* also p. 262; Sprague, VIII, 57; *Journal of Convention*).

Resolution of town meeting, 1773, said to have been directed by him, as were many others (Hazen, pp. 227–28, 262).

*Nathan Davis, Dracut.

Delegate to Const. Conv. 1780 (*Journal of Convention,* p. 171).

*Elisha Fisk, Upton.

Should be Fish, so given in *Boston Gazette,* Sept. 6, 1779.

Delegate to Const. Conv. 1779 (*ibid.*).

*Jonathan French, Andover.

Com. chosen 1780 to join with members of Const. Conv. "to make such remarks and amendments in the Form of the Constitution as they shall think proper" (Bailey, *Hist. Sketches of Andover,* p. 356).

"an active participant in town affairs" (*ibid.,* p. 453). Very probably on other committees.

*Jason Haven, Dedham.

Delegate to Const. Conv. 1779 (Mann, *Hist. Annals of Dedham,*

p. 35; *Journal of Convention*).

Moses Hemmingway, Wells, Me.

Is said to have drawn resol. sent by town committee to Com. of Corres. in Boston. 1774 (Bourne, *Hist. of Wells and Kennebunk*, p. 465).

***Increase Hewins, West Stockbridge.**

Probably delegate to Const. Conv. 1779 (*Journal of Convention*). Is called Captain in list, but was the only Hewins and Rev. Mr. Hewins prayed while clerical members were praying in turn.

***Gad Hitchcock, Pembroke.**

Delegate to Const. Conv. 1779 (Sprague, VIII, 29; *Journal of Convention*).

Daniel Hopkins, Salem.

Delegate to Prov. Cong., 1775. Member of Council, 1778 (Sprague, I, 582).

James Lyon, Machias, Me.

Chairman of Committee of Correspondence (Frederic Kidder, *Military Operations in Eastern Maine and Nova Scotia during the Revolution*, Albany, 1867. Chiefly from orig. documents). Was very ardent.

Samuel Mather, Boston.

On same com. as Chas. Chauncey (see above). Moses Morrill, Biddeford, Me.

Said to have been very influential in town affairs; probably on committees, but no details given (Folsom, *Hist. of Sacco and Biddeford*, pp. 279–80).

John Murray, Boothbay, Me.

Delegate to Prov. Cong. 1775 (*Greene, Boothbay, Southport and Boothbay*, p. 233).

***Phillips Payson, Chelsea.**

Town Com. of Corres. 1775 (Chamberlain, *Documentary Hist. of Chelsea*, II, 683).

Com. May 1780 to consider Canst. and make remarks (*ibid.*, pp. 546, 684).

Delegate to Gen'l Court, 1783 (*ibid.*, pp. 304, 686). Elected 1784 but declined.

Delegate to Canst. Conv. 1787 (*ibid.*, p. 687).

Com. 1783 to address town of Boston on subject of a reunion (*ibid.*, p. 686); on committees of later date.

*Valentine Rathbun, Pittsfield.

Delegate to various county congresses over which he presided (Smith, *Hist. of Pittsfield*, p. 178).

Repres. to Legis. 1777 and several other times (*ibid.*, pp. 178, 356).

Delegate to convocation of Berkshire towns to consider grievances, 1777 (*ibid.*, p. 362).

Com. of Instruction to delegates to Const. Conv. 1779 (*ibid.*, p. 365).

*Joseph Roberts, Weston, not settled.

Com. for enlisting soldiers.

Delegate to Const. Conv. 1779 (Washburn, *Hist. Sketches of Town of Leicester*, p. 92).

Later, repres. to Gen'l Court.

Active in Leicester until 1762, then Weston. Joseph Roby, Lyme.

Com. of Public Safety, 1775 (Lewis and Newhall, *Hist. of Lyme*, I. 340).

*David Sanford, Medway.

Is said to have mingled with assemblies of people and to have taken "leading part in every measure adopted for a vigorous defence against the encroachments of Gt. Britain" (Headley, p. 361).

Probably on committees.

Delegate to Canst. Conv. 1779 (*Journal of Convention*, pp. 8–19, 40).

Zedekiah Sanger, Duxbury.

Repres. to Gen'l Court, 1784 and 1787 (Bradford, *Biog. Notices*, p. 78).

*Daniel Shute, Hingham.

Delegate to Const. Conv. 1779 (Sprague, VIII. 20; *Hist. of Town of Hingham*, I, pt. II, pp. 44–45; *Journal of Convention*).

Delegate to Convention to ratify Federal Constitution 1788 (Sprague, VIII. 20; *Hist. of Hingham,* I, pt. II, pp. 44–45).

Is said to have "used an active influence in forming and guiding public opinion" (*Hist. of Hingham,* I, pt. II, pp. 44–45).

*Wm. Symmes, Andover.

On Com. 1780 with Jonathan French (see above).

*Peter Thacher, Attleboro.

Com. to draw up instructions to delegate, May, 1776 (Daggett, *Sketch of Hist. of Attleborough,* p. 122). Com. to instruct delegate, 1777 (p. 124).

Com. 1778 to discuss Art. of Confederation and instruct delegate (pp. 124–25).

Com. to consider Const. of 1778–1779, 1780 (p. 126).

*Peter Thacher, Malden.

Com. of towp. to draw up instructions to delegate, 1774 (Corey, *Hist. of Malden,* p. 738).

Com. 1774 to see that Commission officers muster inhabitants, etc. (p. 739).

Com. 1774, to prepare agreement respecting obedience to officers to be signed by Alarm and training lists (p. 740).

Com. 1774 to care for money collected for Boston (p. 741).

Com. of Correspondence and Safety, 1775–1776 (p. 730). Probably wrote instructions to delegates, May 27, 1776 (pp. 762–65).

Also much to do with long series of town papers (pp. 721 ff.).

Delegate to Prov. Congress and chosen to write account of Bunker Hill, 1775 (Loring. *Hundred Boston Orators,* p. 125).

Delegate to Const. Conv., 1779–1780 (Corey, pp. 671–72, 780–81; *Journal of Convention;* Loring, p. 125; Sprague, I. 721). Also on other less important committees (Corey, pp. 749, 759).

*Thos. Thacher, Dedham.

Delegate to Const. Conv. 1787–1788 (Mann, *Hist. Annals of Dedham,* p. 37).

John Treadwell, Lyme.

> Com. of Public Safety, 1775 (Lewis and Newhall, *Hist. of Lyme*, I. 340). Com. composed of two ministers of town and one deacon; was "foremost in all the proceedings of town during the Revolution"; probably on many other committees.

*Chas. Turner, Scituate.

> Had been pastor in Duxbury till 1775, then lived in Scituate; not settled. Delegate to Const. Conv., 1779–1780 (Winsor, *Hist. of Duxbury*, pp. 203–204).
>
> Also member of Gen'l Court, 1776; later of Senate (Bradford, *Biog. Notices of Distinguished Men*, p. 403).

*Habijah Weld, Attleborough.

> Town Com. 1778–1779 to consider Const. (Daggett, *Hist. of Attleborough*, p. 126).
>
> Delegate to Conv. to act upon Federal Const. (*ibid.*).

*Samuel West, Dartmouth.

> Delegate to Const. Conv. 1779 (*Journal of Convention*).
>
> Delegate to Convention ratifying' Fed. Const. 1788; influential in both (Sprague, VIII. 40).

*Samuel West, Needham.

> Com. chosen by town in 1780 to consider Const. (Clark, *Hist. of Needham*, p. 168).

*Joseph Willard, Beverly.

> Com. to report on Canst. of 1778 (Stone, *Hist of Beverly*, p. 68).
>
> Com. to draft instructions to delegate giving reason for dissent (*ibid.*).
>
> Com. 1780 to report on Canst. (Thayer, *Address in Beverly*, p. 54).
>
> Is said to have been frequently on committees of town and constantly in consultation with leading citizens.

Elhanan Winchester, Brookline.

> Repres. to Mass. Legis. 1778 (Bolton, *Hist. of Brookline*, p. 248).

Connecticut[3]

Parke Avery, Groton.

Com. of Inspection, 1775 (C. R. Stark, *Groton, Conn.*, pp. 86, 161. 246).

Mem. of Assembly, 1776 (probably the same man). A Baptist.

Ebenezer Devotion, Windham.

Delegate to Gen'l. Assembly, 1765 (Larned, *Hist. of Windham Co.*, II. 54; *Cent. Papers, Gen'l. Conf. Conn.*, p. 69).

Com. of Corres. and various other com. (Probably the same man, may have been his son; *Windham Revol. Records*, pp. 7 ff.).

Elizur Goodrich, Durham.

Had more than 1000 votes from region round about for Governor (Sprague, I. 510).

No details about committees, but very active in neighborhood.

Mark Leavenworth, Waterbury.

Com. app't. by General Assembly to arouse people to "use and exert themselves with the greatest expedition" to reenforce continental army *Cent. Papers, Gen'l. Conf. Conn.*, p. 69).

State Com. for raising troops (*ibid.*).

Samuel Newel, Farmington.

Com. to consider regulations of 15th of March, 1777, and report opinion (Farmington, *Revol. Records*, p. 7). Timothy Pitkin, Farmington.

On same committee as Newel (*ibid.*).

---

3. The few towns and county histories which have been read show that many ministers were very zealous in guiding town affairs, but give no details. Copies of town records in Conn. State Library do not give ministers as members of committees, unless names are given without tiie prefix Rev. In some towns there probably was a layman of the same name as the minister.

Bibliography

Abbreviations

A.A.S.	American Antiquarian Society
B.P.L.	Boston Public Library
C.H.S.	Connecticut Historical Society
C.S.L.	Connecticut State Library
D.C.L.	Dartmouth College Library
J.C.B.L.	John Carter Brown Library
M.H.S.	Massachusetts Historical Society
M.S.L.	Massachusetts State Library
N.L.	Newberry Library
N.H.H.S.	New Hampshire Historical Society
N.Y.P.L.	New York Public Library
Y.C.L.	Yale College Library

Manuscripts

Andrews and Eliot Letters, 1662–1811. M. H. S.

Cole, Nathan. Ye Spiritual travels of Nathan Cole &c. C. H. S. Colman Papers, 2 vols. M. H. S.

Ecclesiastical Papers, vols. XI, XII. M. S. L. Ecclesiastical Papers, vols. VII, VIII, X, XV. C. S. L.

Extracts from Conn. Town Revol. Records, 1774–1784, vols. 1–63. C.S.L. Hollis Papers, 1759–1771. M. H. S.

Letter of Rev. Dr. Richard Salter to William Williams, Jan. 18, 1776. C.H.S.

Letter of Rev. Samuel Cooper to Benjamin Franklin, June 1, 1778.

Franklin Papers, Univ. of Pa. Library. Letters and Papers, 1761–1776. M. H. S. Lexington Town Records.

Oliver, Peter. The Origin & Progress of the American Rebellion to the year 1776 in a letter to a Friend, F. L. Gay Transcripts. M. H. S.

Separate Papers, vol. I, 1733–1772. C. H. S.
Smith, Rev. Hezekiah, Diary, Aug. 1773–April, 1778. M. H. S.
State Papers, Vermont Controversy, 1764–1791. N. H. H. S.
Weare Papers, vol. IV. N.H. H. S.
Wheelock Papers and other MSS. D. C. L.

Newpapers

The Boston Chronicle, Dec. 21, 1767–June 25, 1770. M. H. S.
The Boston Gazette, 1772–1774, 1778–1780. M. H. S.
Boston Post Boy, 1774. M. H. S.
Boston Tifleekly News-Letter, 1740–1741. M. H. S.
Connecticut Courant, 1766. C. H. S.
Essex Gazette, 1770–1775; after 1775, *Independent Chronicle*. M. H. S.
Hartford Courant, 1777. A. A. S.
New London Gazette, Sept.–Dec. 1765. Y. C. L.
Massachusetts Gazette & Boston News-Letter, 1740–1742, 1765–1774, 1775–Feb. 1776. M. H. S.
Massachusetts Spy or American Oracle of Liberty, pub. at Worcester 1775–1780. M. H. S.

Printed Sources

Sermons: Collections

MOORE, FRANK, ed. *The Patriot Preachers of the American Revolution, with Biographical Sketches.* N.Y., 1862. N. L. Sermons by Jonathan Mayhew, Samuel Langdon, Jacob Duche, Wm. Smith, John Zubly, Wm. Gordon, Nath. Whitaker, Oliver Hart, Samuel Stillman, John Rodgers, Geo. Duffield.

THORNTON, J. W. *The Pulpit of the American Revolution.* Boston, 1850. Sermons by Mayhew, 1750; Chas. Chauncey, 1766; Samuel Cooke, 1770; Wm. Gordon, 1774; Samuel Langdon, 1775; Samuel West, 1776; Phillips Payson, 1778; Simeon Howard, 1780; Ezra Stiles, 1783.

Convention Sermons

APPLETON, NATHANIEL. *Faithful Minister of Christ.* Boston, 1743. N. L.

BALCH, WM. *Simplicity and godly Sincerity, in a Christian Minister, the sure Way to Happiness.* Boston, 1760. N. L.

BARNARD, JOHN. *The Lord Jesus Christ the only, and Supream Head of the Church.* Boston, 1738. N. L.

BELLAMY, JOSEPH. *The Law, our Schoolmaster.* Preached before the Association of Litchfield Co., Conn., 1756. New Haven. Y.C.L.

CHAUNCEY, CHAS. *Minister cautioned against the Occasion of Contempt.* Boston, 1744. N. L.

CLARK, PETER. *The Advantages and Obligations arising from the Oracles of God committed to the Church and its Ministry.* Boston, 1745. N. L.

GAY, EBENEZER. *The True Spirit of a Gospel Minister represented and urged.* Boston, 1746. N. L.

HOLYOKE, EDWARD. *The Duty of Ministers of the Gospel to guard against the Pharasaism and Sadducism of the Present Day.* Boston, 1741. N. L.

LOCKE, SAMUEL. *A Sermon Preached before the Ministers of the Province of the Massachusetts-Bay.* Boston, 1772. N. L.

RAND, WM. *Gospel Ministers should be chiefly concerned to please God, and not Men, in the discharge of their Office.* Boston, 1757. N. L.

STILES, EZRA. *A Discourse on the Christian Union, the substance of which was delivered before the Reverend Convention of the Congregational Clergy in the Colony of Rhode Island.* April 23, 1760. Brookfield, Mass., 1799. 1st. ed., Boston, 1761.

TOWNSEND, SOLOMON. *Convention Sermon,* 1771. Newport.

ROWLAND, D. S. *Catholicism.* Providence, 1772.

TUCKER, JOHN. *Ministers considered as Fellow-workers, who should be Comforters to each other, in the Kingdom of God.* Boston, 1768. N.L.

Sermons on Artillery Election Day, to Militia or Army

ADAMS, ZABDIEL. *A Sermon Preached . . . in Lunenburg, New England, on Monday, January 2d, 1775, To a Detached Company of Militia there.* Boston, 1775. J. C. B. L.

BARNARD, THOMAS. *A Sermon . . . to the Ancient and Honourable Artillery Company in Boston . . . June 5, 1758. . . .* Boston, 1758. M.H.S.

BIRD, SAMUEL. *A Sermon, Delivered In New-Haven, April 27th, 1759. To Col. David Wooster, and His Company. . . .* New-Haven, 1759. J, c. B. L.

BRIDGE, EBENEZER. *Artillery Election Sermon,* 1752. Boston, 1752. B. P. L.

CHAUNCEY, CHAS. *Sermon Preached at the Desire of the Honourable Artillery-Company . . . . June 3, 1734.* Boston, 1734. Y. C. L.

CLARK, JONAS. *The Importance of Military Skill, Measures for Defence and a martial Spirit, in a Time of Peace.* Artillery Election

Sermon, June, 1768. Boston, 1768. M. H. S.

COGSWELL, JAMES. *God, The pious Soldiers' Strength & Instruction; A Sermon . . . at Brooklyn in Pomfret, to the Military Company, Under the Command of Capt. Israel Putnam . . . . April, 1757.* Boston, 1757. M. H. S.

COOPER, SAMUEL. *Artillery Election Sermon, 1751.* Boston, 1751. B. P. L.

HOWARD, SIMEON. *A Sermon Preached To the Ancient and Honourable Artillery-Company, in Boston . . . June 7th, 1773.* Boston, 1773. M.H.S.

LATHROP, JOHN. *A Sermon Preached To the Ancient and Honourable Artillery-Company, in Boston . . . June 6th, 1774.* Boston, 1774. M.H. S.

MORRILL, ISAAC. *The Soldier exhorted to Courage in the Service of his King and Country, from a Sense of God and Religion. Sermon at Wilmington, Apr. 3, 1755, to Capt. Phineas Osgood and His Company of Soldiers.* Boston, 1755. M. H. S.

PEABODY, OLIVER. *A Sermon Preached before the Honourable Artiller:,.'Company . . . June 5, 1732.* Boston, 1732. M. H. S.

PEMBERTON, EBENEZER. *A Sermon Preached to the Ancient and Honourable Artillery-Company . . . June 7, 1756.* Boston, 1756. M. H. S.

SHUTE, DANIEL. *A Sermon Preached To the Ancient and Honorable Artillery Company . . . June 1, 1767.* Boston, 1767. M. H. S.

Fast and Thanksgiving Sermons

ADAMS, AMOS. *Religious Liberty an invaluable Blessing.* Two sermons, Roxbury, Dec. 3, 1767. Boston, 1768. C. H. S. (Thanks. Ser.)

ADAMS, WILLIAM. *A Discourse Delivered at New-London, October 23d, A. D. 1760.* New-London, 1761. C. H. S. (Thanks. Ser.)

ALLIN, JAMES. *A Thanksgiving Sermon . . . At Brooklin, Nov. 8th, 1722.* Boston, 1722. C. H. S.

APPLETON, NATHANIEL. *A Thanksgiving Sermon on the Total Repeal of the Stamp Act.* Boston, 1766.

APTHORP, EAST. *A Sermon on the General Fast, Friday, December 13, 1776. . . .* London, 1776. J. C. B. L.

AVERY, DAVID. *Thanksgiving Sermon at Greenwich, in Co_nnecticut, Dec. 18, 1777.* Norwich, 1778. C. H. S. (Chaplain to Col. Sherburne's Regiment.)

BALDWIN, EBENEZER. *The Duty of Rejoicing under Calamities and Afflictions . . . , Preached at Danbury, Nov. 16, 1775.* N. Y., 1776. Y. C. L. (Thanks. Ser.)

CHAMPION, JUDAH. *A brief View of the Distresses, Hardships and Dangers our Ancestors encounter'd, in settling New-England . . . Two Sermons on Gen'l Fast, Litchfield, Apr. 18, 1770.* Hartford, 1770. C. H. S.

CHAUNCY, CHAS. *A Discourse On the good News from a far Country.* Boston, 1766. N. L.

EMERSON, JOSEPH. *A Thanksqiving Sermon Preach'd at Pepperell, July 24, 1766 . . . Boston, 1766.* M. H. S.

FISH, ELISHA. *Joy and Gladness; A Thanksgiving Discourse, Preached in Upton, . . . May 28, 1766.* Providence, 1767. J. C. B. L.

HILLIARD, TIMOTHY. *The duty of a People under the oppression of Man, to seek deliverance from God. The Substance of Two Sermons, Delivered at Barnstable, July 14th, 1774.* Boston, 1774. A. A. S. (Fast Day Ser.)

JOHNSON, STEPHEN. *Some Important Observations Occasioned by, and adapted to, The Publick Fast, . . . December 18th, A. D. 1765.* Newport, 1766. C. H. S.

MAYHEW, JONATHAN. *The Snare broken: a Thanksgiving Discourse . . . May 23, 1766.* 2nd ed. reprinted, Boston, 1766.

PATTEN, WM. *A Thanksgiving Sermon.* Boston, 1766. N. L.

ROWLAND, DAVID S. *Divine Providence Illustrated and Improved. A Thanksgiving Discourse . . . in Providence . . . June 4, 1766.* Providence. J. C. B. L.

SHERWOOD, SAMUEL. *A Sermon, Containing Scriptural Instructions to Civil Rulers, and all Free-born Subjects . . . public Fast, Attgust 31, 1774. With an Address to the Freemen of the Colony. Also, An Appendix, Stating the heavy Grievances the Colonies labour under from several late Acts of the British Parliament, . . . By the Rev. Ebenezer Baldwin, of Danbury.* New Haven. Y. C. L.

SKILLMAN, ISAAC. *An Oration, Upon the Beauties of Liberty, Or the Essential Rights of the Americans. Delivered . . . in Boston, Upon the last Annual Thanksgiving 1772.* (4th ed. carefully corrected, Boston, 1773, signed "A British Bostonian," is attributed both lo Skillman and to John Allen, but by most to Skillman. See p. 276, note 35.) J. C. B. L.

STILLMAN, SAMUEL. *Sermon on the Repeal of the Stamp Act . . . Boston, May 17, 1766.* Boston, 1766. J. C. B. L.

WEBSTER, SAMUEL. *The Misery and Duty of an Oppress'd and enslav'd People, represented in a Sermon Delivered at Salisbury, July 14, 1774.* BostonJ 1774. N. L. (Fast Day Ser.)

WHITNEY, PETER. *The Transgression of a Land punished by a*

multitude of Rulers . . . two Discourses delivered July 14, 1774. Boston, 1774. A. A. S. (Fast Day Ser.)

Election Sermons

The list here given is chronological and includes only those used in this study Others, and especially those of the 17th century, deal also with government. Many can be found in libraries other than those named. Yale, the Boston Public Library, and Mass. Hist. Soc. have especially good collections. The best article on the election sermons is that by Lindsay Swift (*Mass. Col. Soc. Pub.*, I. 388–451). The election, artillery, convention, and other sermons were sometimes printed under a special title, sometimes simply as Election or Convention Sermon.

Connecticut

1674 FITCH, JAMES (Norwich). Y. C. L.

1677 HOOKER, SAMUEL (Farmington). Cambridge, 1677. Y. C. L.

1685 WAKEMAN, SAMUEL (Fairfield). Boston, 1685. Y. C. L.

1686 WHITING, JOHN (Hartford). Y. C. L.

1710 ADAMS, ELIPHALET (New London). *The Necessity of Judgment and Righteousness in a Land.* New London, 1710. Y. C. L.

1711 BUCKINGHAM, STEPHEN (Norwalk). New London, 1711. Y. C. L.

1712 WOODWARD, JOHN (Norwich). *Civil Rulers are God's Ministers, for the Peoples Good.* Boston, 1712. Y. C. L.

1713 BULKLEY, JOHN (Colchester). Y. C. L.

1714 WHITMAN, DANIEL (Farmington). *Practical Godliness the Way to Prosperity.* New-London, 1714. Y. C. L.

1715 MOSS, JOSEPH (Darby). *An Election Sermon . . . The Discourse sheweth, That frequent Readings and Studying the Scriptures and the Civil Law of the Common Wealth, is Needful and Profitable for Rulers.* New London, 1715. Y. C. L.

1716 STODDARD, ANTHONY (Woodbury). New London, 1716. Y. C. L.

1717 CUTLER, TIMOTHY (Stratford). *The Firm Union of a People Represented.* New-London, 1717. Y. C. L.

1718 ESTABROOK, SAMUEL (Canterbury). *A Sermon Shewing that the Peace end Quietness of a People is a main part of the Work of Civil Rulers.* New London, 1718. Y. C. L.

1719 CHAUNCEY, NATHANAEL (Durham). *Honouring God the True Way to Honour.* New London, 1719. Y. C. L.

1720 HOSMER, STEPHEN (East Haddam). 1720. Y. C. L.

1721 MARSH, JONATHAN (Windsor). New-London, 1721. Y.C.L.

1722 BURNHAM, WM. (Kensington). *God's Providence In Placing Men In their Respective Stations & Conditions Asserted & Shewed.* New-London, 1722. Y. C. L.

1723 WILLIAMS, ELEAZAR (Mansfield). New-London, 1723. Y.C.L.

1724 WOODBRIDGE, SAMUEL (Hartford). *Obedience to the Divine Law, Urged on all Orders of Men And the Advantages of it shew'd.* New-London, 1724. Y. C. L.

1725 MATHER, AZARIAH (Saybrook). *Good Rulers A Choice Blessing.* New-London, 1725. Y. C. L.

1726 FISKE, PHINEAS (Haddam). *The Good Subject's Wish or The Desirableness of the Divine Presence with Civil Rulers.* NewLondon, 1726. Y. C. L.

1727 WOODBRIDGE, SAMUEL (Hartford). *Jesus Christ doth Actually Reign on the Earth.* New-London, 1727. Y. C. L.

1728 BUCKINGHAM, THOS. (Hartford). *God's Favour To His Chosen People, in Leading them by the Ministry of Civil & Ecclesiastical Rulers, Well Qualified for the Offices they are Called to Execute.* New-London, 1729. Y. C. L.

1730 RUSSELL, WM. (Middletown). New-London, 1731. Y. C. L.

1731 WHITTELSEY, SAMUEL (Wallingford). *A Public Spirit Described & Recommended.* New-London, 1731. Y. C. L.

1732 EDWARDS, TIMOTHY (Windsor). N. London, 1732. Y. C. L.

1733 ADAMS, ELIPHALET (New London). N. London, 1734. Y. C. L.

1734 CHAUNCEY, NATHANIEL (Durham). *The Faithful Ruler Described and Excited.* N. London, 1734. Y. C. L.

1736 MARSH, JONATHAN (Windsor). *God's Fatherly Care of His Covenant Children.* N. London, 1737. Y. C. L.

1737 COLTON, BENJ. (Hartford). N. London, 1738. Y. C. L.

1738 ELIOT, JARED (Killingworth). *Give Cesar his Due, Or, The Obligations That Subjects are under to their Civil Rulers.* N. London, 1738. Y. C. L.

1740 HEMINGWAY, JACOB (East Haven). N. London, 1740. Y.C.L.

1741 WILLIAMS, SOLOMON (Lebanon). Y. C. L.

1742 STILES, ISAAC (North Haven). *A Prospect of the City of Jerusalem.* N. London, 1742. Y. C. L.

1744 WORTHINGTON, WM. (Saybrook). *The Duty of Rulers and Teachers in Unitedly Leading God's People, Urged and Explained.* N. London, 1744. Y. C. L.

1745 WHITMAN, ELNATHAN (Hartford). *The Character and Qualifications of good Rulers, and the Happiness of their Administration*. N. London, 1745. Y. C. L.

1746 HALL, SAMUEL (N.ew Cheshire). *The Legislatures Right, Charge and Duty in respect of Religion*. N. London, 1746. Y.C.L.

1747 HUNN, NATHANAEL (Reading). *The Welfare of a Government Considered*. N. London, 1747. Y. C. L.

1748 EELLS, NATHANAEL (Stonington). *The Wise Ruler a loyal Subject*. N. London, 1748. Y. C. L.

1749 TONN, JONATHAN (East Guilford). *Good Rulers the Ministers of God, for Good to Men, Or, The divine Original & Authority of Civil Government Asserted*. N. London, 1749. Y. C. L.

1752 WOODBRIDGE, ASHBEL (Glastonbury). N. London, 1753. Y. C. L.

1753 DEVOTION, EBENEZER (Windham). *The civil Ruler, a dignify'd Servant of the Lord, but a dying Man*. N. London, 1753. Y. C. L.

1754 LOCKWOOD, JAMES (Wethersfield). C. S. L.

1755 DICKINSON, MOSES (Norwalk). N. London, 1755. C. H. S.

1756 BECKWITH, GEO. (Lyme). *That People A safe, and happy People, who have God for, and among them*. N. London, 1756. C. S. L.

1757 RAYNOLDS, PETER (Enfield). *The Kingdom is the Lord's; Or, God the Supreme Ruler and Governour of the World*. N. London, 1757. Y. C. L.

1758 THROOP, BENJ. (Norwich). *Religion and Loyalty, the Duty and Glory of a People*. N. London, 1758. Y. C. L.

1759 LOCKWOOD, JAMES (Wethersfield). *The Worth and Excellence of Civil Freedom and Liberty illustrated and a Public Spirit and the Love of our Country recommended*. N. London, 1759. Y. C. L.

1760 FISH, JOSEPH (Stonington). *Christ Jesus the Physician*. N. London, 1760. Y. C. L.

1761 INGERSOLL, JONATHAN (Ridgfield). N. London, 1761. C. S. L.

1762 BELLAMY, JOSEPH (Bethlem). N. London, 1762. Y. C. L.

1763 WHITE, STEPHEN (\i\Tindham). *Civil Rulers Gods by Office and the Duties of such Considered and Enforced*. N. London, 1763. Y. C. L.

1764 WELLES, NOAH (Stamford). *Patriotism Described and Recommended*. N. London, 1764. C. S. L.

1765 DORR, ED. (Hartford). *The Duty of Civil Rulers, to be nursing Fathers to the Church of Christ*. Hartford. C. S. L.

1768 SALTER, RICHARD (Mansfield). N. London. 1768. C. S. L.

1769 WILLIAMS, ELIPHALET (Hartford). Hartford. C. S. L.

1771 COGSWELL, JAMES (Canterbury). N. London, 1771. Y. C. L.

1772 LEAVENWORTH, MARK (Vilaterbury). N. London. C. S. L.

1773 WETMORE, IzRAHIAH (Stratford). Y. C. L.

1774 LOCKWOOD, SAMUEL (Andover). *Civil Rulers an Ordinance of God, for Good to Mankind.* N. London, 1774. Y. C. L.

1775 PERRY, JOSEPH (East Windsor). Ha.rtford, 1775. Y. C. L.

1776 CHAMPION, JUDAH (Litchfield). *Christian and civil Liberty and Freedom considered and recommended.* Hartford, 1776. N. Y. P. L.

1777 DEVOTION, EBENEZER (Saybrook). *The Duty and Tnterest of a People to sanctify the Lord of Hosts.* Hartford, 1777. Y. C. L.

1778 WHITTELSEY, CHAUNCY (New Haven). *The importance of religion in the civil Ruler, Considered.* New Haven, 1778. C. S. L.

1779 DANA, JAMES (Wallingford). Hartford, 1779. C. S. L.

1780 WILLIAMS, NATHAN (Tolland). Hartford. 1780. C. S. L.

1783 STILES, EZRA. Sermon, 1783. N. Haven, 1783.

Massachusetts

1661 NORTON, JOHN (Published 1664). Y. C. L.

1669 DAVENPORT, JOHN. *Mass. Col. Soc. Pub.,* X.

1701 BELCHER, JOSEPH (Dedham). *The Singular Happiness of such Heads or Rulers As are able to Chttse out their Peoples Way, and will also Endeavour their Peoples Comfort.* B. P. L.

1703 STODDARD, SOLOMON (Northampton). *The Way for a People To Live Long in the Land that God Hath given them.* Boston, 1703. B. P. L.

1707 BELCHER, SAMUEL (Newbury) *An Essay Tending to Promote the Kingdom Of Our Lord Jesus Christ.* Boston, 1707. B. P. L.

1710 PEMBERTON, EBENEZER (Boston). *The divine Original and Dignity of Government Asserted.* Boston, 1710. Y. C. L.

1719 WILLIAMS, WILLIAM (Hatfield). *A Plea for God, and An Appeal to the Consciences of a People Declining in Religion.* Boston, 1719. B. P. L.

1722 HANCOCK, JOHN (Lexington). *Rulers should be Benefactors.* Boston, 1722. B. P. L.

1728 BRECK, ROBERT (Marlborough). *The only Method to Promote the Happiness of a People and their Prosperity.* Boston, 1728. B. P. L.

1729 WISE, JEREMIAH (Berwick). *Rulers the Ministers of God for the Good of their People.* Boston, 1729. B. P. L.

1734 BARNARD, JOHN (Marblehead). *The Throne Established by Righteousness*, Boston, 1734. B. P. L.

1736 HOLYOKE, ED. Boston, 1736. N. L.

1738 WEBB, JOHN (Boston). *The Government of Christ considered and applied.* Boston, 1738. B. P. L.

1742 APPLETON, NATHANIEL (Cambridge). Boston, 1742. N. L.

1744 ALLEN, JAMES (Brookline). *Magistracy and Institution of Christ upon the Throne.* Boston, 1744. B. P. L.

1747 CHAUNCEY, CHAS. (Boston). *Civil Magistrates must be just ruling in the Fear of God.* Boston, 1747. B. P. L.

1748 LEWIS, DANIEL (Pembroke). *Good Rulers the Fathers of their People, And the Marks of Honour due to them.* Boston, 1748. B. P. L.

1750 PHILLIPS, SAMUEL (Andover). *Political Rulers Authoriz'd and Influenc'd by God our Saviour, to decree and execute Justice.* Boston, 1750. B. P. L.

1751 WELSTEED, WM. (Boston). *The Dignity and Duty of the Civil Magistrate.* Boston, 1751. B. P. L.

1754 MAYHEW, JONATHAN (Boston). Boston, 1754, N. L.

1756 COOPER, SAMUEL (Boston). Boston, 1756. N. L.

1758 FRINK, THos. (Rutland). *A King Reigning in Righteousness, and Princes ruling in Judgment.* Boston, 1758. B. P. L.

1759 PARSONS, JOSEPH (Brookfield). Boston, 1759. N. L.

1760 DUNBAR, SAMUEL (Stoughton). Boston, 1760. N. L.

1761 STEVENS, BENJAMIN (Kittery, Me.). Boston, 1761. N. L.

1763 BARNARD, THOS. (Salem). Boston, 1763. N. L.

1765 ELIOT, ANDREW (Boston). Boston, 1765. B. P. L.

1766 BARNARD, ED. (Haverhill). Boston, 1766. N. L.

1767 BRIDGE, EBEN. (Chelmsford). Boston, 1767. N. L.

1768 SHUTE, DANIEL (Hingham). Boston, 1768. N. L.

1769 HAVEN, JASON (Dedham). Boston, 1769. B. P. L.

1770 COOKE, SAMUEL (Arlington). Boston, 1770. N. L.

1773 TURNER, CHAS. (Duxbury). Boston, 1773. N. L.

1774 HITCHCOCK, GAD (Pembroke). Boston, 1774. N. L.

1775 GORDON, WM. (Roxbury). Watertown, 1775. N. L.

1775 LANGDON, SAMUEL (Cambridge). Watertown, 1775. Reprinted in Thornton.

1776 WEST, SAMUEL (Dartmouth). Boston, 1776. N. L.

1777 WEBSTER, SAMUEL (Salisbury). Boston, 1777.

1778 PAYSON, PHILLIPS (Chelsea). Boston, 1778. Reprinted in Thornton.

1780 COOPER, SAMUEL (Boston). Boston, 1780. B. P. L.
1780 HOWARD, SIMEON (Boston). Boston, 1780. Reprinted in Thornton.
1781 CLARK, JONAS (Lexington). Boston, 1781. M. H. S.

Vermont

1778 BURROUGHS, EDEN (Hanover, N. H.). *A Sincere Regard to Righteousness and Piety, the sole Measure of a true Principle of Honor and Patriotism.* Dresden, Vt. D. C. L.

Miscellaneous Sermons, Chiefly Political

APPLETON, NATHANIEL. *A Funeral Sermon Occasioned By the Death of the Honourable Spencer Phips, Esq. Preached At the Public Lecture in Boston.* Boston, 1757. Y. C. L.

BACKUS, ISAAC. *The Substance of an Address to an Assembly in Bridgewater, March 10, 1779.* Providence. Y. C. L.

BALDWIN, SAMUEL. *A Sermon, Preached at Plymouth, December 22, 1775.* Boston, 1776. M. H. S.

BAXTER, SIMEON. *Tyrannicide proved Lawful.* Printed in America. Reprinted in London, 1782. J. C. B. L.

BELCHER, SAMUEL. *An Assize Sermon, 1702.* Boston, 1707. B.P.L.

CHAPLIN, EBENEZER. *Civil Government Compared to Rivers, all under God's control, and what People have to do when Administration is grievous. In a Discourse Delivered in Sutton, 2d. Parish, January 17, 1773. Being the Day preceding the Town Meeting, which then stood Adjourned To consider and Act upon the Letter, &c From Boston. . . .* Boston, 1773. M. H. S. First 22 pp. only.

CHECKLEY, SAMUEL. *The Duty of a People to Lay to Heart and Lament the Death of a Good King . . . 1727.* Boston. M. H. S.

CLARK, JONAS. *The Fate of Blood-thirsty Oppressors, and God's tender Care of his distressed People . . . . Preached at Lexing on, April 19, 1776 . . . To which is added, A brief Narrative of the principal Transactions of that Day.* Boston, 1776. M. H. S.

COLMAN, BENJ. *Government the Pillar of the Earth.* Boston, 1730. N. L.

COLMAN, BENJ. *The Fast God hath Chosen.* Boston, 1734. N. L.

COLMAN, BENJ. *The Merchandise of a People Holiness to the Lord.* Boston, 1736. N. L.

COOKE, SAMUEL. *The violent destroyed, and oppressed, delivered . . .* Lexington, Apr. 19, 1777. Boston, 1777. M. H. S.

CROSWELL, ANDREW. *. . . or, A seasonable Defence of the Old Protestant Doctrine of Justifying Faith.* Boston, 1745. Y. C. L.

CUSHING, JACOB. *Divine judgments upon tyrants,and Compassion to the oppressed* ... Lexington, Apr. 20, 1778. Boston, 1778. M. H. S.

Dedham Pulpit: or Sermons by the Pastors of the First Church in Dedham in the XVIIth and XVIIth Centltries. Boston, 1840. D. C. L. One by SAMUEL DEXTER, 1738, and one by JASON HAVEN, 1758.

FINLEY, SAMUEL. *Christ triumphing and Satan raging.* Philadelphia Printed, London Reprinted, 1741. N. L.

FISH, ELISHA. *A Discourse delivered at Worcester, March 28, 1775. At the Desire of the Convention of Committees for the County of Worcester.* Worcester, 1775. J. C. B. L.

FOSTER, DAN. *A Short Essay on Civil Government, The Substance of Six Sermons, Preached in Windsor, . . . October, 1774.* Hartford, 1774. C. H. S.

FOXCROFT, THOMAS. *Some Seasonable Thoughts on Evangelic Preaching* ... Oct. 23, 1740. M. H. S.

FROTHINGTON, EBENEZER. *A Key To Unlock the Door, That lead in, to take a Fair View of the Religious Constitution, Established by Law, in the Colony of Connecticut.* 1767. C. H. S.

GORDON, WM. *A Discourse Preached In the Morning of December 15th, 1774.* Boston, 1775. M. H. S.

GORDON, WM. *Sermon Preached December 15th, 1774, and Afterwards at the Boston Lecture.* Boston, 1775. M. H. S.

HART, LEVI. *Liberty described and recommended; in a Sermon Preached To The Corporation of Freemen in Farmington, at their Meeting* ... *September 20, 1774.* Hartford, 1775. Y. C. L.

HAVEN, SAMUEL. *A Sermon occasioned by the Death of King George the Second* ... *1761.* Portsmouth, 1761. A. A. S.

HITCHCOCK, GAD. *A Sermon Preached at Plymouth Boston, 1775.* M. H. S. December 22d, 1774.

HOLLY, ISRAEL. *Sermon, Preached at Suffield, December 27, 1773. The next Sabbath after the Report arrived, that the People at Boston had destroyed A Large Quantity of Tea ... Rather than to submit to Parliament Acts, which they looked upon Unconstitutional, Tyrannical, and tending to enslave America, ... with some Enlargements.* .... *Hartford, 1774.* C. H. S.

LANGDON, SAMUEL. *Joy and Gratitude to God for the Long Life of a Good King and the Conquest of Quebec.* Portsmouth, 1760. D. C. L.

LATHROP, JOHN. *A Discourse Preached December 15th, 1774.* .... Boston, 1774. M. H. S.

LATHROP, JOHN. *A Discourse Preached on March the Fifth, 1778.* Boston, 1778. M. H. S.

LATHROP, JOHN. *Innocent Blood Crying to God From the Streets of Boston.* Boston, 1771. M. H. S.

LOWELL, JOHN. *The Advantage of God's Presence with his People in an Expedition against their Enemies.* Boston, 1755. D. C. L.

LYMAN, JosEPH. *A Sermon Preached at Hatfield, December 15, 1774.* Boston, 1775. A. A. S.

MATHER, COTTON. *Christian Loyalty.* Boston, 1727.

MAYHEW, JONATHAN. *Christian Sobriety; being Eight Sermons.* Boston, 1763. N. L.

MAYHEW, JONATHAN. *Sermons.* Boston, 1755. N. L.

MAYHEW, JONATHAN. *Seven Sermons . . . 1748.* London Reprinted, 1750. N. L.

MORRILL, ISAAC. *Faith in Divine Providence, the great support of God's people in perilous times, . . . Lexington, April 19, 1780.* Boston, 1780. M. H. S.

PARSONS, JONATHAN. *Wisdom justified of her Children.* Boston, 1742. N.L.

POTTER, ELAM. *A Second Warning to America . . . 1777.* Hartford. C. H. S.

POTTER, NATHANIEL. *A Discourse on Jeremiah 8th, 20th . . . .* Boston, 1758. M. H. S.

ROSS, ROBERT. *A Sermon in which the Union of the Colonies is considered and recommended . . . November Sixteenth, 1775.* New Yark, 1776. M. H. S.

ROWLAND, DAVID S. *Historical Remarks . . . June 6, 1779.* Providence. B. L.

STILES, EZRA. *A Discourse on Saving Knowledge.* Newport, 1770. N.L.

TRUMBULL, BENJ. *A Discourse, Delivered at the Anniversary Meeting Of the Freemen Of the Town of New Haven, April 12, 1773.* New Haven, 1773. C. H. S.

WHEELOCK, ELEAZAR. *Liberty of Conscience, Nov. 30, 1775.* Hartford, 1775. Y. C. L.

WHITNEY, PETER. *American Independence Vindicated. September 12, 1776.* Boston, 1777. A. A. S.

WOODWARD, SAMUEL. *The Help of the Lord, in signal deliverances and special salvations, to be acknowledged and remembered . . . Lexington, April19, 1779.* Boston, 1779. M. H. S.

Pamphlets Other Than Sermons

ADAMS, ZABDIEL. *An Answer to A Pamphlet lately published, intitled, "A Treatise on Church Government."* Boston, 1773. J. C. B. L.

Aged Layman of Connecticut. *A Letter To the Clergy of the Colony of Connecticut.* 1760. Y. C. L.

Aged Minister. *An Answer To A Letter From an Aged Layman, to the Clergy of the Colony of Connecticut.* New Haven. Y. C. L.

The Answer of the Elders and other Messengers of the Churches, assembled at Boston, in the year 1662. To the Questions propounded to them by order of the honorable General Court. N. L.

APTHORP, EAST. *A Review of Dr. Mayhew's Remarks on the Answer to his Observations on the Charter and Conduct of the Society for the Propagation of the Gospel in Foreign Parts.* London, 1765. N. L.

BACKUS, ISAAC. *A Fish caught in his own Net.* Boston, 1768. J.C.B.L.

BACKUS, ISAAC. *A Letter to a Gentleman in the Massachusetts General Assembly, Concerning Taxes to support Religious Worship.* 1771. J. C. B. L.

BACKUS, ISAAC. *Policy as well as Honesty, forbids the use of Secular Force in Religious Affairs.* Boston, 1779. J. C. B. L.

BACKUS, ISAAC. *A Seasonable Plea for Liberty of Conscience, Against some late Oppressive Proceedings.* Boston, 1770. J. C. B. L.

BULKELEY, GERSHOM. *The People's Right to Election or Alteration of Government in Connecticutt.* Phila., 1689. Conn. Hist. Soc. Coll., I.

BULKELEY, GERSHOM. *Will and Doom , or The Miseries of Connecticut by and under an Usurped and Arbitrary Power*, 1692. Conn. Hist. Soc. Coll., III.

CANER, H. *A Candid Examination of Dr. Mayhew's Observations.* Boston, 1763. N. L.

CARE, HENRY and NELSON, WM. *English Liberties, or the Freeborn Subject's Inheritance.* 6th ed. corrected and improved. Providence, R. I., 1774. C. H. S.

CATHOLICUS. *A Letter To A Clergyman, in the Colony of Connecticut from his Friend.* New Haven, 1757. Y. C. L.

CHAPLIN, EBENEZER. *A Treatise on Church-Government, In Three Parts;* Boston, 1773. This was published under pseudonym, "A Neighbor." J. C. B. L.

CHAPLIN, EBENEZER. *A Second Treatise on Church-Government, By a Neighbor.* Boston, 1773. M. H. S.

CHAUNCEY, CHAS. *A Letter to a Friend.* Boston, 1767.

CLAP, THOMAS. *The Answer Of The Friend in the West, To A Letter*

From A Gentleman in the East . . . . New Haven, 1755. Y. C. L.

CLAP, THOMAS. A Brief History and Vindication of the Doctrines Received and Established in the Churches of New England, . . 2nd. ed., New Haven, 1757. N. L. (1st ed., 1755.)

CLEAVELAND, JOHN. *An Essay, to defend some of the most important Principles in the Protestant Reformed System, of Christianity . . . against the injurious Aspersions cast on the same, by Jonathan Mayhew, D.D* . . . . Boston, 1763. N. L.

A Compendium of the Minutes of the Warren Baptist Association, 1767 to 1825. J. C. B. L.

A Confession of Faith . . . of the Churches assembled at Boston in New England, May 12, 1680. Boston, 1772.

COOPER, SAMUEL. *The Crisis*. June, 1754. M. H. S.

COTTON, JOHN. *The Doctrine of the Church*. 2nd. ed., London, 1643. N. L.

COTTON, JOHN. *The Way of the Churches of Christ in New England*. London, 1645. N. L.

COTTON, JOHN. *A Narrative of the Transactions at Middleborough*. Boston, 1746. M. H. S.

DAVENPORT, JOHN. *A Discourse about Civil Government in a New Plantation Whose Design is Religion*. Cambridge, 1663. Y. C. L.

DAVENPORT, JOHN. *The Power of Congregational Churches Asserted and Vindicated*, . . . London, 1672. Y. C. L.

DEVOTION, EBENEZER. *The Examiner Examined . . . In Answer to a Letter, Intitled, The Claim of the Colonies to an Exemption from Internal Taxes imposed by Anthority of Parliament, examined*. New-London, 1766. Y. C. L.

EELLS, EDWARD. *Some Serious Remarks upon the Rev'd. Mr. Jonathan Todd's Faithful Narrative* . . . . New Haven, 1759. Y. C. L.

HART, WILLIAM. *A Letter to a Friend: Wherein some free Thoughts are offered on the Subject of The Rev. Mr. Noyes's Proposed Examination By The Corporation of Yale College.* . . . New Haven, 1757. Y. C. L.

HART, WILLIAM. *Remarks On a late Pamphlet Wrote by Mr. Hobart, Entitled, The Principles of congregational Churches*. New Haven, 1760. Y. C. L.

HOBART, NOAH. *An Attempt To illustrate and confirm The ecclesiastical Constitution Of The Consociated Churches*. New Haven, 1765. Y. C. L.

HOBART, NOAH. *A Congratulatory Letter From A Gentlemen in the West, To His Friend in the East;* . . . New Haven, 1755. Y. C. L.

HOBART, NOAH. *The Principles of Congregational Churches, Relating to the Constitution and Authority of Ecclesiastical Councils, . . .* New Haven, 1759. Y. C. L.

HOMEs, WILLIAM. *Proposals Of Some Things to be done in our administring Ecclesiastical Government . . . .* Boston, 1732. Y. C. L.

LANGDON, SAMUEL. *A Summary of Christian Faith and Practice.* Boston, 1768.

A Layman and Platformist. *A Letter To A Friend, Occasioned By The unhappy Controversy At Wallingford.* New Haven, 1760. Y. C. L.

MATHER, INCREASE. *A disquisition Concerning Ecclesiastical Councils, Proving that not only Pastors, But Brethren delegated by the Churches, have equally a Right to a decisive Vote in such Assemblies.* Boston, 1716. "Congregational Quarterly" Reprint, no. 2, Boston, 1870. N. L.

MATHER, RICHARD and TOMPSON, WILLIAM. *A Modest & Brotherly Answer to Mr. Charles Herle his Book, against the Independency of Churches.* London, 1644. N. L.

MAYHEW, JONATHAN. *A Defence Of the Observations on the Charter and Conduct of the Society for the Propagation of the Gospel in Foreign Parts . . . .* Boston, 1763. N. L.

MAYHEW, JONATHAN. *Observations on the Charter and Conduct of the Society for the Propagation of the Gospel in Foreign Parts.* Reprinted, London, 1763. N. L.

MAYHEW, JONATHAN. *Remarks on an Anomymous Tract, intitled An Answer to Dr. Mayhew's Observations . . . .* Boston, 1764; reprinted, London, 1765. N. L.

A Ministerial Cathechise, Suitable to be Learned by all Modern Provencial Governors, Pensioners, Placemen, etc. Boston, 1771.

Observations Upon the Congregational Plan of Church Government, . . . by the Convention of the Ministers Of the Province of Massachusetts-Bay at their annual Meeting in Boston, May 26, 1773. . . . Boston, 1773. N. L.

PAINE, SAMUEL. *A Short View of the Differences Between the Churches of Christ, and the established Churches in the Colony of Connecticut.* Newport. 1752. Y. C. L.

A Paraphrase on a Passage in A Sermon Preached by the Most Reverend Dr. Markham, Archbishop of York. On the 21st of February, 1777.

The People the Best Governors: Or A Plan of Government founded on the just Principles of Natural Freedom. 1776. Appendix of Chase, *History of Dartmouth College,* vol. I.

A Platform of Church Discipline. Cambridge Platform of 1648. Boston, 1772.

Remarks upon a Discourse Preached December 15th, 1774 . . . and afterwards at the Boston Lecture, By William Gordon. 1775. M. H. S.

The Result of a Council Of the Consociated Churches Of the County of Windham Boston, 1747. Y. C. L.

Result of a Synod at Cambridge, in New-England, 1646. London, 1654. N. L.

The Results of Three Synods Held by the Elders and Messengers of the Churches of Massachusetts Province. Boston, 1725. N. L.

ROBBINS, PHILEMON. *A Plain Narrative of the Proceedings Of the Reverend Association and Consociation Of New-Haven County, Against the Reverend Mr. Robbins of Branford, Since the year 1741. . . .* Boston, 1747. Y. C. L.

The Sentiments and Plan of the Warren Association. Germantown, 1769. J. C. B. L.

SMITH, EBENEZER. *A Letter to a Gentlemen in the Massachusetts General Assembly, Concerning Taxes to support Religious Worship.* 1771. N.L.

Some Remarks on Mr. President Clap's History and Vindication, of the Doctrines of the New-England Churches &c. N. L.

The Testimony and Advice of an Assembly of Pastors of Churches in New-England. At a Meeting in Boston July 7, 1743. Boston. Y. C. L.

TODD, JONATHAN. *A Faithful Narrative, Of the Proceedings of the First Society and Church In Wallingford, in their Calling and Settling The Rev. Mr. James Dana . . . .* New Haven, 1759. Y. C. L.

TODD, JONATHAN. *A Reply To the Reverend Mr. Eell's Serious Remarks, upon the faithful Narrative, &c. . . .* New Haven, 1760. Y. C. L.

The Transactions of The Council, Called for the Ordination of Mr. John Hubbard, At Meriden, December 29, 1767. New Haven. Y. C. L.

Warren Association Minutes, 1769–1862. 3 vols. Boston, 1769–1868.

WHITAKER, NATHANIEL. *A Confutation Of Two Tracts, intitled A Vindication of the New-England Churches; and The Churches Quarrel espoused; Written by the Reverend John Wise, A. M.* Boston, 1774. N.L.

WILLIAMS, ELISHA. *A seasonable Plea For The Liberty of Conscience, And The Right of private Judgment In Matters of Religion, Without any Controul from human Authority.* Boston, 1744. Y. C. L. (Signed "Philalethes," but the author is supposed to be Williams.)

WISE, JOHN. *The Churches Quarrel Espoused.* Boston, 1772, first pub. 1710.

WISE, JOHN. *A Vindication of the Government of New England Churches.* (In same ed. as above; first pub. 1717.)

WOLCOTT, R. *A Letter to the Reverend Mr. Noah Hobart, Windsor, Apr. 25, 1760.* Boston, 1761. N. L.

Collections, Diaries, etc.

ADAMS, JOHN. *Works,* ed. by C. F. Adams. 10 vols. Boston, 1856.

ADAMS, SAMUEL. *Writings,* ed. by H. A. Cushing. 4 vols. N. Y. 1904.

The American Gazette, Numbers I & II. 2nd. ed., London, 1768.

BACKUS, ISAAC. *A History of New England, with Particular Reference to the Denomination of Christians Called Baptists.* 2nd. ed., with notes by David Weston. 3 vols. Newton, Mass., 1871; vol. I. of original pub. 1777; vol. II, 1784. Works. 2 vols., J. C. B. L., includes various sermons, addresses, etc. collected and bound together.

BALDWIN, E. C. *Branford Annals, 1700–1800.* New Haven Colony Hist. Soc. Papers, vol. IV.

BALDWIN, SIMEON E. *Extracts from the Diary of Miss Bethiah Baldwin, 1770.* New Haven. Colony Hist. Soc. Papers, vol. IX.

Belcher Papers, Pt. II. *Mass. Hist. Soc. Coll.,* 6th Ser., vol. VII.

BELKNAP, JEREMY. *History of New Hampshire.* 2 vols. Boston, 1791.

BENTLEY, REV. WILLIAM J. *Diary.* 4 vols. Salem, 1905–1914.

BERDT, DENNYS DE. *Letters, 1757–1770,* ed. by Albert Matthews. Reprinted from *Mass. Col. Soc. Pub.,* XIII, Cambridge, 1911.

Boston Town Records, 1770–1777.

Bowdoin and Temple Papers. Pts. I & II, *Mass. Hist. Soc. Coll.,* 6th Ser., IX, 7th Ser., VI.

CASE, REV. WHEELER. *Poems, Occasioned By Several Circumstances and Occurrencies, In The Present great Contest of America For Liberty.* New Haven, 1778. C. H. S.

CHAMBERLAIN, MELLEN J., Ed. *A Documentary History of Chelsea.* 2 vols. Boston, 1908.

Classified Digest of the S. P. G. Records, 1701–1892.

Connecticut Historical Society Collections. vols. 1–16. Hartford, 1860–1916.

Connecticut, Public Records of the Colony of, (1636–1776). Compiled by J. H. Trumbull and C. J. Hoadly. 15 volumes. Hartford, 1850–1890.

Connecticut, Acts and Lives of His Majesty's Colony of, in New England.

New London, ed. of 1715 and 1769, with supplements tn 1779.

CooPER, SAMUEL, DD., "Diary, 1775–1776," *Amer. Hist. Rev.* VI. 301–411; "Letters to Pownall, 1769–1777," *Amer. Hist. Rev.*, VIII. 301–30.

Danvers Historical Collections, VII.

EDWARDS, REV. MORGAN. *Materials for a History of the Baptists in Rhode Island.* Written 1771 and incomplete. *R. I. Hist. Soc. Coll.*, VI, 301–70.

Fitchburg, Old Records of the Town of, Fitchburg, 1898.

FORCE, PETER. Ed. *American Archives*, IV Ser., I & II. Washington, 1837.

FRANKLIN, BENJAMIN, *Calendar of the Papers*, I–VI, in the Amer. Philos. Soc., ed. by I. Mims Hays. Phila., 1908.

FRANKLIN, BENJAMIN. *Complete Works*, ed. by John Bigelow. 10 vols. 1887–1888.

GIBBES, R. W., Ed. *Documentary History of the Americm Revolution.* N.Y. 1855.

GORDON, WILLIAM. *The History of the Rise, Progress, and Establishment of the Independence of the United States of America.* 2 vols. 2nd. Amer. ed., N. Y. 1794. Much original material.

GREEN, S. A. *Groton during the Revolution.* Groton, 1900. Much original material.

GRIFFITH, WILLIAM. *Historical Notes of the American Colonies and Revolution from 1754 to 1775.* Burlington, N. J., 1843.

INGERSOLL, JARED. "A Selection from the Correspondence and Miscellaneous Papers," ed. by F. B. Dexter. *New Haven Colony Hist. Soc. Papers*, vol. IX.

MANN, HERMAN, Ed. *Historical Annals of Dedham.* Dedham, 1847.

Massachusetts Colonial Society Publications, I, III.

Massachusetts Historical Society Collections, 1st S., VIIi; 2nd S., X; 3rd S., V; 4th S., I, IV, V; 5th S., VII, LXXIV.

Massachusetts, The Journals of Each Provincial Congress of, in 1774 and 1775, and of the Committee of Safety, with an Appendix containing the proceedings of the County Conventions. Boston, 1838. M.S. L.

Massachusetts Bay, Journal of the Convention for Framing a Constitution of Government for the State of, from the Commencement of their first session, September 1, 1779, to the close of the last session, June 16, 1780. Boston, 1832.

MATHER, COTTON. "Diary 1709–1724." *Mass. Hist. Soc. Coll.*, 7th S., VIII.

New Hampshire Historical Collections. IV, V, IX.

New Hampshire Provincial Papers, VII.

New Hampshire Provincial and State Papers, X.

New Hampshire State Papers, VIII, X.

New Hampshire Town Papers, IX, XI, XII, XIII.

NILES, H., Ed. *Principles and Acts of the Revolution in America.* Baltimore, 1822.

PARKMAN, REV. EBENEZER. *Diary,* ed. by Harriette M. Forbes. Westborough, 1899.

PASCOE, C. F. *Two Hundred Years of the S. P. G. An Historical Account, 1701–1900.* Based on a digest of the Society's Records. London, 1901.

PERRY, WM. STEVENS. *Historical Collections relating to the American Colonial Church,* vol. IV.

Plymouth Church Records. 2 vols. N. Y., 1920.

Plymouth. Records of the Town of, vol. I. Plymouth, 1889.

PRINCE, THOS., JR. *The Christian History, containing Accounts of the Revival and Propagation of Religion in Great-Britain & America.* For the Year 1743, Boston, 1744. For the Year 1744, Boston, 1745. M.H. S.

Records of the Presbyterian Church in the U. S. of America, 1706–1788. Phila., 1904. Also Minutes of the Gen'l Convention of Synod of Phila. & N. Y. and the Consociated Churches of Conn., 1766–1775.

Records of the Town of Plymouth. Vol. I. Plymouth, 1889.

SEWALL, SAMUEL. *Letter-Book.* 2 vols. *Mass. Hist. Soc. Coll.,* 6th Ser., vols. I, II. Boston, 1886.

SMITH, REV. THOMAS. *Journals of the Rev. Thomas Smith and the Rev. Samuel Deans,* ed. by Wm. Willis. 2nd. ed. of Journal of Smith, Portland, 1849.

STILES, REV. EZRA. *Extracts from the Itineraries and Other Miscellanies, 1755–1794, with a selection from his correspondence,* ed. by F. B. Dexter. New Haven, 1916.

TRUMBULL, BENJAMIN. *A Complete History of Connecticut Civil and Ecclesiastical from the Emigration of its first Planters . . . to the year 1764.* 2 vols. 1st ed., London, 1818.

TURELL, EBENEZER. *The Life and Character of the Reverend Benjamin Colman,* D.D. Boston, 1749.

WASHINGTON, GEORGE. *Writings,* I–XII, ed. by J. Sparks. Boston, 1837.

WHITEFIELD, GEORGE. *Works,* I–IV. London, 1771.

Biographies and Miscellaneous Writings

ADAMS, JAMES TRUSLOW. *The Founding of New England*. Boston, 1921.

ADAMS, JAMES TRUSLOW. *Revolutionary New England, 1691–1776*. Boston, 1923.

ALLEN, WILLIAM. *An Account of the Separation in the Church and Town of Pittsfield*. Pittsfield, 1809. M. H. S.

ALLEN, WILLIAM. *The American Biographical Dictionary*. 3rd ed., Boston, 1857.

ALLISON, W. H. *Inventory of Unpublished Material for American Religious History in Protestant Church Archives and other Repositories*. Washington, 1910.

BALCH, G. W. "Some Account of Rev. Benjamin Balch." *Danvers Historical Collections*, VII.

BALDWIN, ROGERS. "A Bit of College History" in *Mag. Atner. Hist.*, XXVIII. 281–83.

BARBER, JOHN WARNER, Ed. *Connecticut Historical Collections, Containing a General Collection of Interesting Facts, Traditions. . . .* 2nd. ed., New Haven, 1836. C. S. L.

BARRY, JOHN STETSON. *The History of Massachusetts*. 3 vols. Boston, 1855.

BATES, A. C. "Fighting the Revolution with Printers' Ink in Connecticut." *New Haven Colony Hist. Soc. Papers*, IX.

BELCHER, J. *George Whitefield*. American Tract Soc., 1857.

BELKNAP, JEREMY. *American Biography*. Boston, 1794–1798.

BLAKE, S. L. *The Separates or Strict Congregationalists of New Eng land*. Boston, 1902.

BOYLSTON, E. Q. *Historical Sketch of the Hillsborough County Congresses, Held at Amherst, N. H., 1774–1775*. Amherst, 1884.

BRADFORD, ALDEN. *Biographical Notices of Distinguished Men of New England*. Boston, 1842.

BRADFORD, ALDEN. *Memoirs of the Life and Writings of Jonathan Mayhew. Boston, 1838.* Much original material.

BRADFORD, ALDEN. *History of Massachusetts, . . . from the year 1620 to 1820*. Boston, 1835.

BRADFORD, ALDEN. *History of Massachusetts, 1764 to 1820*. 3 vols. Boston, 1822–1829.

BREED, W. P. *Presbyterians and the Revolution*. Phila., 1876.

BRIGGS, C. A. *American Presbyterianism*. N. Y., 1885.

BRUCE, W. C. *Benjamin Franklin Self-Revealed*. 2 vols. N. Y., 1917.

CHASE, ELLEN. *The Beginnings of the American Revolution.* 3 vols. N.Y., 1910.

CHASE, FREDERICK. *A History of Dartmouth College and the Town of Hanover, New Hampshire.* 2 vols. Cambridge, 1891. Much original material.

CLARK, J. S. *A Historical Sketch of the Congregational Churches in Massachusetts, from 1620 to 1858.* Boston, 1858.

COBB, S. H. *The Rise of Religiotts Liberty in America.* N. Y., 1902.

COGSWELL, WM., Ed. *New Hampshire Repository.* 2 vols. Gilmanton, N.H., 1846.

Connecticut, Centennial Papers Published by Order of the General Conferences of the Congregational Churches of, Hartford, 1877.

Connecticut, Contributions to the Ecclesiastical History of, ed. by Wm. Kingsley. New Haven, 1861.

Connecticut Historical Society, Collections, vols. 1–16. Hartford, 1860–1916.

Connecticut, List of Congregational Ecclesiastic Societies Established in, before October 1818 with their Changes, ed. by A. C. Bates. Hartford, 1913.

CRANDALL, A. W. *The Religious Sects in Rhode Island during the Revolutionary Period.* Master's Thesis, Univ. of Chicago, 1920.

CRANE, JOHN C. *Peter Whitney and his History of Worcester County.* Worcester, 1889.

CROSS, A. L. *The Anglican Episcopate and the American Colonies.* N.Y., 1902.

CUSHING, H. A. "The People the Best Governors." *Amer. Hist. Rev.,* I. 284–87.

DEXTER, F. B. *Biographical Sketches of the Graduates of Yale College, with Annals of the College History.* First, Second, and Third Series, N.Y., 1885.

DEXTER, F. B. "Thomas Clap and His Writings." *New Haven Colony Hist. Soc. Papers,* V.

DEXTER, F. B. "Notes on some of the New Haven Loyalists including those graduated at Yale." *New Haven Colony Hist. Soc. Papers,* IX.

DEXTER, H. M. *Congregationalism: What it is; Whence it is; How it works;* . . . 4th ed., rev. & enl., Boston, 1876.

DEXTER, H. M. *The Congregationalism of the Last Three Hundred Years, as Seen in its Literature.* N. Y., 1880.

Fairfield County Historical Society, Reports of. Bridgeport, 1895.

Fairfield East and Fairfield West, The One Hundred and Fiftieth Anniversary of the Consociations. Bridgeport, Conn., 1886.

Fairfield East Association and Consociation, Historical Sketches and Rules of, With Statistical Notices of the Consociated Churches. New Haven, 1859.

FAŸ, BERNARD. *L'Esprit révolutionnaire en France et aux États-Unis, à la fin du XVIIe siècle.* Paris, 1925.

FORBES, HARRIETTE M. *New England Diaries, 1602–1800.* 1923.

GARVER, AUSTIN S. *Peter Whitney: A Discourse.* Worcester, 1888.

GILLIES, JOHN. *Memoirs of the Life and Character of the late Rev. George Whitefield, A.M.* 2nd ed., Dublin, 1811.

GIPSON, LAWRENCE H. *Jared Ingersoll: a Study of American Loyalism in Relation to British Colonial Government.* New Haven, 1920.

GREENE, M. LOUISE. *The Development of Religious Liberty in Connecticut.* Boston, 1905.

Groton, Proceedings of the Centennial Celebration at, 1876.

GUILD, R. A. *Chaplain Smith and the Baptists.* Phila., 1885.

GUILD, R. A. *Life, Times and Correspondence of James Manning, and the Early History of Brown University.* Boston, 1864. Both have many documents.

HALE, E. E. *The Centennial of the Constitution.* Boston, 1880.

HEADLEY, J. T. *The Chaplains and Clergy of the Revolution.*

HODGES, A. C. "Yale Graduates in Western Massachusetts." *New Haven Colony Hist. Soc. Papers,* IV.

HOLLAND, J. G. *History of Western Massachusetts.* 2 vols. Springfield, 1855.

HOLLISTER, G. H. *The History of Connecticut.* 2 vols., Hartford, 1857.

HOVEY, ALVAH. *Memoir of the Life and Times of the Rev. Isaac Backus,* A.M. Boston, 1859.

LAMB, MARTHA J. "Judge Charles Johnson McCurdy, 1797–1891." In *Mag. Amer. Hist.,* XXVI, 32–40.

LAWRENCE, R. F. *The New Hampshire Churches.* Claremont, 1856.

Lexington, Proceedings and Addresses Commemorative of the Two Hundredth Anniversary of the Incorpomtion of the Town of, 1914.

LORING, J. S. *The Hundred Boston Orators, 1770–1852.* 2nd ed., Boston, 1853.

LOVE, W. DELOSS, JR. *The Fast and Thanksgiving Days of New England.* Boston, 1895.

M'CLURE, DAVID and PARISH, ELIJAH. *Memoirs of the Rev. Eleazar Wheeloclk, D.D . . . . to which are added, Copious Extracts from Dr. Wheelock's Correspondence.* Newburyport, 1811.

MCLAUGHLIN, A. C. "The Social Compact and Constitutional Construction." *Amer. Hist. Rev.,* V, 467–91.

MATHEWS, L. K. *The Expansion of New England.* Boston, 1909.

MOORE, J. and FARMER, J., Eds. *Collections, Topographical, Historical and Biographical Relating Principally to New Hampshire.* 3 vols. Concord, 1822.

MORISON, S. E. *A History of the Constitution of Massachusetts Reprinted from the Manual for the Constitutional Convention of 1917.* Boston.

MORISON, S. E. "Massachusetts Constitutional Conventions." *Mass. Hist. Soc. Proc.*, L.

MURDOCK, K. B. *Increase Mather.* Cambridge, 1925.

New England Historical and Genealogical Register.

New Haven Colony Historical Society Papers, I–VIII.

PALFREY, J. G. *History of New England.* 5 vols. Boston, 1890.

PARKER, E. P. "The Congregational Separates of the Eighteenth Century in Connecticut." *New Haven Colony Hist. Soc. Papers*, VIII.

PARSONS, F. "Elisha Williams: Minister, Soldier, President of Yale." *New Haven Colony Hist. Soc. Papers*, VII.

PIERCE, BENJ. *A History of Harvard University.* Cambridge, 1833.

PLUNKETT, MRs. H. M. "The Fighting Parson." In *Pittsfield Sun.* Oct. 20 and 29, 1898. M. S. L.

PURCELL, R. J. *Connecticut in Transition, 1755–1818.* Washington, 1918.

QUINCY, JOSIAH. *The History of Harvard University.* 5 vols., Cambridge, 1840.

REED, S. M. *Church and State in Massachusetts, 1691–1740.* Urbana, Illinois, 1914.

Reports of the Fairfield County Historical Society. Bridgeport, 1895.

REYNOLDS, T. B., FISHER, S. H., WRIGHT, H. B., Eds. *Two Centuries of Christian Activity at Yale.* N. Y., 1901.

Rhode Island Imprints . . . between 1727 and 1800. Providence, 1914.

RICE, JOHN L. "The New Hampshire Grants." *Mag. Amer. Hist.*, VIII, 1–23.

RILEY, I. WOODBRIDGE. *American Philosophy, The Early Schools.* N. Y., 1907.

SABINE, LORENZO. *Biographical Sketches of Loyalists of the American Revolution, with an Historical Essay.* 2 vols. Boston, 1864.

SILL, E. E. "A Forgotton Connecticut Patriot." *Pub. Conn. Soc. Order of the Founders and Patriots of Amer.*, No. 4. New Haven, 1901.

SPRAGUE, W. B. *Annals of the American Pulpit.* 8 vols., N. Y., 1866–1877.

STACKPOLE, E. S. *History of New Hampshire.* 4 vols. N.Y.

STICKNEY, A. F. "John and Ebenezer Cleaveland." *Mag. Amer. Hist.*, XXVIII, 391–92.

STORRS, R. L., Ed. *Proceedings at the Centennial Celebration of the Incorporation of the Town of Longmeadow.* 1884.

SWIFT, LINDSAY. "The Massachusetts Election Sermons." *Mass Col. Soc. Pub.*, I, 388–451.

THACHER, REV. THOS. *A Biographical Memoir of the Rev. Dr. West.* Boston, 1808. M. H. S.

THAYER, C. T. *An Address Delivered in the First Parish Beverly.* Boston, 1868.

TRACY, JOSEPH. *The Great Awakening.* Boston, 1842.

TRUMBULL, J. H. *List of Books Printed in Connecticut, 1709–1800.* Hartford, 1904.

TRUMBULL, J. H. "Sons of Liberty in 177S." In *New Englander*, XXXV, pp. 299–313. New Haven, 1876.

TUDOR, WM. *The Life of James Otis.* Boston, 1823.

TYERMAN, L. *Life of the Rev. George Whitefield.* 2 vols. London, 1876.

TYLER, M. C. *The Literary History of the American Revolution.* 2 vols. N.Y. 1897.

VAN TYNE, CLAUDE. *The Causes of the War of Independence.* N.Y., 1922.

VAN TYNE, CLAUDE. "Influence of the Clergy and of Religious and Sectarian Forces on the American Revolution." *Amer. Hist. Rev.*, XIX, 44–64.

WALKER, WILLISTON. *The Creeds and Platforms of Congregationalism.* N. Y., 1893. Many documents.

WALKER, WILLISTON. *A History of the Congregational Churches in the United States.* Amer. Church Hist. Series, III. N. Y., 1894.

WINSOR, JUSTICE. *Narrative and Critical History.* 8 vols. Boston, 1881–1889. (Especially val. VIII.)

Town and County Histories

Often much original material is to be found in these histories. Many others of little or no value have also been consulted.

ALLEN, F. O. *The History of Enfield, Connecticut. Compiled from all the Public Records of the Town Known to Exist, Covering from Beginning to 1850.* 2 vols. Lancaster, Pa., 1900.

BAILEY, S. L. *Historical Sketches of Andover.* Boston, 1880.

BARRY, WM. *A History of Framingham.* Boston, 1847.

BITTINGER, J. Q. *History of Haverhill, N. H.* Haverhill, 1898.

BOURNE, E. E. *History of Wells and Kennebunk.* Portland, 1875.

BOUTON, NATHANIEL. *History of Concord.* Concord, 1856.

BUARTER, N. F. and FOWLER, T. L. *History of Pembroke.* Concord, 1895.

CHAFFIN, WM. L. *History of the Town of Easton.* Cambridge, 1886.

CHANDLER, C. H. *The History of New Ipswich.* Fitchburg, 1914.

CHASE, G. W. *The History of Haverhill.* Haverhill, 1861.

CLARKE, G. K. *History of Needham, Mass.* Univ. Press, 1912.

COLE, J. R. *History of Washington and Kent Counties, Rhode Island.* N.Y., 1889.

COREY, D. P. *History of Malden, Mass.* Malden, 1899.

CROWELL, R. E. *History of the Town of Essex.* Essex, 1868.

DAGGETT, JOHN. *A Sketch of the History of Attleborough.* Boston, 1894.

Dartmouth, Old, Historical Sketches, 1903–1909. no. 7.

DAVIS, C. H. S. *History of Wallingford, Conn.* Meriden, 1870.

DWELLEY, J. and SIMMONS, J. F. *History of the Town of Hanover, Mass.* Hanover, 1910.

EATON, CYRUS. *History of Thomaston, Rockland and Soutth Thomaston, Maine.* 2 vols. Hallowell, 1865.

FITTS, J. H. *History of Newfield, N. H.* Concord, 1912.

FOLSAM, GEO. *History of Saco and Biddeford.* Saco, 1830.

GREEN, F. B. *Boothbay, Southport and Boothbay Harbor.* Portland, 1906.

HAZEN, HENRY. *History of Billerica.* Boston, 1883.

Hingham, History of the Town of. 3 vols. Hingham, 1893.

HUDSON, CHAS. *History of the Town of Lexington.* Revised and continued to 1912 by the Lexington Historical Society. 2 vols. Boston, 1913.

HUNTINGTON, E. B. *History of Stamford, Conn.* Stamford, 1868.

HURD, D. H., Ed. *History of Middlesex County, Mass.* 3 vols. Phila., 1890.

HURD, D. H., Ed. *History of New London County.* Phila., 1882.

JAMESON, E. O. *The History of Medway, Mass., 1713 to 1886.* Providence, 1886.

JUDD, SYLVESTER. *History of Hadley.* Springfield, 1905.

KENT, J. C. *Northborough History.* Newton, 1921.

KIDDER, FREDERIC. *History of New Ipswich.* Boston, 1852.

LAMB, MARTHA. "Lyme." *Harper's Mag.,* Feb. 1876, pp. 313–28.

LARNED, ELLEN D. *History of Windham, County, Conn.* 2 vols. Worcester, 1874, 1880.

LEWIS, ALONZO and NEWHALL, J. R. *History of Lynn.* 2 vols. Lynn, 1890.

LYFORD, J. O., Ed. *History of Concord, N. H.* 2 vols. Concord, N. H., 1903.

MARVIN, A. P. *History of the Town of Lancaster.* 1879.

MCDUFFEE, FRANKLIN. *History of the Town of Rochester, N. H.* 2 vols. Manchester, 1892.

MORRISON, L. A. *History of Windham, N. H.* Boston, 1883.

PALMER, C. J. *History of the Town of Lanesboro.*

PARKER, C. S. *Town of Arlington.* Arlington, 1907.

PIERCE, F. C. *History of Grafton.* Worcester, 1879.

READ, BENJ. *History of Swanzea.* Salem, 1892.

RUNNELS, M. T. *History of Sanbornton.* 2 vols. Boston, 1882.

SCALES, JOHN. *History of Strafford County, N. H.* Chicago, 1914.

SHATTUCK, LEMUEL. *History of Concord.* Boston, 1835.

SMITH, FRANK. *History of Dover.* Dover, 1897.

SMITH, J. E. A. *History of Pittsfield, Mass., from the year 1734 to the year 1800.* Boston, 1869.

STARK, C. R. *Groton, Conn., 1705–1905.* Stonington, Conn., 1922.

STEINER, B. C. *History of the Plantation of Menunkatuck and of the Original Town of Guilford, Conn.* Baltimore, 1897

STONE, E. M. *History of Beverly.* Boston, 1843.

SWAYNE, L. L., Ed. *The Story of Concord, Told by Concord Writers.* Boston, 1906.

TAPLEY, H. S. *Chronicles of Danvers (Old Salem Village), Massachusetts.* Danvers, 1923.

TEELE, A. K., Ed. *History of Milton, Mass., 1640 to 1889.* Boston.

WASHBURN, EMORY. *Historical Sketches of the Town of Leicester.* Boston, 1860.

WATERS, T. F. *Ipswich in the Massachusetts Bay Colony.* 2 vols. Ipswich, 1917.

WELLS, D. W. and R. F. *History of Hatfield.* Springfield, 1910.

WHEELER, G. A. and H. W. *History of Brunswick, Topsham and Harpswell, Maine.* Boston, 1878.

WHEELER, R. A. *History of the Town of Stonington, Conn.* New London, 1900.

WINSOR, JUSTIN. *Memorial History of Boston.* 4 vols. Boston, 1881.

WINSOR, JUSTIN. *History of the Town of Duxbury.* Boston, 1849.

CPSIA information can be obtained at www.ICGtesting.com
Printed in the USA
LVOW01s0819110115

422314LV00003B/5/P